THE REMNANT CHURCH

THE COMPLETE VOLUME

THE SUM TOTAL OF ALL THINGS

Bishop Ronald D. Roston

The Remnant Church, The Sum Total of All Things:
The Complete Volume
Copyright © 2023 Ronald Roston

Cover Design: C Marcel Wiggins

All rights reserved. No part of this publication may be reproduced, distributed or transmitted in any form or by any means, without prior written permission. Unless otherwise identified, scripture quotations are from the King James Version of the Bible.

Publisher
Dreamer Reign Media, LLC
P.O. Box 291354
Port Orange, FL 32129

www.dreamerreign.com

For Worldwide Distribution
Printed in the U.S.A.

ISBN: 978-1-952253-24-9

CONTENTS

Dedication & Acknowledgements 4

Preface 5

Intro 9

Foreword 14

Chapter One: The Remnant 17

Chapter Two: Why A Remnant Church? 69

Chapter Three: The Sum Total & The Remnant 119

Chapter Four 157

Chapter Five 197

Chapter Six 247

Chapter Seven 283

Chapter Eight 333

Chapter Nine 353

Endnotes 379

Work Cited 388

DEDICATION

In addition to Jehovah, Jesus, and The Holy Spirit, I dedicate this work to the Body of Christ, my spiritual family; the Church... the living organism which the Father has chosen to be co-laborers with Jesus Christ, harbingers of the deliverance, grace, and mercy of the Ancient of Days.

ACKNOWLEDGEMENTS

I thank God for my beloved wife, LaCreece, who encouraged me to birth this body of information, and her shared concern for the saints to have access to this material. I bless the Father for giving me a "good thing" to walk with me in ministry.

I bless the Most High for the Servant Warriors with whom I share ministry: Bishop C.A. Roston; Bishop Jamar Suber; Bishop Roy Etienne Smith; Bishop Cardijn Mokube; Elder Keith Cash; Rev. Elliott Hampton, and Rev. Michael Harris. I love these brothers dearly, and appreciate the gifts and graces they contribute to the Church.

Last, but not least, I devote this project to my natural and spiritual sons and daughters worldwide. My hope and prayer is that this material will help them mature into the children of God they are predestined to become by His grace.

I am grateful that Jehovah commissioned me to "do the work."

PREFACE

Having been led by the Spirit of God, and in obedience to Him, I pen these words and thoughts. I merely lend myself as a vessel of expression for Him to use. I yield my gifts, talents, and graces to Him to use (as He will) to accomplish His purposes in the earth. This literary work has nothing to do with my abilities, but everything to do with His direction and inspiration upon my thinking. It is my response to His impression on some critical issues we must examine, as this earth and time heads for a collision with God and eternity.

There appears to be a condition in the Church which is causing a misrepresentation among unbelievers, as to just who the Body of Christ is. There are some general misconceptions as to the identity of "the called out one," what they look like, how they function, and just what they do and do not possess. It can also be said that these same types of issues and concerns can be found within the Body of Christ, itself. There is a need for clarity because of these misnomers, and the resulting effect they have on the lives of society. Humanity's response, or lack of response, to the Master's invitation to come out from among them and be ye separate, makes it necessary to begin to distinguish what is and what is not Christianity. This situation drives us to examine Christianity, as it lines up to how God has called the Church to function, and address what God calls the Church to look like.

The very nature of this type of examination will surely cause eyebrows to raise and cries of, "how dare you stand in judgment of the Body of Christ" being heard from every corner of Christendom. "Who gives you the right" will ooze off of the lips of saints and sinners alike, as this work attempts to draw a line in the sand. As we set up examination criteria as a means of determining if the Church is in fact living up to God's expectations of her, there will be criticism from both far and wide. I can remember my father teaching me a lesson, when I was newly saved. He said, "If you are walking down the street and you see a man run out of the bank with a stocking cap covering his face, a gun in his hand, and a sack of money thrown over his back, you do not have to make a judgment that he is a bank robber. The facts that are blaring in your face clearly tell you that he is a bank robber.

There are times when we are confronted with "in your face" facts that plainly confirm what you believe to be true. As such, you are not judging when you form your opinion; you are merely standing in agreement to what the facts validate as truth. Such is the case as we begin this examination as to where the Church presently stands in terms of its current behavior, and how it correlates to how God says the Church should be functioning here at the end of time. Yet, we dare ask the question, "Is it not the responsibility of the senior members of this organism, this live, functioning body of believers, to take an inventory to determine if the Church is on point?" Is she on schedule? Is she on task? Is she living up to God's mandate for us to be an extension of the ministry of Jesus Christ in the earth? Are we fulfilling our responsibility to replicate the actions of the author and finisher of our faith? Is our face and actions set to the task of destroying the works of the devil, and reconciling the world unto God? Do we have the propagation of the advancement of the principles of the Kingdom of God in the earth, as our central motivation and number one priority? Are we determined to keep the unity of the Spirit in the bond of peace? Is the love of God the driving force behind all that we do? Or do we come up lacking in these areas? Is the Body "missing the mark" when it comes to these things? These are questions we have to answer affirmatively if we are to function in our destiny and purpose, as we operate at the end of time. If the Church is not meeting these benchmarks, what needs to be done to insure that the Body does what's necessary to come up to speed?

If it is not the Body of Christ that asks these soulsearching questions, if it is not the saints of the Lord God Jehovah, creator of heaven and earth, who push the envelope to determine these critically needed answers in the time of the global crisis in which the world finds itself, then who will sincerely take on this task? If not us who; if not now, when? It is the duty of those who claim relationship to the Ancient of Days, to take an honest inventory of just how successful the "ecclesia" is doing in operating in her God appointed capacity. Do we truly exist to reconcile the world unto Jehovah, wage war against the kingdom of darkness, and function as duly authorized designated representatives and delegated authorities of Christ? We must take a painstaking evaluation of the Church, her motives and objectives, if we are to truthfully answer these questions. They must be answered without trying to safeguard our reputation or hide any apparent flaws, if we are ever to be the end time body of believers that actually serves as an extension of the ministry of Christ in the earth.

As this work begins to examine those types of questions, it

is not the author's intention to make a judgment of the Church. Conversely, it is our intention to stimulate the Body to critically examine our condition, as an attempt to foster a catalyst for positive change. Our desire is to motivate those who seek to emerge out of the mundane rote worship and existence that has invaded Christendom, to implement the changes necessary to catapult the Church to a state of functionality, that separates her from the "Church as usual" body and transforms her into "the remnant Church."

Know that you are loved, empowered and ordained; as the family of God, we are predestined to become "THE REMNANT CHURCH"

I love you in Jesus' name!

Your brother in arms,

Apostle Ronald D. Roston, D. Min. - ROMI

International Presiding Bishop & General Overseer

Restoration Oasis Ministries International

Senior Pastor - Times of Refreshing Ministries

Founder/Chief Facilitator

Apostolic Kingdom Covenant Ministries / AKC Ministries

INTRODUCTION

As we barrel towards the last day, our world of time is encompassed by catastrophic events of nerve-shattering proportions. We watch helplessly as nature collides with God's timeline; and devastating events that have been predestined in eternity past, come to fruition in our here and now. We stand in awe, as seemingly improbable eruptions of weather and political & economic upheaval rock the very basis of our belief systems; leaving us demoralized, hopeless, and at an all-time low in regards to our faith. We have begun to have serious doubt as to whether God is able to deliver us from these calamities. Can God counteract these events, their impact, and the subsequent panic that has been created by their existence? Yet a portion of the Body of Christ remains undaunted in their faith and commitment to seeing the agenda of God fulfilled in the earth. They remain focused on advancing the Kingdom of God, for the name's sake of Jesus, the Christ. They are known as "The Remnant Church." They are the focus group to whom this work is seeking to identify, call forth, and encourage.

Recently, we have witnessed so many events that have left us speechless, that nothing really comes as a shock to us anymore. We have seen the collapse of the Berlin Wall, the end of the Cold War, and the breakup of the Soviet Union. We have watched as a long list of dictators and blood-letting terrorists have been disposed of. Josef Stalin, Adolf Hitler, Benito Mussolini, Vladimir Lenin, Mao Tse-Tung, Emperor Hirohito, Idi Amin, Ayatollah Khomeini, Moammar Khadafi, Kim Youg il, Kim II Sung, Ho Chi Minh, Tojo Hideki, Saddam Hussein, Pol Pot, Imad Mughniyah, Osama bin Laden, Mohammed Atef, Fazul Abdullah Mohammed, Ayman Al-Zawahiri, Ahmed Mohammed Hamed Ali, Sheikh Ahmed Swedan, Imad Mughniyah, Abu Hasan al Muhajir, and Abu Bakr al-Baghdadi just to name a few. We have experienced the presidency of a reality TV star. We have lived through a historical time; in which the United States has been the most polarized ever.

We experienced nuclear meltdowns; the devastation of tsunamis in Indonesia, Hawaii, and Japan; nation-wrecking earthquakes in Turkey, Haiti, Indonesia, Japan, Chile, Mexico, New Zealand and the Philippines; American hurricanes Andrew, Hugo, Charley, Katrina, Patricia, Harvey, Irma, Alex, Earl, Maria, Florence, Michael, and Dorian will forever standout in our minds; as well as the volcanic eruptions of Shinmoedake in Japan, Mt St Helens in the state of Washington, Pinatubo in the Philippines, Nevada del Ruiz in Columbia, and El Chichon in Mexico, and wildfires all throughout the state of California. There have been so many natural disasters that it would not be feasible for us to try to name them all. Can't you hear the Lord clearly speaking out of Matthew 24, "And as he sat upon the mount of Olives, the disciples came unto him privately, saying, Tell us, when shall these things be? and what shall be the sign of thy coming, and of the end of the world? And Jesus answered and said unto them, Take heed that no man deceive you. For many shall come in my name, saying, I am Christ; and shall deceive many. And ye shall hear of wars and rumours of wars: see that ye be not troubled: for all these things must come to pass, but the end is not yet. For nation shall rise against nation, and kingdom against kingdom: and there shall be famines, and pestilences, and earthquakes, in divers places. All these are the beginning of sorrows."

The world watched as God blinked and allowed the collapse of the American stock market in 2008, sending the country into a recession, which had all the symptoms of a depression. We saw the ripple effects in the housing industry failure, the automobile industry failure; and the major collapses of other worldwide money markets, such as England, Greece, China, India, Russia, and Brazil. As a result, there was skyrocketing inflation and dramatic increase in the price of gasoline and other petroleum-based products. All of these events gave us a snapshot of how easy it would be for a global economic failure to open the door for a one world money system. This one world economic system will be accompanied by a one world government to oversee the one world-wide currency. How easy it will be to institute the mark of the beast, without which no one will be able to buy, sell, or trade.

Then in 2020, the entire world was paralyzed as the whole globe was afflicted by the COVID 19 pandemic. We watched in horror as hundreds of thousands of the inhabitants of the world died from this calamity. We stood in utter disbelief as millions contracted this horrific disease as the whole of humanity struggled to overcome and survive this global crisis. Yet there was no worldwide repentance.

Here in the United States of America, we also stood witness to one of the most unthinkable events in modern history. In a country that is only a little more than officially two hundred and forty years old, where people of African descent were brought to its shores solely for the purpose of providing "free" labor, a major upset of the social balance took place. In an economy built upon the enslavement of a race of people, a practice which was indulged and protected by the federal government, the course of history was changed. Contrary to legislation written to prohibit such; the son of a slave was elected to highest office in the land. An African American was chosen to serve as the president of a county only 156 years removed from slavery.

It is against the backdrop of such a myriad of natural and supernatural calamities that we find the Church struggling to maintain value, purpose, and integrity. Whether as a result of the impact these events have had, or not; there is an ever apparent identity crisis that can be seen within the framework of the Body of Christ. We cannot decide if we are going to equip or entertain; instruct or tell stories; set order or maintain tradition; discuss strategies for spiritual warfare or philosophy over denominational dogma. We have not determined if we are going to produce relationships or memberships. The verdict is still out as to whether we will march towards the new testament model of the first century Church, or will we remain steeped in our tradition of "church as usual." We have split decisions as to what we should do; so we are caught up in a "tug of war" about just how we should proceed from this point.

There is a pressing need for a clarion voice to give legitimate direction to the Body of Christ; which reflects the perspective of the Kingdom Government of God; and also advances His principles in the earth. This work is an attempt to be a part of the collective voice whose purpose is to fill that void. While we recognize that this is by no means the only voice that needs to be heard, we do believe that it is a legitimate voice, which has some God appointed and anointed information to contribute on the subject. We would not be presumptuous enough to think that we have a corner on the market, so to speak, relative to this discussion; but we do think this is a conversation that you need to hear; and allow the Spirit of God to shed illumination on the revelatory truths found within the pages of this discourse. While we acknowledge that there is no private interpretation of the Holy Scriptures, we do believe that sometimes, it is necessary to examine the Logos from a perspective that is free from traditional denominational influences.

With that being said, we invite you to delve into the pages of this study with an open mind. Free yourself from any preconceived notions as to what the Church should look like at this juncture. Allow the Holy Spirit to minister to you just how He wants the Church to operate, here at the end of time. Be open to the fact that end-times ministry should duplicate the ministry that was in the first century Church. As we understand that Jesus is coming back for the same kind of Church He spoke of when He said to Peter, "Upon this rock I build My Church; and the gates of hell shall not prevail against it." This will allow us to assume our rightful position as "The Remnant Church."

God bless you. Be all that God says you are! Until He returns ...EMERGE!

FOREWORD

In the current state of the world and the church, it is vital that we are made aware of the seriousness of our commitment to Christ and our assignment to this generation of believers. The crisis hasn't just begun; it has gotten louder and bolder. Leaders are against leaders; friends are against friends. Church, for many, has a negative connotation and has lost much esteem. The reality of scripture that "the love of many has waxed cold" is quite evident. If this is the final hour of a "system" in destruction. In the midst of the ruins, there yet remains a remnant of those who stand uncompromised in their faith. They know who they are and why they are. The very Kingdom of God is at hand.

The disciples were given a momentous responsibility to go into the world making disciples of all men. They were truth seekers; they were God-revealers. Nevertheless, modern expressions of God are distorted and mixed for the self-interest of those who claim to be His representatives. These counterfeit disciples are immersed with power, prestige, and position. Their egotistical endeavors have brought chaos and not change—ravenous wolves with humble appearances to comfort their cause. Amazingly, all have not been bitten; all have not been compromised. A culmination is occurring, and wheat and tares are being disjointed.

In this book, Bishop Ronald Roston takes readers on a journey of exploration into the heart of God and His true intent for His church. If you are a part of His remnant, you will feel strengthened to fight, and encouraged to stand. Regardless of our individual theological view points, all believers should keep praying and remain equipped to defend this truth—that Jesus Christ is LORD and reigns forever. May we all continue to abound in His grace and the finished work of Calvary's cross.

-Dr. Roy Etienne Smith
President of Isaiah University & Seminary

"Even so then at this present time also there is a remnant according to the election of grace. And if by grace, then is it no more of works: otherwise grace is no more grace. But if it be of works, then is it no more grace: otherwise work is no more work."

Romans 11:5-6

Chapter One
The Remnant

"Remnant: the part of something that is left when other parts are gone." The definition for this word is so simplistic, yet it represents an extremely complex and detailed idea that involves the notion of something smaller being used to accomplish that which the larger part failed to accomplish. The idea that something which is void of its other parts, parts which appeared to be necessary, is still able to function in the purpose and role for which it was created, and intended to be used. The remnant is a mystery that causes us to wonder how that which remains still has the power and capacity to fulfill the mission that was assigned to the whole—the remnant!

The remnant is a concept that really has not received a lot of attention from the Church until recently. However, it seems to be circulating in the group of saints with whom I am associated and gaining increasing popularity. It is a concept I have been espousing since 2011. Although this conversation may be considered to be in its infancy, it is yet a concept that is crucial to our understanding just how God will deal with humanity, here at the end of time. This idea is so central to Christianity, that the theme is interwoven into the entire Bible story in one form or another.

As we examine the lineage of the children of Adam and Eve. It can be found in the account of Noah and the flood. Look again and you will see it in the call of faithful Abram. Obviously, we see it in the narrative of Isaac and Ishmael. How could we miss it as we study the rift between Jacob and Esau? How evident it is when viewing the separation of Joseph from his brothers? What about the group of African Edenic Hebrews that left Egypt in the "Exodus," and the separation God allowed as He split the camp with venomous vipers? It is easy to note as we see the descendants of Abraham split into the two kingdoms of Israel and Judah.

As we become aware of the Jews who remained faithful to Jehovah as their kings exposed them to pagan worship and deities, and while in exile remained faithful; we find "the remnant."

The concept is as prevalent in the New Testament as it is in the Old Testament. Although the physical word may not be present in a lot of the Biblical text, to try to comprehend God's relationship with man, without giving credence to this notion, would be a mistake of grave proportions. The impact of God dealing with some things or persons that have survived destruction or a separation of some sort, tells the story of many of the Bible's central characters. There has always been a remainder or residue from a particular group after the majority of that group has been removed in one way or another. This constitutes a remnant. Even as we rehearse the familiar concept of "the rapture" or "the catching away," however you choose to term it; the notion of a remnant is completely intertwined in that discussion.

"For we shall not all sleep, but we shall be changed in a moment, in the twinkling of an eye. And those of us who do remain (the remnant) shall be caught up to meet him in the air..." 1 Corinthians 15:52

The Holy Spirit speaks a singular message to the Body of Christ; He speaks it plainly, succinctly, and repeatedly. Those who have an ear to hear, listen to what the Spirit of God is speaking to the Church. Understand what the remnant represents and why it is critical to end times ministry and the role of the Church at the end of the age. As we witness an unprecedented "spirit of compromise" in the Church, as we witness the erosion of some central core values and beliefs among believers, there is a remnant being formed. As the Church rocks and reels from scandal after scandal, and previously solid progenitors of "the faith" begin to waiver on fundamental issues, a remnant is being formed. As the government seeks to impose its sanctions on freedom of speech over the electronic airways, on TV, and radio, and remove basic rights of the Church to use the name of Jesus, a remnant is being formed.

As groups within the Body of Christ justify behavior and practices that are in direct contradiction to the tenets of the faith that were passed onto us by the patriarchs and apostolic fathers of this great Christianity, a remnant is being formed! Think about it, it was the remnant of Adam's sons that God chose to deal with—Seth. Out of all the other sons he had, the Bible only records Seth and his descendants as having any consequential impact upon the future of mankind. In fact, it was only after Seth grew up and had a son named Enosh/Enos that people first began to worship Yahweh by name. The King James Bible refers to it like this,

> *The Holy Spirit speaks a singular message to the Body of Christ; He speaks it plainly, succinctly, and repeatedly. Those who have an ear to hear, listen to what the Spirit of God is speaking to the Church.*

"And to Seth, to him also there was born a son; and he called his name Enos: then began men to call upon the name of the Lord." Genesis 4:26

It was through the lineage of Seth that Lamech, the father of Noah, was born. Imagine the whole of humanity so continually inclining their thoughts toward evil that they were willing to enter into negotiations with the fallen angels.

CHAPTER ONE: THE REMNANT

"And it came to pass, when men began to multiply on the face of the earth, and daughters were born unto them, That the sons of God saw the daughters of men that they were fair; and they took them wives of all they chose."
Genesis 6:1-2

They were arranging for these beings, which had lost their heavenly estate, to marry the daughters of men. This foul union produced the race of giants. These creatures, upon their death, released what we know as "familiar spirits" into the earth. God was so sorry that He even created mankind; He chose to destroy the entire world. He only chose a remnant of humanity to experience His mercy and grace: Noah, his wife Mrs. Noah, Noah's sons: Shem, Ham, and Japheth, and their wives. The entire known world was decimated because of their unbelief, the entire creation was destroyed; only eight people were left over; a remnant!

"And all flesh died that moved upon the earth, both of fowl, and of cattle, and of beast, and of every creeping thing that creepeth upon the earth, and every man: All in whose nostrils was the breath of life, of all that was in the land, died. And every living substance was destroyed upon the face of the ground, both man, and cattle, and the creeping things, and the fowl of the heaven; and they were destroyed from the earth: and Noah only remained alive, and they that were with him in the ark." Genesis 7:21-23

Japheth and Ham both left the place that represented the second cradle of civilization, the place where God had decided to reestablish His creation. Japheth went north, (his sons and their families) Tarshish (Italy), Javan, Tiras, Gomer (Turkey,

Russia, Ukraine, Bulgaria), Ashkenaz, Lud, Meshech, Dodanim (Lebanon), Tubal, Togarman, Hamath (Syria), Greece, Cyprus, Romania and settled what would ultimately become known as Europe. Ham moved south, (his sons and their families) Put, Lehabim, Lubim, Mizraim (Egypt), Cush (Sudan), Seba (Ethiopia), Sheba, Dedan, (Saudi Arabia), Ophir, Pathrusim, Havilah (Saudi Arabia), Raamah, Libya, Malta, Tunisia, Algeria and settled what would ultimately become known as (Africa). Only Shem, his sons and their families, rested in the land where the Ark settled. (Saudi Arabia, Jordan, Iran, Iraq, Pakistan, Afghanistan, India). Not only did he settle what was to become known as the Holy Land, but he also became the progenitor of the line that would produce Messiah Jesus; Jesus Ha' Mashiach. God used what was left over, He used what remained, Shem, to fulfill the promise He had made in the Garden of Eden. In Eden, the Creator spoke of there being enmity, hostility, mutual hatred, antagonism, animosity, rivalry between the offspring of the devil and the offspring of the woman. Hostility would bruise the heel of the Messiah, but it would crush the head of the devil.

"And I will put enmity between thee and the woman, and between thy seed and her seed;" Genesis 3:15

Could God have possibly known what would happen between the fallen angels and the daughters of men, in Noah's day? Of course He did; He knows the end from the beginning. Could He have known about the offspring that would be created as the fallen angels saw the daughters of men, that they were pleasant, and took as they would for wives? Did He have foreknowledge of the demons and familiar spirits which were to be released on mankind and how they would war for the souls of men? Of course He did. This is why He prophesied in the Garden of Eden about the warfare that would take place between these groups.

"And I will put enmity between thee and the woman, and between thy seed and her seed; and it shall bruise thy head, and thou shalt bruise his heel."
Genesis 3:15

There is nothing that is a surprise to God. There is no way for us to fool Him; yet He still allows us to have a "free will" and exercise the privilege of choice He bequeaths upon us as a gracious father bestows gifts upon his children. Abram was what was left over after the languages were confused at Babel. Another remnant, he now stood as the only one in the whole earth having access to the Lord God Jehovah; Yahweh.

"Go to, let us go down, and there confound their language, that they may not understand one another's speech. So the Lord scattered them abroad from thence upon the face of all the earth: and they left off to build the city. Therefore is the name of it called Babel; because the Lord did there confound the language of all the earth: and from thence did the Lord scatter them abroad ..." Genesis 11:7-9

"Now the Lord had said unto Abram, Get thee out of thy country, and from thy kindred, and from thy father's house, unto a land that I will show thee:"
Genesis 12:1

He arose out of the confusion, to now stand as the only

man having total exclusivity to a Heavenly Father, that had once been available to all mankind. Out of the midst of a creation of whom ALL had access to God, only he and his descendants alone, could now claim to have covenant relationship with the Ancient of Days. If anyone else wanted to have relationship with Jehovah, they had to become a part of Abraham's people in order to worship the God who Abraham worshipped. As God transitioned from absolute inclusivity, He transformed Himself to being exclusively the God of the Hebrews. Only Abraham, Isaac, and Jacob could now claim to be the recipients of having communion with the God of creation. If anyone else wanted to have communion with God, they had to be in covenant relationship with Abraham and his descendants, that was the exception they had to fulfill. It was only Abraham's descendants, and those who would become proselytes of what would come to be known as Judaism, who could hope to benefit from the grace and mercy God was extending from heaven to earth. They were the remnant.

> *"There is nothing that is a surprise to God. There is no way for us to fool Him; yet He still allows us to have a "free will" and exercise the privilege of choice..."*

"And I will make of thee a great nation, and I will bless thee, and make thy name great; and thou shalt be a blessing: And I will bless them that bless thee, and curse him that curseth thee: and in thee shall all families of the earth be blessed." Genesis 12:2

CHAPTER ONE: THE REMNANT

Then, there is David, the youngest of Jesse's sons. The whole group of Jesse's male offspring was presented before Samuel the prophet. Samuel was tasked to choose the Lord's anointed servant to replace Saul as the king of Israel.

I Samuel 16:1-13. The entire collection of Jesse's sons passed by the eye of the prophet, yet the future king was not in their midst. So, the questions were asked, "What's left over, what remains, who is the remnant that I have not yet seen?" [Surely God did not lie when He told me that I would find the chosen king of Israel among your sons, Jesse. Where is the balance of your sons, where is the one that yet remains to be seen? Bring me the remnant Jesse, so God's Word and promise can come to fruition.]

There is a Church rising out of the Church, one Church that has not yet been seen. There is a body of believers so dedicated to the doctrine passed on to us by the apostolic fathers of the first century Church, that they would rather stay hidden, and be ridiculed for their non-conformity. They refuse to buy into the ethical and moral compromise the Church has allowed to seep within her walls. They are a group that yet remains to be seen and identified as progenitors of the Christian faith. They are more concerned with equipping the saints to endure to the end, rather than entertaining them to make them think they have a "religion they can feel." This remnant is not concerned with title and position, but rather is bound to the concept of "functionality" as the gauge of one's position in Christ. They have been blessed with a deposit of righteousness and steadfastness that will make Israel jealous of the zeal that they possess for the

God of the Hebrews. God is waiting to reveal this remnant to the nations.

Invariably, as we begin a discussion about the concept of the remnant, we must first acknowledge that in order for the remnant to exist, there must first be a main body of people or things out of which this remnant has been extracted. That being said, it is impossible to talk about the remnant of the Church or the remnant of Israel without first acknowledging the veracity or authenticity of those two bodies. A remnant is usually a small part, member, or trace remaining, a small surviving group—often used in plural, an unsold or unused end of piece goods, still remaining. The Middle English, contraction of remenant is from Anglo-French remanant, which is from the present participle of remainder.

Remainder means to remain: to be a part not destroyed, taken, or used up; to be something yet to be shown, done, or treated; to stay in the same place or with the same person or group; especially to stay behind, to continue unchanged.

We are speaking of a group of people who possess the full virtues and attributes of the original group. They have embraced the purpose for which the original group even had existence. Although a smaller group numerically, it is a group that is as large in vision and purpose as the original one. The larger group is the one that has had their vision and purpose changed—compromised. This smaller group, this remnant, remains steadfast, unmovable, always abounding in the work of the Lord, with the knowledge that their labor of love is not in vain. This remnant is sold out to the same type of sacrificial love that Messiah Jesus had as He voluntarily left His home in glory, allowed Himself to be fashioned in the image of human man, took upon Himself the role of a servant, and yielded to the cruel death of the cross.

This group continues to operate in the purpose for which it was created. It continues to demonstrate the trait that identifies it as being disciples of the Christ. "Sacrificial love" permeates everything the remnant does. It is the driving motivation that permits them to endure the disassociation from the larger group. It is the bedrock upon which their faith is built, and the substance that sustains them as they refuse to change from operating in the foundational principles upon which this great Church was built. It is the anchor that keeps the remnant within the veil as they continue unseen, unchanged and faithful to the dictates of the Father.

It is from the latter definitions that we would like to center our discussion of the concept of "The Remnant Church." We contend that the remnant is something that is yet to be shown or done. It is a manifestation of the Church that has stayed behind, despite the contemporary shifts in our presentation of Christianity, to exist as the Church that "continues" unchanged. As one of my great contemporaries, the late Bishop Otis L. Carswell once stated, "The old Church is dying and must do so. The true Church of our Lord and Savior Jesus Christ is EMERGING out of that old Church; that old system of doing things." The Church triumphant is that Remnant Church; the Church that has stayed in place and continued in the Apostle's doctrine as recorded in Acts 2:42,

"And they continued steadfastly in the apostles' doctrine and fellowship, and

THE REMNANT CHURCH

in breaking of bread and in prayers."

It is a small part or body of believers. It is the unused part that has not been destroyed by the contemporary shifts, which have been responsible for causing the Church to look like the world. Those shifts which have made it hard to distinguish whether you are listening to gospel music or the latest releases from the world of hip hop, rhythm and blues, and jazz. These attempts to make the Church "palatable" and appealing to the world have made it hard to recognize if you are listening to a presentation of the gospel message, or to a re-iteration of the latest world news or an emotional presentation of social doctrines. The remnant is that "trace" which remains committed to look and act like the original body from which it was extracted; not the current Church, but the original Church. It is the sign or evidence of the past state in which the Church operated, known as holiness. It is a minute and sometimes barely detectable amount or indication of the place of power in which the Church was initially birthed. The remnant is that tiny speck of power that has not been compromised by the wiles of the enemy, as he attempts to make the testimony of the saints null and void. This group refuses to be invalidated and made of non-effect, because of her allowance of the operating principles of this world to influence her look and sound. She remains true to the stature from which she was formed, and will not allow her mold to be broken. Every fiber of her being smells with the sweet aro-

> *"The remnant is that tiny speck of power that has not been compromised by the wiles of the enemy, as he attempts to make the testimony of the saints null and void."*

ma of the presence of the Spirit of God; that same presence that was so obvious on the Day of Pentecost.

The concept of a remnant deals with the idea of a "balance" or something left over. It endorses the idea of a "remainder" or put another way, an amount in excess; especially on the credit side of an account. "Leftovers," as it were, refer to something that remains unused or unconsumed; especially leftover food served at a later meal. That's what the remnant is, something that remains unused or unconsumed by the current trends which are causing the Church to be "blended" into the world. Those practices which make Christianity an item that easily fits into the category of being a "cross-over" commodity, mandates that a balance of uncompromised leftovers exist in order to perpetuate the true mission of the Church...to come out from among them and be ye separated, says the Lord of Hosts. The remnant has to be that unconsumed leftover food that can be used to satisfy the hunger of a dying, emaciated world as it cries out, "What must I do to be saved?" There has to be a balance of something left over, that truly represents the flavor and consistency of the original fodder, which was left in place to satisfy the hunger of a sin-sick world.

The main priority in which the Church was established centered on reconciling the creation back to the Father, and ministering deliverance from the grips of the evil one. Both of these are representative of what Jesus was charged to do. This is what He did as He left eternity and made His incursion into our dwelling sphere known as time.

"For this purpose the Son of God was manifested, that He might destroy the works of the devil."
I John. 3:8b.

What are "the works of the enemy?" In the onslaught that happened in the Garden of Eden, the enemy was able to separate the creation from the Creator. Man was created in perfect harmony with God. They were united by the Spirit of God, which Jehovah breathed into His creation, a creation crafted from the dirt of the earth. Man was perfect and had no knowledge of evil. When Adam and Eve partook of the fruit, they were exposed to the knowledge of good and evil. Evil is disobedience to the Word, or law, of God. This knowledge contaminated their Spirit, and caused it to be disconnected from the Spirit of God. Man's spirit became dead, hence the condition known as "spiritual death" came into the world. Consequently, the need arose for man to be "born-again;" man needed a spiritual rebirth.

The work that the enemy of our soul was able to accomplish was to change the nature, or spirit, of man from being holy and perfect. He performed a "spiritual assassination," which resulted in the admittance of mental & physical sickness, and spiritual & physical death into this sphere known as time on this place known as earth. Jesus came to undo all that satan had accomplished, and has commissioned His Church to do the same. This mandate to destroy the works of the enemy serves as the reason the Church was birthed, and how she has been instructed to operate until Jesus returns to rapture her. Where is the remnant? Where are those who will season the world with the flavor of

God? Where are the people that will stand in the gap to preserve the creation? Where are those who will replicate the compassion the Father had for His deceived creation? For God so loved the world that He gave. He gave the best that Heaven had to offer. He gave Himself. He allowed His creative component known as "The Word" to fulfill prophecy, manifest out of eternity and be housed in human flesh; live a sinless life; die a substitutionary death, and be resurrected from the dead. He did all of this in order to redeem His creation from the sentence of death imposed upon them as a result of "the fall."

Jehovah could have condemned the creation because of their disobedience, destroyed them, and started all over again from the beginning, but He didn't. Instead, He made the ultimate sacrifice; He allowed Himself to carry the "sin of the world" in a human body of flesh. He separated Himself, and turned His back on that sin ladened God-man, known as Jesus of Nazareth. He Himself paid the penalty for the crime that was committed in the Garden. His act of kindness provided a pardon for mankind and subsequent access to God again, by giving the creation the free gift of eternal life. Who wouldn't serve a God like our God?

The remnant doesn't blend into the look and sound of the presentation of Christianity that is trying to seduce the world into salvation by sending that oh so dangerous message, "See, we are just like you." The remnant is not saying, "The only difference between us is that we have accepted Jesus Christ as our personal Savior." Our message is uncompromised, and parallels the original Good News that was presented, with repentance as the requisite; we are labeled as "odds and ends." The remnant is seen as miscellaneous articles and small matters to be attended to. We don't really count; we are remnants. The remnant is not a part of the larger whole; it is even considered to be cultish, because it doesn't agree or buy into the popular notion of Christianity currently being espoused by men and women who command the attention of a large national and international audience.

I would much rather be a remnant, than to be a part of a large body of believers who are missing the purposes of God, and walking in a manner that is not becoming that of being a royal priesthood and a holy nation. I would much rather be a miscellaneous article that is "peculiar" and distinguished, than an unrecognizable part of a larger group that is missing the mark originally intended for the ecclesia. Call me crazy, but I would much rather be a leftover than something that is consumed and all used up. The remnant can ill-afford to function in a capacity that is not in alignment with the original purpose of the initial Church.

There is an inherent danger in not functioning in accordance to one's purpose. One of the most prolific Bible teachers of our time, Dr. Myles Monroe, said it this way, *"If something is not functioning according to its purpose, then abuse is inevitable."* Since God is ultimately in control of everything, and there is nothing that is a surprise to Him, once He has decided that it is time for the remnant to emerge, it must function in accordance to the purpose that the Father has assigned to it. If the stage has been set for the present-day conformist, deceived, compromised Church to move aside in deference to the remnant, then the remnant must operate in its own purpose. Otherwise, the remnant will be confused as being the current conformist-Church. It will not be recognized as different from it.

The danger in operating outside of purpose is that something cannot fulfill the destiny for which it was created. If the remnant fails to fulfill its purpose, it will not be able to accomplish the things that God has decreed it to do here at the end of the age. Therefore, not walking in purpose has the potential of elongating the time table for the fulfillment of all things purposed by the Ancient of Days. In addition to sending a confusing message to the unsaved, by not operating according to God's purpose for it, the remnant also has the potential to cripple Christians who are discontent with the conformist, deceived, compromised Church, and are looking for a God-given alternative. Unless the remnant is operating in its God-given purpose, it will not be the agent of continuity, reflecting the exousia (authority) and dunamis (ability) of the first century Church, the Church that adhered to the apostle's doctrine. This doctrine that was passed on to the apostles by the Christ of God Himself.

The "remnant" has been challenged to abide: to wait for the coming change. She is commanded to await the arrival of the metamorphosis that will transform her into the Church triumphant: the reflection of the New Testament Church that was in the earth and "turned the world upside down." Thus, the remnant must endure without yielding. She must endure the criticism and ridicule that labels her as "holy rollers" who are too stiff to conform to the compromising rendition of Christianity prevalent here at the end of the age.

The remnant must remain steadfast, unmovable, holding fast to the profession of her faith and to the principles that were handed down to her by the Church fathers, and the apostles who crafted the framework, built upon the foundation laid by Christ. She cannot yield to the temptation to give in to the pressure, lower the standard of holiness, and adorn the garments of carnality and sensuality. She has been commissioned to abide, to remain anchored in the hope of her expectation that God has called her to a position of righteousness that is realistic and attainable. The remnant must withstand the enticement to water down the Gospel of the Lord in an attempt to coerce the unbelieving world to accept the concept of a loving God that will not chastise His creation. She must bear patiently, the weight of the mantle that has been placed on her. She must tolerate, and accept without objection, the hatred the world has for her, because of her stance for righteousness and her adherence to the doctrine that was handed down to her by the first century apostles and prophets.

The remnant must remain steadfast in her determination to replicate the ministry of Jesus Christ in the earth. As she recognizes that her objective is to be a mirror image of the ministry of reconciliation provided by Jesus, it will serve as the mortar that cements her in the role God has predestined her to play in end-times ministry. She must buy into the fact that the Church is fixed in a state of transition, as she blossoms into the Church that forcefully shakes the kingdom of darkness in this present age.

The Church is not standing still; she is in constant motion. She is on a journey that will return her to her original state of power. Though it might seem that she is afflicted and stagnant, she is constantly being restored and healed. She is headed back to her position of prominence in the affairs of this world. Change is an absolute truth that cannot be ignored. The fact of the matter is that the Ancient of Days is returning the Church back to her original state of power. The fire and zeal that were present in the first century Church, as she turned the world upside down with the presentation of the Gospel message, accompanied by signs and wonders, shall once again be the evidence by which the true Body of Christ in the earth is identified.

When the Roman government made Christianity the official religion of the Roman Empire, it snatched the leadership of the Church out of the hands of the Jewish apostles, and launched the Church into a decline. We refer to this as the dark ages of the Church; her spiritual vitality began to decline. She remained in decline until the Protestant Reformation. It was at this time that God began to restore moves of His Spirit back into the Church. This restoration will continue until the full-blown emergence of the remnant. This emergence will be the time that the Church has returned to the place of power and effectiveness that was so noticeable after the Day of Pentecost.

The remnant must continue in this place of transition as she sojourns as strangers and pilgrims in this world. She cannot forego the pruning and perfecting that God has determined as necessary to remove the dross, and allow the pure gold to rise to the top. She does this with the knowledge that her citizenship is not of this world, but has foundation in the realm of eternity, and in fact this realm is the place to which her spiritual existence will be physically translated. Although the Church operates in the sphere of time and the limitation it imposes, her existence in the sphere of eternity provides the basis for the supernatural power she possesses, and her ability to perform the miraculous. If her citizenship and power were grounded in this world of time, she would not have the capacity to alter physical and mental situations—representative of healing, miracles, and deliverance.

The Church, nor the remnant, should allow the secular world to dictate how they operate, or set their guidelines and goals. Therefore, their reality should not be framed by the dictates of this world, but rather by the dictates of heaven. Their governance should come subject to the eternal standard of God, as opposed to submitting to the standards of this world. These ecclesiastical bodies must be governed by the principles of the place where their citizenship has been established: the eternal dwelling place of God, eternity. For example, if you try to run a non-profit organization by the rules that are used to run a for-profit corporation, mayhem will ensue. You cannot effectively operate an organism with mandates designed and intended for an organization from a completely different category. In order for either of those two bodies of believers to experience any modicum of success, there must be synergistic dynamics in play between the eternal Kingdom of God, the Church, and the remnant.

The remnant actually has its purpose founded upon the original purpose of the first century Church. The fact that the contemporary Church is conformist verifies the reality that she has not operated within the guidelines of her original purpose.

Subsequently, it is the responsibility of the remnant to step up to the plate, and fulfill the original purpose for which the Church was left in the earth.

Therefore, it is safe to say that these two institutions are dependent on each other. The contemporary conformist-Church needs the remnant to exist in order for the original purpose of the Church to be actualized and fulfilled. However, the remnant has no existence without the Church being conformist, and thereby substantiating the need for a Remnant Church. Both of them are dependent upon being governed by eternal citizenship and the laws of the Kingdom of God, versus being governed by secular citizenship and the laws of this world. This earth is merely the place where they subject themselves to the laws of their place or origin and citizenship, in order to fulfill the purposes of God in allowing them to be here. They are His delegated authorities and designated representatives in the earth. They are to be fruitful, multiply, replenish the earth with their kind, subdue the earth, and have dominion over it.

There is a mind-bending fact we have to be aware of, and it poses a somewhat troublesome reality. This is the fact, "The remnant is a 'remaining' group, a part or trace of a larger portion, a number left after a subtraction, the final undivided part after division that is less than the original divisor." The remnant is not a large, ominous body, but it is the leftovers. Then, by definition the remnant is not considered to be a large, robust, ample portion, but conversely, it is usually thought to be lacking quantity and sometimes, quality. It is often categorized as not being enough to generate satisfaction. The remnant is not something that is coveted or sought after. It is not an item that is usually desired. It is not an object of obsession for those who are in search of being fully satisfied.

So, the obvious question is how can this remnant be capable of carrying out what needs to be accomplished by the end time Church? How can this body of believers, who are only a small portion of the larger body, have the strength, resources, and physical bodies to do the work of reaping the end time harvest before the second coming of Jesus Christ? These are pertinent questions which need a believable answer, if the remnant is expected to shoulder up under the heavy responsibility associated with its mandate to reap the harvest. We shall attempt to bring some clarity to these questions as we progress deeper into this discussion.

As we explore these questions and look for a viable answer, the only spiritually logical explanation we can give centers around what Jesus told His disciples as they returned from town and saw Him conversing with the Samaritan woman, at the well. When asked if He needed nourishment for His body, His response was that His meat was to do the will of the One who sent Him, and finish His (Jehovah's) work. In other words, the thing that sustained Him, energized Him, provided Him with everything He needed to carry out the tasks assigned to Him, was doing the will of the Father.

Jesus was not dependent on natural sources to provide Him with what He needed to accomplish His assignment. He was dependent on His faith. According to the definition of faith provided by the TRM/ROMI School of Ministry, "faith is unquestioning confidence and trust in the Word we had heard from God." It was His faith and obedience to fulfill His purpose, which were the nutrients that energized Him and made it possible for Him to walk in His destiny. He knew that in order to set a good example and pattern, for us, of how to be totally dependent on God, He would have to place doing the will of God as the priority in His life. Regardless of what others perceived as a deficit, He was able to maintain forward movement because His motivation was to please the Father, to accomplish and fulfill the purpose for which He had been established in the earth. Despite what appeared to be an apparent lack of adequate supply and energy, He was able to minister because His obedience proved to be a source of sustenance. When the natural nutrients and resources were not in place to carry Him on, it had to be doing the will of the Father that continued to drive Him forward, and subsequently energize Him to complete His assigned task.

It is and shall be with the remnant. Although the natural eye will consider her inadequate, understaffed, under-financed, ill-equipped according to this world's standards, she will prevail. Despite her numerical deficiencies, her faith and commitment to obediently fulfill the Father's prophetic agenda will be all she needs to walk in her destiny. These attributes of faithful obedience will not only sustain her, but they will propel her in the proper direction, at the proper time, and with the proper persons to accomplish every aspect of the will of God. He needs the remnant to succeed.

In order to help bring about the close of the age, the remnant must be single focused in trusting that God has deposited in them everything they need to succeed. Their size and physical resources, or lack thereof, are not enough to hinder them from being the vehicle God uses to complete what the conformist-Church failed to fulfill. In fact, it is exactly their lack of what the natural man considers to be necessary to achieve this monumental task, which actually positions them to be just the vessel God needs to do this. It is their apparent lack that will contribute to the onlookers recognizing that it is only by the empowerment of God Himself that they are able to do what they do.

> *"It is imperative that we understand that the existence of the Remnant Church is a deliberate and purposeful act of God."*

Their lack will force people to glorify God for what they are able to do, realizing that it is He who is the force by which everything is accomplished. The faith and knowledge that the Ancient of Days is poised to provide them with every type of resource they need is the very thing that sustains the Remnant Church, and empowers her. When we speak of the remnant, we address the concept of a residue or something that remains after a larger part is taken away or separated. The remnant is the part that is designated to remain after the majority portion has been removed.

The Remnant Church is not a coincidental byproduct of the conformist-Church's failure to perform. She is not a happenstance or after thought of God, as He pondered how to deal with the compromise that has been able to creep into the contemporary Church. The remnant does not exist merely because God didn't know what to do about the enemy's ability to de-claw the Church

CHAPTER ONE: THE REMNANT

and render her powerless because of her authority being undermined by conforming to this world's standards. The remnant is not an unintentional, accidental mishap that just happens to come into existence just in the nick of time, to save God from the embarrassment of a failed strategy. It is really the polar opposite of those suppositions.

The Remnant Church is the organism that has been elected, chosen, and selected to stay behind, stay put, and continue in operation long after the conformist, deceived, compromised Church has outlived her usefulness. She is the vehicle that the Ancient of Days has nominated to linger in the earth until the fulfillment of all things. It is imperative that we understand that the existence of the Remnant Church is a deliberate and purposeful act of God. It reflects a decision that was made in the annals of eternity. She is a group of saints that have been elected by Jehovah to continue in the apostle's doctrine long after the conformist-Church has abdicated her position of power and authority. She has been chosen to help fulfill the plan of the Father to reconcile the world to Himself, and bring the institution known as "time" to an end. Time also exists to give mankind an opportunity to escape the final judgment against evil, which will take place as God blends time into eternity. Time is a period that has been set aside for something to begin, happen, and end. It currently represents the period that God has allowed for man to once again have access to eternal life, the same eternal life he had in the Garden of Eden.

In this period allotted for the reconciliation of mankind, God has selected the Remnant Church to insure that His original purpose in establishing the Church in the earth is fulfilled. Even though the original vehicle will not bring mankind to its expected end, the conformist-Church will catapult a designated group of believers to a precipice of decision. Knowing the end from the beginning, God has decreed that a segment of the conformist-Church will remain faithful to the doctrine and purpose of the first century Church; it is God's ram in the bush; it's called the Remnant Church. The remnant is the part that is still in place after the completion of a process. It is the part that is still intact after all of the changes and transitions have taken place in the original structure. It is still planted and anchored in its original position, with all of its original power and virtues in place.

After God has allowed the conformist-Church to decline and settle into just a shadow of its original greatness, the Remnant Church emerges to carry out the dictates of Jehovah, and accomplish His initial purpose for the ecclesia. She rises as His representation in the midst of an evil and chaotic time. She manifests stability and power in an environment where the inhabitants of the earth are searching for a physical manifestation of the one true invisible God.

After God allows the completion of the process, which depletes the conformist-Church of all of her usefulness, the Remnant Church surges forth in the power and authority of the Apostolic Church that was birthed on the Day of Pentecost. She begins to boldly operate in the power of The Holy Spirit, as the magnet that will draw mankind to repentance before that great and terrible Day of the Lord. She remains as a designated authority of the Lord, a strong tower into which those seeking salvation can run and find refuge. The Remnant Church has not been moved off her mark; she has maintained her position and is operating exactly in the place where she has been commanded to have dominion. She has not been swayed by the winds of change or the doctrines of men; she has remained faithful to the Great Commission.

The remnant can also be said to be "the rest of;" it is the something that remains over, after the other part has been extracted. When the conformist-Church has been moved out and taken out of the way; the Remnant Church stands as that which was chosen to be separated from the conformist-Church, and designated as adequate enough to remain in content and substance as the fullness of what the original was. She has been delegated to successfully operate in the void of power and purpose which resulted from the conformist-Church's failure to fulfill her original purpose. She represents the balance, or the stability, of the essence of the Church. She functions in the fundamental nature and core values of the organism that Christ left in the earth to finish His work of reconciliation. The Remnant Church is the personification of God and operates in His Spirit to fulfill the real meaning of the word Christian. She is the physical embodiment of His character, the epitome of His love for the creation, and the exemplification of His concern for mankind, and His ultimate desire for mankind to have eternal life.

After the procedure or course of action takes place that separates the pretenders from the real, the false from the true, the weak from the strong, what is left in place, is actually of a higher quality then that from which it was taken. The Remnant

Church emerges as a body which has a greater propensity to use the anointing of God, simply because it is what is left in place when the impurities of the conformist-Church are removed from the Body of Christ. She stands as a purged and pruned organism, free of defect, free of obstacles that could block the flow of the anointing, but most of all, dedicated to fully accomplish the purpose of God. She is of a higher quality because she has truly crucified her agenda. The remnant has put their agenda to death. They have not covered it, they have not masked it, they have not hidden it; they have killed it. They have completely destroyed it, lest in a situation when their flesh wants to be in control, their agenda should try to rise in opposition to God's agenda. Therefore when the imps of hades come to perpetuate compromise against God's agenda, there is nothing for them to anchor onto because every vestige of the remnant is in subjection to God's agenda. There is no wiggle room. There is no room for leaven.

So, the quality of the remnant is greater because she has a genuine predisposition to carry out God's commands. She has a greater inclination to be in total alignment with the vision of God, and will not deviate from the plan which He has instructed her to follow. While the conformist-Church has a penchant or weakness to give in to the things that will bring her acclaim, the remnant has a predilection or preference to avoid those things, and she has a tendency to only do the things that will bring glory to God. As the fire separates the dross from the gold, so the Lord's pruning process for establishing the remnant will serve as a refining and perfecting of those chosen to be the harbingers of God's peace and wrath at the end of the age. As the Father allows

CHAPTER ONE: THE REMNANT

the winds of secular change to blow on the conformist-Church, the internal struggle she experiences will prove to be the thing that causes the remnant to be weighted down with the mantle of holiness.

As the spiritual foundation of the contemporary conformist-Church begins to crack and crumble, as the effect of compromise begins to take its toll on her, the members who accept that conforming compromise will become more visible. They will become as noticeable as the dross that floats on the molten precious ore during the refining process. They will not be as substantial as the valued gold which is hidden because of the content of its substance. The refining process will render them good for nothing, but to be separated from the valuable, prized adherents to the apostolic tenets of faith.

It is the compromised Church's struggle to accept the ways of the world or maintain the apostle's doctrine that will precipitate the separation of the remnant from the conformist. It is the battle to hold the plumb line of holiness as a standard operating procedure that will cause the rift, much like the separation that happened with serpents in the wilderness camp of Israel.

"And the people spake against God, and against Wherefore have ye brought us up out of Egypt to die in the wilderness? for there is no bread, neither is there any water; and our soul loatheth this bread. And the Lord sent fiery serpents among the people, and they bit the people much of Israel died. Therefore the people came to Moses, and said, we have sinned against the Lord, and against thee; pray unto the Lord, that He take away the serpents from us. And Moses prayed for the people. And the Lord said to Moses,

Make thee a fiery serpent and set it upon a pole: and it shall come to pass, that everyone that is bitten, when he looketh upon it, shall live. And Moses made a serpent of brass, and put it upon a pole, and it came to pass, that if a serpent had bitten a man; when he beheld the serpent of brass, he lived."
Numbers 21:5-9

In order for the remnant to effectively engage in end-times ministry, she must be proven, battle-ready, pressure tested Servant Warriors of Jehovah. She has to know what it means to "go through," "pray through," and "persevere." She cannot faint at the slightest test, trial, or tribulation. The remnant can ill-afford to be weak at heart. She must know how to engage in spiritual warfare, and she must have experience using her weapons, and not merely have mental knowledge of them. The Remnant Church must continually have her senses exercised to discern good and evil by reason of use, and be committed to see the war through until the end. She cannot have an "escapist mentality," but she must stand ready to see the mission through to its final conclusion. The remnant cannot be "wishy washy." They cannot be on fire and in the heat of the battle today, and tired, worn out and on the sidelines tomorrow. She must have gone through the seasoning process. The Remnant Church must be marinated in the cauldron of hardship, thereby proving and strengthening her faith. It is this "seasoning process" that establishes her as "ready" to shoulder the awesome responsibility of being an active participant in end-times ministry. This process is necessary in order for the remnant to be equipped, prepared, and organized to be geared up for the battle that is in front of her. She must have

CHAPTER ONE: THE REMNANT

practiced using all of the weaponry at her disposal in order to be adequately prepared to vanquish her formidable foe.

Her foe is not just a run of the mill anti-God entity. He was the most powerful angel in heaven; he guarded the throne of God, and he led the angelic host in praise. He was deceitful enough to influence one-third of the angels, who only knew holiness and perfection, to follow him in an active rebellion against the Lord God Jehovah. He had the ability to persuade supernatural beings, who had no knowledge of evil, to transgress the hierarchy of heaven, and compromise their loyalty to the one true living God. Lucifer's success in getting those angels to compromise should serve as an example of just how little of a match mankind is for him, apart from the power of the Holy Ghost. This should also allow the remnant to recognize how easy it was for him to introduce compromise into the midst of the conformist-Church. These are beings who themselves are not supernatural in origin, but only have access to natural power. There is only one way mortal beings, which have been infused with the power of God, can combat and defeat this ancient foe. This foe has been waging war against the Kingdom of God from before the foundation of the earth. The remnant has to be well versed in the spiritual weapons and armament that is available to them. They must also be extremely adept at effectively using the weapons of their warfare. They must be able to receive and follow orders and instructions. They must be mature enough to trust their leadership and move synergistically as one, armed force moving in one direction, and moving with one purpose. This state of being does not happen by osmosis. It is not a condition that one accidentally stumbles into. It happens by design, and is achieved intentionally by going through the process intended to purposefully bring about this stature in the organism.

We can also visualize the remnant to be the part of a testator's estate remaining after the satisfaction of all debts, charges, allowances, and previous devises or bequests. After every financial settlement of an estate's outstanding condition has been taken care of, there is a balance that is unused and is yet available to be used for any additional situations that have to be dealt with. This is the purpose the remnant serves: the unused portion that still has functionality. They are the unused portion that yet has value. Jesus is the testator and the Church being the estate, the picture should be clear. There is a larger portion of the Church which has been exhausted; it has been used to cope with what the Church has had to struggle against up to this point. The Remnant Church has to be careful not to stand in condemnation of tradition and denominationalism; she must guard against pride and false humility. The Remnant Church is the outgrowth of these two establishments. These portions of the testator's estate were absolutely necessary to provide the springboard from which the remnant could be launched. The fact of the matter is that had there not been any denominations or tradition, there would

> *"The Remnant Church has to be careful not to stand in condemnation of tradition and denominationalism; she must guard against pride and false humility. The Remnant Church is the outgrowth of these two establishments."*

be no remnant. The fact that there is a remnant is a direct result of the fact that these two institutions of denomination and tradition existed and continue to exist. Since the remnant is a by-product of these things, they can ill-afford to decry them. These institutions were necessary as a foundation from which the remnant could emerge. They are the place that the remnant transitions from. If they do not exist, then the remnant has no place from which to claim its origin. Therefore, we must value the institutions of tradition and denominationalism. Although they might not be the things we need to empower us in end-times ministry, they were definitely needed as the things to launch us into end-times ministry.

This is the reason that we should not refer to ourselves as non-denominational; we should correctly label ourselves inter-denominational. If the truth is to be told, we are truly comprised of a little bit of all of them. They have all played a part in the development of Christianity, and the growth of the Universal Church. The conformist-Church was not always conformist, she morphed into that state. The fact of the matter is that she was a powerhouse at her inception. She was walking in the power and authority of her role model, Jesus the Christ. Even in her infancy, she was a power to be reckoned with. She was actively duplicating the works she had witnessed Messiah Jesus perform. She was bold, confident, confrontational, compassionate, and committed. As she ascends and recovers from her plunge into the dark ages, she is continually being built line upon line, precept upon precept. This descent of the conformist-Church was due to her apostolic leadership being stolen by Rome as Constantine declared Christianity the official religion of the Roman Empire.

Dr. Bill Hamon, in his magnanimous work, "The Eternal Church," succinctly describes the attention to detail the Father used, as He restored moves of His Spirit into the Church. Dr. Hamon gives us an account of how the various "movements" the Church experienced as a result of the Protestant Reformation were indicative of God bringing her back to vitality, operational functionality, and power. As God began to send wave after wave of His anointing into the Church, she began to return back to her place of origin. She began to look more and more like the first century apostolic body of believers who personified the image and character of Yeshua. As she climbed out of the hall of Roman Catholicism, the enemy increased his campaign to invalidate her claim to holiness and taint her testimony by constantly enticing her with the principle of compromise.

Satan interjected compromise into every facet of Christian living. From immorality to greed, from in-fighting to apathy, the enemy has attempted to thwart the growth of the Universal Church by lulling her to sleep by way of compromise. He has attempted to steal the vigor and zeal of the redeemed, by enticing them with compromise and then condemning them for giving into it. Though his efforts have been somewhat successful, the outcome was not a surprise to God.

Though the Church may have been momentarily incapacitated, she was not totally debilitated. Our God does know the end from the beginning; He is ever mindful of what we need before we need it. That's why it is called provision. It is the resource provided and put in place before the need arises for its usage. It is a product of God's anticipation of what is required to fulfill the mission, based on His omniscience, and His commitment to not allow His Word to return to Him void. This causes Him to have everything the Remnant Church needs for her success in place, exactly when she needs it. In order for the remnant to fulfill her purpose, there are "operations of the Spirit" that must be in place and available to do battle against the forces of hell. There are supernatural powers, which only God can provide, that must be utilized in this end-time battle against evil, and the evil one. There are armaments, the remnant must possess, that are specifically designed and intended to defeat the ramped-up offense of satan at the end of the age. Again, because He knows the end from the beginning, Jehovah strategically provides everything the Remnant Church needs to win the war, and places them at her disposal exactly when they need to be in place for her to bring into usage.

The righteous people of God, those in right relationship with Him, comprise the Remnant Church. In a time when there has been a major infiltration of the Church, by the devices of Lucifer, there must remain a people who are upright, honorable, virtuous, and blameless. A people that have the moral fiber to decry the "popular forms of worship" that send mixed messages to the unbelievers, and confuse them as to whether they are in church, or at the club. There must be a remnant who is dedicated to the original mission of the Church—*salvation from the penalty of sin, and deliverance from the practice of sin.* This must be the catalyst for all she does in ministry, at the end of the age. She must be focused on spiritually educating her members, and strengthening them so that they are strong enough to spiritually reproduce themselves. A people that are committed to fasting, prayer, holiness, and deliverance are a formidable foe against the kingdom of darkness. Those who have not compromised, have not conformed to the deception injected into the Church by the "prince of the power of the air," are the righteous remnant. They are those that are left over after His divine judgment. They are the ones who escape, survivors, and those who have been loosed from their bonds.

All of these aforementioned phrases are concepts expressed by Hebrew words in the Old Testament, to convey the idea of the remnant. Objects or people may be separated from a larger group by selection, assignment, or destruction. The Ancient of Days views the components of the conformist-Church and makes a collective choice of people to comprise the remnant. He makes an allocation of the resources in the conformist-Church to those people who have decided not to deviate from the original purpose for which the Church was left in the earth. Jehovah delegates His righteous people to carry on the ministry and work of His Son. He deputizes them [in a manner of speaking] to execute His judgments in the earth. He appoints the remnant; He entrusts and authorizes them to serve as His ambassador, or envoy. They become His agent, and a duly authorized emissary with the ability to speak on His behalf, and decree His rulings and decisions.

The Remnant Church exists because Elohim has designated her to exist. The only wise God has chosen her, selected her, and elected her to operate as the portion of the body of believers that helps restore the Church back to her original place of prominence. He does this by obliterating the conformist-Church; He eliminates her influence. He shifts the world's focus from her by reducing her importance to nothing. He wipes out her ability to speak on His behalf, and bequeaths that to the remnant. When we speak of the Father's annihilation of the conformist-Church, we are merely talking about His intent to extinguish, smother, snuff out and turn off her ability to distract unbelievers, and believers alike. We are referring to His strategy to prohibit the conformist-Church from presenting a false image of Christianity. We are alluding to His plan to allow the true image of His Church to shine forth by removing the conformist-Church from the spotlight, and placing His chosen vessel that accurately reflects who He is at center-stage. God is able to do this by devastation of the character of the conformist-Church; He exposes her for who she is. He ruins her reputation and wrecks her influence by shifting the world's attention to focus on the group that correctly represents Him: The Remnant Church.

The God of Abraham, Isaac, and Jacob must orchestrate demolition of the conformist-Church. He must knock down and pull down the foundations and traditions which are the result of the Roman government's successful overthrow, if you will; of the apostolic leadership Jehovah, through Jesus Christ, set in place to govern the Church. As previously stated, when Rome embraced Christianity as the state-religion, she was able to wrestle the governance of the Church from the hands of the apostles.[1] She replaced apostolic leadership with secular leadership, and thus set in motion the events that began to thrust the first century Church into her decline. God must undo this. He must demolish the effect of the conformist-Church; He must destroy her influence. What is left over when He does this is the residue or remnant, the Remnant Church.

The remnant can also be described as those who remain after an epidemic, war, or some other type of cataclysmic event. What happened when Rome incorporated Jewish Christianity into Roman government can be seen as an epidemic. An epidemic is a plague.

- ◊ It is a disease that is accompanied by infection.
- ◊ It is a curse, an outbreak, with the subsequent eruption of a rash which is contagious.
- ◊ It is communicable, transmittable and has the ability to contaminate and pollute.
- ◊ It is also associated with the corruption of that which is whole and healthy.
- ◊ It is often seen as a scourge: a blight or bane that is endemic in nature, and viewed as something that is a common, widespread and extensively deadly disease.

This sums up what happened when the apostles, who were left in charge to administer the Church, were replaced by a government that removed the concept of conversion as a result of repentance. Rome replaced the foundation of repentance and baptism by immersion with the notion that one could become a Christian simply by being sprinkled with water, or being born into a family that was already a part of the Church. This practice lives up to all the references we made to the epidemic which ensued, or developed, when Rome took over the governance of the first century Church. The Great I Am must totally decimate the negative impact that the loss of apostolic leadership had on the Church. The way He will do this is to take the conformist-Church off of center-stage and replace her with His delegated authority and designated representative...the Remnant Church.

The contemporary conformist-Church is on an inescapable road to an internal conflict. It is headed into an inevitable war within itself that will serve as a line of demarcation between those who desire to maintain the tenets upon which the Church was birthed, and those who are open to accept the spiritually compromising ways of the world. The ways of the world are those which are designed to make the Church appealing to people who want to be self-indulgent, yet claim to be submitted to God.

One of the main pillars of Christianity rests upon our conscious decision to abdicate the "throne of our life," and instead, allow God to sit in that place of authority. This war focuses on our willingness to do the things that are pleasing to Him, in deference to doing the things that give us pleasure, and making pleasing Him our number one priority.

1. It will be a universal general war.
2. It will not be isolated to a particular country or culture.
3. It will not be relegated to a certain economic or social class.
4. It will affect the entire Body of Christ.
5. It will serve as a sword to divide the holy from the carnal; the surrendered from the self-serving, and those committed to the "old" ways from those intent on replacing those old holy values with "new" ones; that are more current and socially

THE REMNANT CHURCH

> *"Just as Israel experienced a judgment for their apostasy, so the conforming Church will be evicted and thrown out of her place of world influence."*

acceptable.

One might even call those new ways "politically correct." In order for God's Word to be fulfilled and His agenda to be accomplished, there must be a "great falling away" from the principles of faith upon which the Church was established. In order for prophecy to be fulfilled there must be an abandonment of the apostolic principles that founded the Church. We must remember that the apostle's doctrine, which served as the basis for these principles, was merely a duplication of the instruction they had received from Christ. Those principles sustained the Church through the persecution of the Roman government. Those are the same principles that helped her through the Protestant Reformation. Through the subsequent ages, as God began to restore her back to her original state, it has been these same principles that built her, and are now the target of the contemporary conformist-Church. These principles are in the cross-hairs of conformity, because they stand as a promoter of holiness, instead of an advocate for the endorsement of moderation. This upcoming civil war will be known as The Great Apostasy.

The Remnant Church represents the fully restored Church. In order for the Church to be translated, she must first be restored to her original place of ultimate dominance. In order for Jesus to receive her and offer her up to the Father, she must first be in the position where she is unified. She must be a measure of the stature of the fullness of Christ. The remnant represents the culmination of the restoration of all of the doctrines, truths and spiritual experiences with which God will bless the Church. He has been constantly restoring her through all the different "movements," which have helped to move the Church out of her decline. The Protestant Reformation Movement, the Holiness Movement, the Pentecostal Movement, the Charismatic Movement, and the Prophetic-Apostolic Movement comprise these moves of God.

The great apostasy is a great rebellion against God Himself. It is an aggressive climatic revolt against God that will prepare the way for the appearance of the man of sin.

"Let no man deceive you by any means: for that day shall not come, except there come a falling away first, and that man of sin be revealed, the son of perdition. Who opposseth and exalteth himself above all that is called God, or that is worshipped, so that he as God sitteth in the Temple of God, showing himself that he is God." II Thesselonians 2:3-4

The great apostasy represents a specific act of rebellion that embodies the supreme opposition by the forces of evil to the things of God. Satanic deception, which caused the fall of man, will characterize the end of the age. Satan is the one who deceives the whole world [2] and is the power behind the beast and the false prophet.[3] The time is coming when professing Christians will reject the truth to embrace the doctrines proclaimed by false teachers.[4] Let us examine this term, "apostasy." According to Webster's Dictionary, apostasy is the renunciation or abandonment of a former loyalty. It is renouncing, rejecting, repudiating, or denying something to which you previously had allegiance or faithfulness. It is an abandonment or desertion of something to which at one time you had devotion and fidelity. The result is that you end up leaving behind and neglecting an ideal to which you had previously been committed.

The Old Testament speaks of it in terms of falling away, such as deserting to a foreign king. Associated ideas include: religious unfaithfulness; rebellion; cast away; trespass, and backsliding. As we examine the Scriptures,[5] we see numerous accounts of Abraham's descendant's unfaithfulness to Jehovah. Time and time again, they cast away the worship of the Great I Am, and exchanged it for the worship of the false gods of their neighbors in surrounding lands. They constantly rebelled against His ways, trespassed His laws and statutes, and were commonly referred to as "backsliders." In a manner of speaking, they deserted their king and sovereign, and cast their lot with the great deceiver. They chose the guardian of the throne, as opposed to choosing the One who sits upon the throne. Although the word "apostasy" was not used to describe their condition, it certainly applied. The definition of apostasy accurately connotes what these Hebrews were guilty of doing. They were abandoning and leaving behind their foundation principles, for that which did not have the power to sustain them.

The prophets picture Israel's history as one filled with apostasy. They continually turned from God to "other gods." As a result of their apostasy, they experienced "exile." Until recently, 1948 to be specific, the Jewish nation was still experiencing the result of being scattered to the nations. They had been

CHAPTER ONE: THE REMNANT

dispossessed of their land, and had no homeland to speak of. They were scattered to the wind, separated from their inheritance, the land of Canaan, and were a people without a country. As a result of their disloyalty, their sovereign had released them from their place of prominence.

The natural consequence of abandoning your king is to be banished, sent away, and separated from the benefits associated with being under his covering, or being a part of his kingdom/government. When one chooses to reject or deny the government standards to which they had a former allegiance, it should not be a surprise when they are deported, and separated from their previous position. Just as Israel experienced a judgment for their apostasy, so the conforming Church will be evicted and thrown out of her place of world influence. She must be forced out and pushed out of the way to make room for the Remnant Church. The remnant must have room to fully operate in the power of the Spirit without being in competition with another group posing as the lawful representative of the Almighty. Therefore, the conforming Church must be ejected out of her place as the mouthpiece of Jehovah. The Father has to set her aside, not only because she has conformed, but also because she has failed to maintain adherence to the principles of holiness, upon which the Church was founded. Generally speaking, in the New Testament, apostasy is considered to be the act of rebelling against, forsaking, abandoning, or falling away from what one has believed. It is condemned in the Epistle of Jude.

"So I want to remind you, though you already know these things, that Jesus[b] first rescued the nation of Israel from Egypt, but later he destroyed those who

did not remain faithful. And I remind you of the angels who did not stay within the limits of authority God gave them but left the place where they belonged. God has kept them securely chained in prisons of darkness, waiting for the great Day of Judgment. And don't forget Sodom and Gomorrah and their neighboring towns, which were filled with immorality and every kind of sexual perversion. Those cities were destroyed by fire and serve as a warning of the eternal fire of God's judgment."
Jude 5-7 (NLT)

> *"Satan's strategy is to make the Church comfortable adopting a policy of moderation, founded in the principle of self-satisfaction."*

Apostasy is derived from the Greek word apostasia. The New Testament speaks of it in terms of, "to stand away from." The Greek noun only occurs twice in the New Testament;[6] though it is not translated as "apostasy."

"But the Jewish believers here in Jerusalem have been told that you are teaching all the Jews who live among the Gentiles to turn their backs on the laws of Moses. They've heard that you teach them not to circumcise their children or follow other Jewish customs."
Acts 21:21

"Let no man deceive you by any means: for that day shall not come, except there come a falling away first, and that man of sin be revealed, the son of perdition;" II Thessalonians 2:3

II Thessalonians addresses those who believed that the Day of the Lord had already come. However, Paul was clarifying that an apostasy would proceed that Day. He was letting them know that one of the telltale signs the Day of the Lord was upon them would be the apostasy and the revealing of the son of perdition. In I Timothy. 4:1, the Spirit had explicitly revealed this falling away from the faith.

"Now the Spirit speaketh expressly, that in the latter times some shall depart from the faith, giving heed to seducing spirits, and doctrines of devils;"
I Timothy 4:1

In latter times, such apostasy will involve doctrinal deception, moral insensitivity, and ethical departures from God's truth.[7] God is acutely aware of the fact that the enemy is intent upon deceiving the Church. Our foe is deliberately introducing seductive doctrines designed to sway the Church from the principles of holiness. Satan's strategy is to make the Church comfortable adopting a policy of moderation, founded in the principle of self-satisfaction. His desire is to manipulate the Church into a state where pleasing God is equated with pleasing ourselves. He wants to convince the Church that it is justifiable behavior to not be so rigid and adherent to the call to holiness, that it doesn't take "all that." It is the conforming Church's acceptance of these principles that is the very thing that disqualifies her to be the conduit of the "power of the Spirit" necessary to accomplish the end-time mandate for the Church. It is exactly why the conforming Church must be moved aside to make room for the Remnant Church; she must be exiled in order for the remnant to emerge.

Apostasy is a Biblical concept that has fueled a lot of debate. The biblical warnings against it should cause us to recognize that while God does have the ability to keep us, man still has a "free will." Free will positions man to have the ability to ignore God's commands, and potentially reject His salvation and dictates. There must be a realization that apostasy, by nature, is subject to a cause and effect relationship. The actions one takes, or doesn't take, produces a direct effect on the status of the relationship. When one freely chooses to disregard the standards by which their organism was birthed and by which it grew, there are consequences.

When one chooses to compromise the morals and ethics by which the Church has maintained her reputation and integrity, as the delegated authority and designated representative of God, one leaves themselves vulnerable and exposed. In reality, one has positioned themselves to experience the judgment of God. This judgment might conceivably look like being moved aside, so that a more qualified representative can occupy that position of honor.

There is an inherent danger in religious unfaithfulness that necessitates exile. When one does not correctly reflect the values of their sovereign, one for whom you are supposed to be an ambassador, there is no justification for allowing that entity to continue being seen as a legal representative of said sovereign. While the contemporary conforming Church was duly charged and elected to be Jehovah's envoy, by exercising her "free will" to accept the devil's compromise, she voluntarily made herself a candidate for exile, and ultimately replacement. While "free will" is a wonderful gift given to us by the Father, it also poses a threat to those who misuse it, or use it without the proper filter. Since man is not an android or robot, there has to be a conscious exercise of free will to maintain adherence to the faith that was passed on to us by the founding apostolic fathers.

The conforming Church has to either decide to repent and return to her apostolic origins, or face the penalty of apostasy. Apostasy ends up with her being placed aside and no longer being used as the harbinger of the Gospel message. If the conforming Church does not exercise her free will to return to the position occupied by the first century Church, she leaves God no alternative but to replace her with a Church that will maintain His standards. She forces the Father to cause a division to take place within her ranks or an extraction so to speak. What remains is a Church that refuses to be seduced into compromising the old landmarks that have come to frame the integrity of the Body of Christ.

This extraction is known as the Remnant Church. There has always been a remnant. All throughout the Holy Scriptures one has always been able to find the concept and example of the remnant. Both of the divided kingdoms of Judah and Israel can be said to have experienced circumstances which qualified them to be classified as having a remnant.[8] While this thought is typically associated with the nation of Israel, there are specific examples of individuals that can also be pointed to as fitting the classification as a remnant. Noah and his family can be said to have been survivors, remnants, of the divine judgment God executed against the whole of humanity when He smote the earth with the Great Flood.[9] The exact same thing can be said of Lot, as he escaped the destruction of Sodom and Gomorrah.[10]

We dare not forget Jacob's family as they fled to Egypt to find refuge from the famine and drought that had plagued humanity.[11] This small surviving group became the nucleus of Hebrews that God used to fulfill His prophetic promise to Abram. He assured faithful Abram that the sign, that Jehovah had cut a covenant with him, would be the enslavement of Abram's descendants in a foreign land for over 400 years.[12] While Joseph's brothers didn't have to sell him into slavery in order for God to position him as the second most powerful man in the then known world, it was God ordained for them to do so. They unwittingly helped God's covenant promise to Abram to come into fruition. Elijah and the 7000 faithful followers of Yahweh represent yet another example of the remnant, as they would not bow their knees to Baal and the wicked King Ahab and Queen Jezebel.[13] The whole nation was steeped in Baal worship, yet there was a faithful remnant to the God of Abraham, Isaac, and Jacob. Can we fail to mention Daniel,[14] Shadrach, Meshach, and Abednego; I think not.[15]

> *"God is merely looking for a Church that will stay faithful to the assignment for which she was chosen."*

There are countless other heroes of the faith, who stand as an example of those who were left over, escaped, survived or were loosed from their bonds either by selection, assignment or destruction of the larger group. They stand as monumental pillars of faith and testimonies to the concept of the remnant. Whether they were selected or assigned, they serve to demonstrate to us that God doesn't need a great crowd. Rather, a faithful few, such as Gideon's three hundred.[16] The prophet Isaiah is one of the strongest vocal proponents of "the remnant." He was so committed to the idea that he named one of his sons Shear-Jashub, meaning "a remnant shall return."[17]

Isaiah understood that while exile, as a consequence of disobedience, was inescapable, God always allows the opportunity for repentance and redemption. Let me be absolutely clear of this one thing, when God exiles the conforming Church, it is not to destruction with no hope of redemption. It is merely a process where He shifts the emphasis, and world attention, from the Church that has been seduced into compromise. His desire is to make the non-conformist-Church, which has chosen to remain true to the tenets of the first century Church, the primary focus of this world. If the conforming Church sees the error of her ways, and repents, she can be grafted into the remnant.

God is merely looking for a Church that will stay faithful to the assignment for which she was chosen. God is willing to allow the truly repentant to be restored back to usefulness. While there will be some in the conforming Church that will never repent, there will be those who yield to the conviction of The Holy Spirit and return to their first love. God's intention has always been to have "a people" that would voluntarily serve and love Him. Many of Isaiah's remnant passages are closely tied to the future king who would be the majestic ruler of those who would seek His mercies, the Messiah. These passages have a strong eschatological thrust, expecting future generations to be the remnant. Other passages looked to the remnant to be in Isaiah's day. However, the passages in the latter part of the book have a very evident future orientation. They intimate that there would be a new people, a new community, a new nation, and an extremely strong faith in one God.

The Messianic Jews and the first century New Testament Church are an example of the concept of the remnant. As Israel moved from the dispensation of Law through the dispensations of Grace and Kingdom, there had to be a new group that would emerge from the old. There had to be something that was taken out of the old group as a remainder or left over. Though Israel had progressed from the Dispensation of Promise through the Dispensation of The Law, she still had not reached her final destination. She still had not evolved into the form necessary to catapult God's body of believers to the end of the age. One has to recognize that in order for a remnant to emerge, there must be an erosion of sorts in the original body.

The changes that happened in Judaism and the Jews' strict adherence to the Law were necessary for God's plan to be fulfilled. Her legalism and legalistic religious practices were necessary in order for the Messianic Church to be birthed. Those practices were the reason that certain Jews were willing to receive John's baptism of repentance, and subsequently sever their relationship with the temple and the nation of Israel. Those Jews that stepped into the Jordan to be baptized of John knew that they were voluntarily separating themselves from the main body of the Jewish community, and that they would be ostracized because of their decision. They didn't cower in fear, as they readily made them-

CHAPTER ONE: THE REMNANT

selves the remnant. They were those who were separated from the larger body, yet had a more powerful relationship with their God, Jehovah.

While the Jews, that group who had exclusivity when it came to relationship with Jehovah, were moved aside in order for the focus to shift onto the first century Church; they were not completely thrown away. The Jews continue to be God's chosen people, even today. The time clock for our world centers upon them. Apocalyptic prophecy revolves around that small Middle Eastern nation. In addition to all of that, they still have the ability to be saved. God has not forgotten them, and has made provision for them to repent and be grafted into the Remnant Church.

The Gentile Church is supposed to provoke the Jews to jealousy, and make them want to enter into the same covenant relationship with Jehovah, which the Gentile Church has. The Ancient of Days, the God of the Hebrews, is simply amazing, and His love for His creation is unsurpassed.

The greater number of the other prophets may not have been as explicit as Isaiah was in their usage of the term "remnant." Nevertheless, their works are replete with the idea that only a few of the Jews would survive judgment, as a result of their repentance, and God would use them to raise up a new community or nation. Amos, Micah, Ezekiel, Jeremiah, and Zechariah[18] all prophetically alluded to the notion that there would be a small group of leftovers that would survive the exile, return to the Promised Land, resettle Jerusalem, rebuild the Temple, and establish God's new community of covenant believers. Jehovah

THE REMNANT CHURCH

always had and will always have a "remnant."

Chapter Two
Why a Remnant Church?

According to Dr. Bill Hamon, author of "The Eternal Church," there is a process that the Church has gone through since her inception. It is a process marked by an inception full of power and authority. Through a series of events, she declined in both areas, and began to see a restoration to her initial state as she experienced the Protestant Reformation.

Dr. Hamon's work leads one to believe that the Church must be fully restored before Jesus comes back to offer her up to the Father. There were some foundational spiritual truths and experiences that were lost as the Church slipped into her "dark ages." Without going into the causes of those losses here, we will say that they were an integral component of the fiber and fabric that vested the Church in her power. These doctrines, truths, and spiritual experiences were active ingredients in the recipe that yielded the signs and wonders that gave the Church credence. They are the very things that God wants to bring to the forefront in the Remnant Church, as a means of validating her, and substantiating her right to operate in the earth as His delegated authority and designated representative. They are components that are currently missing in the conforming, deceived, compromised Church, and must be operational and visible in the Remnant Church.

If the remnant is going to garner the attention it needs to serve as a magnet for the "final harvest," these first century apostolic signs and wonders must be fully operational and noticeably visible. There is a restoration of lost doctrines, truths, and spiritual experiences that must take place for the Remnant Church to justify her existence as the legal replacement of the conforming Church. The remnant cannot simply decry the conforming Church's seduction and claim to be her replacement without a demonstration of signs, wonders, power, and authority. Otherwise, why would there be a need for a remnant? Why would we attempt to replace that which already has longevity, without being able to justify the replacement based on operational functionality? In order for the Father to substantiate the need to move the conforming Church out of the limelight and shift the focus onto a more qualified spokesperson, He must endow that replacement with the virtue that will cause it to be a true reflection of His character and His power. There is only one reason for there to be a Remnant Church, and that is to fulfill purpose and accomplish what the conforming Church could not fulfill, and failed to accomplish. Thus, the Remnant Church must exist as a fully functional and operational organism; reflecting the character of God and the first century Apostolic Church. If the remnant fails to do this, she is guilty of fraud, character assassination, and spiritual homicide. Hence, the Remnant Church cannot afford to be a replica of the conforming, compromised Church it is intended to replace.

As we examine the notion of a Remnant Church, we must first understand the how, the why, the origin, and birth of the first century New Testament Church. Many will tell us that the Church was birthed on the Day of Pentecost, when the Father made The Holy Spirit available to dwell within the creation. No longer would the Spirit of God be dispatched from heaven to rest upon an individual person to perform a specific task, but now God's Spirit would be available to all of creation on an on-going basis. What about Jesus breathing The Holy Spirit into His disciples on Resurrection Day? We will address this fact a little later on. However, we must consider that fact. While the actual birth of the Church may be a topic for conversation, we can be assured of this one thing, the Day of Pentecost certainly represents the day that the Church became a noticeable physical reality. We can definitely mark this as the day that the Holy Spirit of God became available to ethnic Jew and non-ethnic Jew alike. As we consider the Church's birth through the eyes of the Spirit, we will have to concede that she was birthed in the eons of eternity; long before the foundation of the world.

"Blessed be the God and Father of our Lord Jesus Christ, who hath blessed us with all spiritual blessings in heavenly places in Christ: According as He has chosen us in Him before the foundation of the world, that we should be holy and without blame before Him in love."
Ephesians 1:3-4

After the fall, the Messianic race (descendants of Abraham, the Jews) was born and continued in existence; in order to bring forth the Messiah. God's chosen people, the Hebrews, were selected to be the seed through which the Father would redeem creation. God's plan to reconnect the creation to Himself centered on creating a group into which He could deposit the inhabitants who freely exercised their will to worship Him, and receive His free gift of salvation. That group, or body, is known as the universal Church, the ecclesia, the called-out ones. The vessel in which these inhabitants were initially housed, known as "the Church," was first made available to and comprised of His chosen people; the Jews. Long before the fall; long before the Tower of Babel; long before the separation of the races, based on similarity of speech; Jesus was predestined to be a Jew. The original recipients of God's extension of grace to mankind, based on mankind's need for redemption, were always going to be the descendants of Noah's son Shem. The choice of the Hebrew nation to be the progenitors of the patriarchs and the Messiah was not an after-thought of God; as He decided how to deal with what happened in the Garden of Eden. Messiah Jesus was always predestined to be of Jewish descent; a practicing Jew.

The first century New Testament Church was always predestined to be an outgrowth of Judaism. Since our God knows the end from the beginning; none of what happens in the affairs of men is a surprise to Him. We must understand that the spiritual container which God had designed to hold those who responded to His call for repentance and conversion is the place that He commissioned the Messiah to create; it is known as the Church. This spiritual container was first made available to the descendants of Abraham, Isaac, and Jacob.[19] It is the receptacle for those whom God has mercifully spared from the eternal wrath which is to come upon the inhabitants of the world; who refuse to receive God's free gift of salvation. That receptacle originated out of the Jewish people, was shared with the Gentile world, and will ultimately stand as the vessel that once again houses God's chosen people; when all of Israel shall be saved.

"And so all Israel shall be saved: as it is written: There shall come out of Sion the Deliverer, and shall turn away ungodliness from Jacob."
Romans 11:26

The Church is built upon the foundation of the apostles and prophets; Jesus Christ Himself being the Chief Cornerstone.[20] The government of the body of believers who worship

Jehovah had moved from Mt. Sinai to Mt. Zion. There had been a transition from the Old Covenant to the New Covenant. God had moved His dwelling place from the Temple in Jerusalem to bodies of men and women; their bodies had become the temple of The Holy Spirit. Even though the New Covenant supersedes the Old Covenant, it exists just as Jesus did. Messiah stated that He didn't come to do away with the Law; He came to fulfill the Law. While the New Covenant brings fullness to the Old Covenant, it does not invalidate nor disinherit the recipients of the Old Covenant. The New Covenant offers entrance to the participants of the Old Covenant, while simultaneously offering admittance to those who previously had no access to the provisions of the Old Covenant. Again, we worship the God of the Hebrews, the God of the Jews. We have accepted a Jewish Messiah, and we belong to the Messianic Jewish body of believers; known as the Church. We have been grafted into her!

What about the early Church? Let's talk about her for a moment. During her first three hundred years, she was governed by Jewish apostles. She was the object of massive persecution, and the slaughter of thousands of Christians. Perhaps even hundreds of thousands of Christians were slaughtered. The fact is that the Roman Empire, under which the Church was birthed, outlawed Christianity from 100 A.D. until 313 A.D. We don't really know what happened be-

> *"While the New Covenant brings fullness to the Old Covenant, it does not invalidate nor disinherit the recipients of the Old Covenant."*

CHAPTER TWO: WHY A REMNANT CHURCH?

tween 68 A.D. and 100 A.D. because there was no written Church history during that time period. In fact, there was no written record of the Church for the fifty years that followed Paul's death. Judaism, the Jewish faith from which the Church was born, also even participated in her early persecution. According to the Book of Acts, we do know that after Pentecost, there was major persecution of the Church by the Jews; which is evidenced by the young zealous Pharisee named Saul. We also find the first recorded martyr of the New Testament Church, Steven, coming by the hands of the original body of people, the Jews, which had produced the remnant Church of the first century. We find the earliest writing of the Church fathers around 120 A.D. So, we can see that the early Church suffered massive persecution under the Roman government, and under the religious organization known as Judaism.

The last recorded persecution of the Church by the Roman Empire happened between 303 A.D. and 310 A.D. This remnant first century New Testament Church that was birthed out of Judaism, under the watch of the Roman Empire, had persecution as a tool that helped her maintain the integrity of her membership. No one would claim membership to an organization that had the potential to be responsible for causing one to lose their life; unless they were serious about their commitment to Christ. Being a part of that first century New Testament remnant was not popular, convenient, or glamorous. It was taken very seriously, and was not considered something that was "én vogue." Membership had its privileges, but it also had its costs. The persecution that the remnant received at the hands of the

THE REMNANT CHURCH

religious body that birthed her, along with the onslaught from the secular government which kept her under thumb, served as a screening filter to help determine those who were serious about changing their lifestyle. However, all of that was about to change due to the Battle at the Stone Milvian Bridge, at the Tiber River. On October 27, 312 A.D., just outside of Rome, facing his enemy Maxentius, tradition tells us that Emperor Constantine had a vision as he was about to go into battle.

As the sun was setting, he saw a vision of a cross; with the caption of, "in this sign conquer" written above it. As a result, he fought that battle under the banner of Christianity, and won. We must note however that as he recounted the vision, the description that he gave of the cross was actually that of the Egyptian occult sign known as an ankh.[21] It was this very image that he had placed on the shields of his soldiers. After his victory, Constantine declared himself a Christian and sprinkled his troops in baptism.[22] Subsequently, Constantine made Christianity the religion of his court and encouraged his subjects to embrace it as a religion. The aristocrats and wealthy persons refused to do so, and as a result, Constantine moved his capital from Rome to Byzantium and renamed it Constantinople. This became the capital of the new Christian empire. Invariably, this led to a conflict between Rome and Constantinople for the role of the leadership of Christendom. This eventually resulted in the formation of the Eastern Orthodox Church and the Western Roman Catholic Church.

In 313 A.D. Emperor Constantine passed the now famous "Edict of Toleration" and the "Edict of Milan." In these pieces of legislation, Constantine sanctioned the practice of Christianity in the Roman Empire, made Christian worship a lawful act, and ceased all persecution of Christianity by the Roman Empire. It was this very act that represented a spiritual coup, and began the process to wrestle the leadership of Christianity from the hands of the Jewish apostles; to whom the Christ had left in charge. This was the beginning of the formalized Church of Rome. It signaled a dominance of Roman government over the affairs of the Church. This dominance lasted unopposed for twelve hundred years; until the Protestant Reformation of the 15th century. After robbing the apostolic Jewish leadership of their governance of the first century New Testament Remnant Church, the next fifteen centuries of Christianity were practiced under the auspices of some form of Roman Catholicism. To make matters worse for the spiritual remnant first century Church, some seventy years later, the Roman Emperor Theodosius mandated Christianity to be the state religion of the Roman Empire. His decree forced all Roman subjects to formally accept Christianity in order to maintain their citizenship, hold public office, and conduct business in the Roman Empire. This single act undermined the notions of voluntary repentance and conversion, conviction of sin, spiritual rebirth, and a transformed lifestyle. These things were no longer necessary to become, or live as a Christian. Theodosius also forcibly suppressed all other religions and prohibited idol worship.[23]

The first century New Testament Remnant Church had become a political organization that reflected the spirit and pattern of the Imperial Roman Empire. In order to appease some pagans who had forcibly been made to accept Christianity as the "state religion," some compromises were made. Some traditional Jewish holidays were replaced with pagan holidays; while other pagan holidays were merely thrust upon the Church. One of notable mention is Christmas. The Roman sun-worshippers celebrated the birthday of the Sun-god on December 25th. To maintain this holiday for the pagan Romans, who were forced into Christianity, the new Church headed by the Roman government substituted the celebration of Christ's birthday on this day. Another example is how Constantine officially recognized and named the weekly meeting day for the Christians "the venerable day of the sun." We now call it Sunday; this day versus the traditional days that the Jews celebrated Sabbath; being Friday evening into Saturday evening.[24]

So, what started as a pure remnant, from a tainted religion that failed to recognize her Messiah, was transformed into a deceived compromised body. There was also a major circumstance that contributed to the mutation that happened as a result of the exchange in Church leadership; from the hands of the apostles to the hands of the Roman government. You have to brace yourselves to understand the significance of what I'm about to share with you.

"In the city of Antioch, in Syria, true believers were making 'exact' copies of the original manuscripts. From Antioch the Christians sent missionaries down to Egypt to teach the people living in Alexandria; the second largest city in the world. This was located in the land of Isis (the Queen of Heaven) and Horus (the Sun god). At that time it was the seat of Baal worship. Some of the world's greatest minds were living in Alexandria. These men were proud

of their great wisdom. They called themselves 'Gnostics.' [25] *These Gnostics formed a school of religion and philosophy; that became the 'Center of Christian Learning and Culture."*

However, they didn't believe in a real heaven or hell. When they got hold of the Bible manuscripts they started making changes. A great student, Origen, became head of this school. He didn't believe that Jesus was God Almighty, so he and others chopped I John 5:7 out of the scriptures. He was an Arian, he believed Jesus was a lesser God. He was mightily used by satan to corrupt Bible manuscripts.[26]

Constantine, who still secretly worshipped the sun god, ordered a man named Eusebius (the Bishop of Caesarea) to make him fifty Bibles. Eusebius had a choice of using the Greek manuscripts from Alexandria or from Antioch; to make up his fifty Greek Bibles. Since Eusebius believed the same way Origen did, he did not use the manuscripts from Antioch. Rather, he used the corrupted manuscripts from Egypt to make his Bibles for the Roman Catholic Church.[27] The Latin Vulgate Bible, written by Jerome, (Bible for the Roman Catholic Church) came out of the fifty Bibles made up by Eusebius. This became the official Bible for all Roman Catholics; all others were outlawed.[28] This is a sad commentary on the history of the first century New Testament Remnant Church transition into Roman Catholicism.

Another great change that affected the compromised, deceived Church that came out of the apostolically governed first century New Testament Remnant Church is mind boggling. The pagans were allowed to bring their statues and idols of Semiramis (the Queen of Heaven) and Nimrod (Baal, the Sun god) into the Church. The names were changed to the Virgin Mary, Queen of Heaven, and little baby Jesus. Baal worship, started by Semiramis and her husband-son Nimrod had successfully moved into the Roman Catholic institution. An interesting note is that by 1950, the Roman Catholic Church had raised the Virgin Mary to a goddess with the power to be co-savior and co-redeemer with Christ; exactly like Semiramis. The Doctrine of the Immaculate Conception says Mary was born without original sin—1854; The Dogma of the Assumption of Mary into heaven means she never died—1950.[29]

The Bible clearly forbids the worship of the Queen of Heaven in the seventh and 44th chapters of Jeremiah. Just for clarity's sake, we need to take a closer look at the origin of Baal worship. Another sad commentary is what happened to the 15th century New Testament Remnant Church, which was formed as a result of the Protestant Reformation. She also became a deceived compromised body; necessitating the emergence of an end-times Remnant Church.

We now stand at that precipice; poised and ready for the remnant to stand up and be counted. We will examine the transition of the apostolically governed first century New Testament Remnant Church to the Roman governed third century Church. We will then follow her descent and subsequent ascent from the fifteenth century Church. We ultimately will look at her progression to the end-times Remnant Church. As we follow her journey, we will simultaneously examine the nation of Israel, and the impact she has had on the world. With great detail, we will examine the relationship between the Remnant Church and the nation of Israel.

Paul makes mention of the concept of the "remnant" to the New Testament Church.[30] However, we are mindful that when he did, he was speaking of covenant promises made to ethnic Jews.

"I say the truth in Christ, I lie not, my conscience also, bearing me witness in the Holy Ghost, That I have great heaviness and continual sorrow in my heart. For I could wish that myself were accursed from Christ for my brethren, my kinsmen according to the flesh: Who are Israelites; to whom pertaineth the adoption, and the glory, and the covenants, and the giving of the law, and the service of God, and the promises; Whose are the fathers, and of whom as concerning the flesh Christ came, who is over all, God blessed forever. Amen." Romans 9:1-5

He quotes Isaiah as an assurance to the Christian community living in Rome.[31] He reminds them that Yahweh's covenant promise is yet extended to His chosen people, the Jews.[32] Even though the Jews had refused to accept their Messiah, Jesus of Nazareth, God still had intentions on making salvation, deliverance from the works of the devil, available to the nation of Israel.[33]

As we look all around us, we see Jews everywhere. Orthodox Jews, Hassidic Jews, Reformed Jews, Conservative Jews, Messianic Jews; there are all kinds of Jews everywhere. They yet remain God's chosen people. Contrary to that false teaching of "Replacement Theology," God did not replace His

THE REMNANT CHURCH

> *"Contrary to that false teaching of 'Replacement Theology,' God did not replace His covenant choice of the Jews with the Church."*

covenant choice of the Jews with the Church. While the Church may "represent spiritual Israel," God's intention yet remains to honor the covenant He made with the Jewish nation. The Church is merely a branch. She did not replace the root; she was grafted into the root. God will use the Gentile branch to make the Jewish root jealous enough to lay claim on the free gift that was originally intended for the descendants of Abraham, Isaact, and Jacob.[34] [35]

Eventually, the Jews will realize what they have forfeited and come running to the feet of the Master; begging to be embraced and received by The Beloved.[36] Paul, who had formerly been a chief persecutor of the Church, was reminding the saints in Rome that even though there was concern about the fate of the Jewish nation, and their decision not to receive Jesus of Nazareth as the Messiah; there was still a reason to hope for salvation. The idea that there would be a portion of those chosen people who would still be redeemed in spite of the nation's rejection of Christ, was directly associated with the idea of there being a remnant.

In a time when the majority of the Jews had actively and consciously decided to refuse acceptance of Jehovah's answer to the problem of the "sin nature," there was still a remnant according to God's grace. This remnant represented an assurance that God will always leave Himself a "witness." He will always allow a portion to remain who will reflect His nature and purpose. God elects a group to represent Him in accordance to their possession of the holiness and integrity necessary to influence non-believers to accept the free gift of salvation; in all of its fullness and with all of its benefits. God will always have a group that will not bow to the pressure of the world to have the Church conform to "worldly mores and values." There will always be a remnant that will maintain the faith handed down to us by the saints, and not succumb to the deceptive devices of satan.

There will always be a group of "leftovers" who will not bow their knee to Baal. This just serves as another example to illustrate for us that although the Church is the recipient of some of the covenant promises God makes in His Word; she is only a recipient because of her relationship with the Jews. It is only because the Church has been made members of the commonwealth of Israel that she can boast of inclusion into these provisions of grace. Despite the winds of change that blow upon the ecclesia, there will always be a remnant that stays the course, and remains true to the model that was left in the earth by the Christ, and His chosen leadership.

Why the concept of a Remnant Church? I am painfully aware that the concept of the "remnant church" does not appear verbatim, as written script in the Holy Bible. However the "idea" of the remnant church is present in numerous places in the Word of God. Although this concept is not included in the dogma of major denominations and non-denominational organizations, the reality of it cannot be understated. As a result of the prevailing escapist mentality in the Body of Christ, the

THE REMNANT CHURCH

idea of a remnant church is not a popular notion, nor a major teaching. In fact, this idea is rarely presented, if at all, because it intimates that the Church will be in the earth after the great tribulation has taken place. This idea is definitely taboo among most conservative and evangelical Christians. The reality is that most church bodies teach that the saints will be raptured before the great tribulation, or at best, in the middle of it. The concept of the remnant church is actually an affront to most Christians, due to the fact that it contradicts the message being propagated by the popular "Left Behind" series.

However the fact remains that the idea of a remnant Church can be seen throughout the Bible. While it can be argued that the Old Testament references to "the remnant" are a direct reference to the nation of Israel, we must deal with the mention of that idea in the New Testament.[37] Additionally, attention must be given to the reality that the first century New Testament Church also symbolically represents spiritual Israel, and in and of itself can be considered a remnant. It is the remainder or leftover part of the original descendants of Abraham, who were looking for the advent of the Messiah. This is the piece that continued in the hope of His coming, and actually received the fact that He had come. So, the concept of the remnant, a smaller portion left behind after the larger portion has been removed, definitely applies to the first century New Testament Church.

After the prominence was removed from Judaism and shifted to Christianity, that new group could properly be referred to as a remnant. Although this group was the original "Church," they were still only what resulted once a portion was subtracted

CHAPTER TWO: WHY A REMNANT CHURCH?

and separated out of the larger body; known as followers of Judaism. This body was comprised of ethnic and non-ethnic Jews.

Although primarily composed of Jewish believers, the number of Gentiles who practiced Judaism, which were added to the Church on the Day of Pentecost, cannot be overlooked. We must remember that the initial group of believers who responded to the gospel message on the Day of Pentecost was ethnic Jews, and non-ethnic persons who practiced Judaism. I believe that the contemporary Body of Christ has severely missed the fact that the majority of the Holy Scriptures were primarily written by Jews for Jews. We often lose sight of the fact that we actually worship Yahweh, the God of the Hebrews, or Jews, and that our Savior is the Jewish Messiah; Yeshua Ha'Mashiach.

Therefore, as we begin our discussion of the Remnant Church, we must start from the perspective of that Church being intrinsically related to the people of Israel. To explore the concept of a remnant, as it pertains to the first century New Testament Remnant Church and the modern-day conformist-Church, one must acknowledge her inherent Jewish foundation. There is an inescapable attachment of the Church to Israel. To attempt to ignore this is ludicrous. Too often, the modern-day Church has been guilty of not acknowledging that she worships the God of the Hebrews; the God of the Jews. In times past, she has sometimes tried to act like Christianity has an access to God that precludes in association with Israel. Sometimes she forgot that without the nation of Israel, and God's attachment to her, the Gentile Church would be non-existent. She has been guilty of trying to disassociate her future from the destiny of Israel. She has tried to interpret apocalyptic prophetic scriptures without having the Jewish nation as the central focus of those prophecies. Thanks be to God that He is currently, actively correcting that erroneous presumption on the part of the modern-day Church. He is making it abundantly clear, on many different platforms, that His plan for the end of the age and the Church, cannot come to pass without Israel playing a major part in it.

In times past, many people and ethnic groups have viewed the Jews as enemies of humanity; greedy, selfish, and self-promoting. Anti-Semitism would attempt to have us believe the blessing that is upon these chosen people as something they themselves control. The Jews are the recipients of the blessing of Jehovah, and will always be the recipient of that blessing. Just as the descendants of Ishmael (the Arabs), Abraham's first born[38] received the inheritance and blessing of the first born, and in spite of their religious error are still a blessed people.[39] Even so, the Jews, in spite of rejecting their Messiah, are still a blessed people. The Church has been fortunate enough to have been grafted into her, and now receives the same covenant blessings and promises reserved for the "seed" of Abraham.[40] Now that she is composed of persons of faith, the Church is also the "seed" of Abraham.[41]

One cannot speak of the New Testament Church without intentionally correlating her to the root from which she springs, Israel; the Jewish nation. It is impossible to examine eschatological truths without admitting the fundamental Hebrew composition of the Prophets, Apostles, supporting cast, and central figure of this great ensemble of characters. In its birth, as the first century Church moved out of Judaism, Jehovah was leading her from the bondage of the Law into the liberty of the Spirit. As I heard Bishop William L. Washington, say in 2000, "Just because you are free doesn't mean you have to be loose." Although the Law bound those Jewish believers, it also kept them until the Messiah was manifested, and could endow them with the power of The Holy Spirit. It is the power of the Holy Ghost that provides the means for living within the context of the Kingdom of God. The Law was intended to point the Jews to the Messiah, while simultaneously showing them that they did not have what it took to observe all 613 statutes of the Law, the Mitzvot. As the early New Testament Church emerged from Judaism, she was to be faced with many perilous times.

However, the most perilous time she was about to face was not the long period of persecution. It was the "looseness" she was about to experience as she grew and matured. Quite to the contrary of the persecution she had suffered, it was her acceptance as the state religion of Rome that would prove to be her most perilous time. Her being blended into a system full of sun-worshippers would thrust her headlong into a period of deception and compromise. Throughout the history of Israel, there has always been a remnant. From Genesis through the Revelation of Jesus Christ, given to John the beloved disciple, the concept of the remnant has always been present. It has stood as a monument and memorial to commemorate the fact that there has always been a group that has either gone on to a different place; or has been left behind in the same old place. *There has always been a deposit in the earth that was representative of the pure purpose of God. He has always made sure that there would be a smaller part left after the larger part was gone. His plan and purpose insured that the smaller part would still have the power and capacity to fulfill the mission that had been assigned to the larger part.*

In the Old Testament the "remnant" represented God's chosen people, the Jews. Abraham and his descendants were the smaller group that remained after God separated the human race at the Tower of Babel. As mankind built a tower into the heavens, to escape another flooding of the earth should God have decided to send one, they began to try to govern in an area where God had not given them jurisdiction. The command to Adam was, *"be fruitful, multiply, replenish the earth, subdue it, and have dominion over it."*[42] Nowhere in that command is there any mention of having dominion over the heavens. They were seeking to establish themselves in an area that was reserved for spiritual dominance. So, out of the whole of all the inhabitants on the earth at that time, God separated one man, and gave that man exclusive access to Himself.

Prior to the Tower of Babel, the whole of creation had access to Jehovah. He had made Himself available to anyone who would seek him. He was an all-inclusive God; no particular group of people could claim sole ownership or access to Him. He was a God of everyone, and for everyone. After the Tower of Babel, Jehovah became the God of the Hebrews. After He confused the languages, He separated Himself a remnant out of that mass of confusion, Abram, and made Himself exclusively available to Abram and his descendants. That remnant became the portion of creation that would be responsible for nurturing a relationship with the living God, and housing the bloodline that

CHAPTER TWO: WHY A REMNANT CHURCH?

would bring forth the Savior for the whole world. That small group of people would ultimately be responsible for saving the whole of creation. That remnant would maintain a right relationship with God, while the rest of the world would fall victim to the god of this world; who deceived its inhabitants with the "I, Me, My Syndrome." Israel would be the remnant that would not conform or be seduced into the deceptive ways of "the kingdom of self;" invariably known as the kingdom of darkness.

In the New Testament the "remnant" represented God's chosen people, comprised of the Jewish and Gentile (non-Jewish) believers who have accepted Jehovah's Messiah, Jesus of Nazareth, as the Christ of God. It is interesting to note, and one should pay close attention to the fact that I am always referring to the remnant as, "God's chosen people." We must be mindful of the fact that remnant always exists by election or selection. The remnant does not "will" itself into existence, but rather exists at the pleasure and by the will of the Father. The Remnant Church does not accidentally come forth, trip into purpose, or stumble into destiny. The Remnant Church is a deliberate, ordained, selected group of people. They have a pre-ordained purpose, a pre-planned course of action, and a predestined destination. They exist as an extension of God's continual plan to perfect the Church, and insure that she lives up to His original purpose for her. God has always been in search of a people who would voluntarily serve Him, obey His command, and seek to do His will. He has always been pursuing the remnant; a people with a passion for serving God's agenda.

So, after God demonstrated to man that mankind was

incapable of maintaining innocence, living by conscience, being constrained by human government, or keeping the law; He had to make another intervention. He had to initiate a time of grace, where He would extend mercy to sinful man; by the sacrifice of His dear son, Jesus of Nazareth. Virgin born Jesus, who fulfilled prophecy, lived a sinless life, died a substitutionary death, was raised from the dead after three days, and now calls men everywhere to repent.

> *"In the New Testament the 'remnant' represented God's chosen people, comprised of the Jewish and Gentile (non-Jewish) believers who have accepted Jehovah's Messiah, Jesus of Nazareth, as the Christ of God."*

When the ethnic Jews and the non-ethnic Jews who practiced Judaism realized that they could not keep the Law as a means of maintaining relationship with Jehovah; they submitted to God's plan for them to become a remnant. As they received the message of salvation on the Day of Pentecost, and responded with a repentant acceptance of the Messiah, a remnant was birthed. The first century New Testament Remnant Church, those Jewish Disciples of Christ and the three thousand added on the Day of Pentecost, emerged out of the exclusive religion of Judaism, and the Creator was once again inclusively available to all of creation.

Whether Old Covenant or New Covenant, there has always been a remnant associated with the Hebrew people, and there will always be a remnant associated with the Jewish nation. The idea of a remnant is necessary as a way of God preserving the purity of His intentions, and the accomplishment of His purpose. Despite the constant attempts, and success, of the enemy to pollute what God has intended to be a reflection of His holiness; there will always be a portion of the original group that refuses to bow down, refuses to compromise, and refuses to accept the deception, the remnant. Throughout the history of God dealing with His people, He has always made provision for an elected portion of the whole to remain true to the call, true to the vision, true to the mission of accomplishing His purpose, the remnant. In His foreknowledge, God is acutely aware of the fact that leaven will seep in to try to sidetrack His purpose, defeat His ultimate strategy of redeeming the world to Himself, and perpetrate the deception of satan upon the creation. Jehovah selects a people, and makes the option of non-compromise available to them. Some choose that option, while others choose the compromise. In any event, there is always a group that will stay on task; a group that will not give in; a group that will stay the course, the remnant.

God's Word, which proceeds out of His mouth, will not return unto Him void. It will prosper, and accomplish the purpose whereunto it has been sent. In order for this foundational truth to remain constant, there must be a way to circumvent the enemy's attack on this vital truth. This truth is central to the Christian's ability to take God at His Word. It is at the core of the believer's ability to have unconditional confidence and trust in the Word they have heard from God; which is what faith is. It is the essential component, and platform, upon which the Church is built; for if the Word of God is not able to perform what He promises; then God is a liar, and cannot be trusted. In order to safeguard His Word, and guarantee the manifestation of everything He has spoken, God has put a stop-gap in place. There is an instrument that will insure the fulfillment of His Word, His intentions, and His purpose, the remnant.

God is a covenant giving God, and a covenant keeping God. Covenant is the context in which God has extended relationship to His people. Blood covenant, in particular, is the mandatory context in which man must relate to his God, Jehovah, the Ancient of Days, the Great I Am; the God of the Hebrews. It is the thing that made Able's sacrifice superior to Cain's; sacrifice; it is what made Able's sacrifice acceptable. It is steeped in the notion of obedience. Without the shedding of blood, there is no forgiveness of sin.[43] Blood covenant is a mutual and binding agreement between two or more parties, and is made at the incision where the blood flows. It reflects the nature of our relationship with the Creator, and is overshadowed with the concept of reciprocity. There are certain provisions that must be kept, certain terms of covenant that must be maintained in order for the Church to receive what God has promised her. Some of the promises of God are unconditional, other sare definitely conditional. We call these "conditional promises" "terms of covenant." God has positioned the provision of "the remnant" in place to insure that the terms of covenant are kept, thereby providing Him the ability to keep His Word, and bring to fruition the promises He has made to His people.

God honors His Word above His name, He will go to great lengths to make sure that His Word is kept, and His prom-

CHAPTER TWO: WHY A REMNANT CHURCH?

ises are delivered.

"I will worship toward thy holy temple, and praise thy name for thy loving-kindness and for thy truth; for thou hast magnified thy word above all thy name" Psalm 138:2

The Remnant Church is a means of God ensuring that the purity of His intentions and Word are actualized. So, throughout the Old and New Covenants He has made sure that there was, and will be, a remnant to remain true to the expressed purpose that has proceeded out of His heart, mouth, and mind. Therefore, in the Old and New Testaments of the Bible, you will always find the concept of "the remnant."

Since the Old Covenant is the covenant that God made with Abram and his descendants; it is God's covenant with the Hebrew, or Jewish nation. Since the New Covenant is the covenant God made with those who accepted the Messiah sent to the Jews; it is God's covenant with the Messianic Hebrew or Jewish nation, and all that have been grafted into her; the Gentile Church, the "seed" of Abraham.[44] The question is not so much whether we recognize, or accept, the impending existence of The Remnant Church, as much as it is do we recognize the significance of The Remnant Church.

Whether or not we recognize the existence of this Church does not invalidate her being; or discourage God from causing her to emerge. God will not allow anything or anyone to prevent His purpose from being accomplished. He will be undaunted by the world's refusal to recognize the provision He has established; to allow all of His prophetic Word to be fulfilled. He is impervious to our unbelief; or lack of acceptance of the notion of a Remnant Church. He understands that there must be a body of believers in place, who are not influenced by this world system; a group of people who will not buy into the compromise. He knows that if there is to be a group of believers who are not deceived by the enemy's allurement to be socially and politically correct; there has to be a Remnant Church. There has to be a Church that will maintain the principles of, "touch not the unclean thing..., come out from among her, and be ye separate..." Even though as a "labeled" entity, she may not appear in Scripture; as a concept, she is clearly visible, and has never been hidden. He also knows that the emergence of the Remnant Church is paramount to dispelling the idea that He is okay with compromise, and is in agreement with a Church that will not stand her ground on the extreme issues. He has no pleasure in a Church that is looking to establish herself in the middle of the controversial issues; a Church that would rather be non-offensive than be one which causes polarization.[45]

As was stated previously, there are a couple concepts that are not literally mentioned in the Scriptures, yet they are fundamental truths upon which many people's faith is built. If you look for these words in the Bible, you will not find them. Yet the reality of what they represent is inescapable, and is a much valued tenet in the Christian belief system of many people. Words such as rapture and trinity cannot be found on the written page, but are concepts printed in the hearts and minds of many believers. Additionally, they are concepts clearly defined, and represented on the written pages of the Bible. So too is the concept of The

CHAPTER TWO: WHY A REMNANT CHURCH?

Remnant Church. It is much like the example that Jesus used with Nicodemus; as He explained the wind.

"The wind bloweth where it listeth, and thou heareth the sound thereof, and cannot tell whence it cometh, and whither it goest: so is everyone who is born of the Spirit."
John. 3:8

While you cannot literally see the wind, its affects are unmistakable. So, it is with the Remnant Church, even though we don't see her literally mentioned on the written page; her impending emergence and cataclysmic impact are undeniable. God doesn't break His pattern; He changes not. He will always allow that portion to remain, which will accomplish His purpose.

What is the significance of the Remnant Church?

What is her importance, meaning, and worth?

What is the implication of having a Remnant Church in the earth?

What is the consequence and impact of having this body of believers around the world?

If we compare this end-times Remnant Church to the first century New Testament Remnant Church, the significance is earth changing, and has implications that will disrupt life in the highest places of government. If the end-times Remnant Church is a time-span parallel of her former self, then the world needs to be prepared to be turned upside down. As it was in the beginning, so shall it be at the end. It is safe to say that the latter shall be greater than the former.[46]

THE REMNANT CHURCH

There are some Scriptures that are specifically written to ethnic Jewish people. There is no way that we can dispute this fact. The thing we need to begin to understand is that as the Church, we have been grafted into that primarily Jewish body. How dare we forget that the majority of the crowd who heard the Pentecost message was Jewish? The Church started with the Jews, and will end with the Jews. The time is fast approaching when all of Israel will be saved. Their blessings are our blessings; their curses are our curses. We have become a part of them; in totality. Our destiny is linked to them; so that wherever they go, so goes the Church. We are simply amazed that theologians want to separate the prophetic promises made to Israel from the prophetic promises made to the Church. The Church has no promises save the ones that are associated with Israel. The Church can ill-afford to let Replacement Theology cause her to think that there is one set of promises for Jews, and another set of promises for Gentiles. There are only promises for believers and promises for non-believers. Promises for the faithful, (Abraham's seed) and promises for the faithless. There are provisions for the Body of Christ, which is one body, and lack of provision for those belonging to the kingdom of darkness. There is neither Jew nor Gentile, bond nor free, male nor female; all are one in Christ Jesus.

> *"Words such as rapture and trinity cannot be found on the written page, but are concepts printed in the hearts and minds of many believers."*

CHAPTER TWO: WHY A REMNANT CHURCH?

"There is neither Jew nor Greek, there is neither bond or free, there is neither male or female: for ye all are one in Christ Jesus."
Galatians 3:28

We must bear in mind the simple fact that the end-times Remnant Church, which reflects the power, authority, and nature of her first century counterpart, will be the vehicle that sparks Israel to jealousy. She will be the vessel that reminds the Jews that salvation was to the Jew first, and then to the Gentiles. ⁴⁷The Remnant Church will provide the spark that causes the light to come on for the nation of Israel. She will be the catalyst that prompts the Jews to finally understand that Christianity is the grown up child of Judaism. Israel will ultimately accept that Christianity is the result of the whole world recognizing Jehovah, the God of the Hebrews, as the one and only true living God. They will be prompted by the end-times Remnant Church to finally see that Jesus of Nazareth, whom they crucified, is in fact the Jewish Messiah that the nation of Israel was waiting for. The Remnant Church will be responsible for ushering in the great end-time harvest of Jewish converts to Christ. This cataclysmic event alone will change the course of human history. Our finite mind cannot begin to fathom the impact this change of religious position will have upon human government. The ripple effect that this will have on the course of mankind is mind-boggling. The world will truly be turned upside down; just as it was in the days of the first century Church. There will be major re-alignments of world governments. The Islamic holy jihad will have new fuel for its fire. The hatred of the alliance between the

United States and Israel will heighten to levels not even imaginable. The stage will be set for the greatest war of all times. The appearance of The Remnant Church will also signal a drastic intensification in the level of spiritual warfare conducted by the Body of Christ.

The compromised, deceived, conformist-Church will no longer be in a position of power to block the move of the Holy Ghost in the earthly body of believers; those empowered to be God's delegated authority and designated representative in the earth. The remnant will be an agent in the earth duly authorized to do battle against the kingdom of darkness, and intent on doing just that. A cadre of Servant Warriors dedicated to function in the same manner as their Commander in Chief, Jesus; the author and finisher of our faith.

"Looking unto Jesus the author and finisher of our faith; who for the joy that was set before Him endured the cross, despising the shame, and is set down at the right hand of the throne of God." Hebrews 12:2

An army of believers equipped to wage war against the darkness; with a sworn commitment to destroy the works of the enemy.

"He that commiteth sin is of the devil; for the devil sinneth from the beginning. For this purpose the son of God was manifested, that He might destroy the works of the devil."
I John 3:8

CHAPTER TWO: WHY A REMNANT CHURCH?

The emergence of the end-times Remnant Church represents a return to the fiery vigor and vitality that was present as the Holy Spirit of God made Himself available to dwell in the physical earthen bodies of as many as would receive Him. She represents a well-oiled, fighting machine, with a single driven focus to wreak havoc upon her archenemy; satan, the imps of hell, and the kingdom of darkness.

The word remnant is also usually associated with the idea of a portion that is left over. We commonly label "leftovers" as things that are not as good as the principals that served as their original source. They are typically seen with a negative connotation. Leftovers are commonly viewed as something less desirable than the main course; from which they are the remainder. They are usually served in an attempt to clean out the refrigerator, or rid the shelves of excess; in preparation to receive a new shipment. They are often sold at a discount price, due to their lack of size or perceived inability to fill a significant space in a large room. It signifies something that remains after the rest of the whole has been depleted, exhausted or otherwise used up. In other words, remnants are perceived as that which remains after the best part has been utilized, and the finest resources have been drawn upon. Stated another way, the remnant is construed to be that which is left over when the preeminent assets have been brought into play, and applied to the situation. It has inherent in its definition, the idea of not being complete; or in some way being deficient. Leftovers are deemed not to be complete, full, or comprehensive. They are usually associated with not being ample. Likewise, the remnant is all too often perceived as being scarce, lacking, underprovided, undersupplied, and wanting. It is not typically related to the notion of completeness, nor is it normally perceived as a positive attribute.

None of the worldly attributes mentioned above apply to the remnant of our discussion. The Remnant Church that emerges at the end of the age is the antithesis of all the things alluded to in our discussion of "leftovers." In fact, the remnant is the exact opposite of these things, and stands in direct contrast to the images envisioned when we speak of leftovers. She represents the preeminent resources; this is why she has been called forth. She has what the compromised, deceived, conformist-Church is lacking. The Remnant Church has the provision. She has the supply, and an abundance of it. She is complete, and full of the power of God. She is totally comprehensive, and capable of fulfilling the divine purpose for which the Church was established. She IS the best part of the Church, and is the finest resource that God has to offer this sin-sick generation. The remnant is ample; as a matter of fact she is more than enough. If enough is that which satisfies, she is more than satisfaction; she is fulfillment. The Remnant Church is not lacking in size, or ability to fill the void that has been created by the deceived, conformist-Church. The remnant is abounding in the flavor of God, and has the ability to preserve the world in the midst of the onslaught of evil; that will be experienced as this present darkness intensifies.

As we explore the remnant in the Old Testament, we do it from the perspective of understanding that the remnant is the part of something that is left when other parts are gone. It is

CHAPTER TWO: WHY A REMNANT CHURCH?

something smaller being used to fulfil that which the larger part failed to accomplish. It reinforces the idea that something which is void of its other parts, parts which appeared to be necessary, is still able to function in the purpose and role for which it was created, and intended to be used.

If we start with the lineage of the children of Adam and Eve, we can see the principle of the remnant in operation. We find a situation that begins with an account of all of Adam and Eve's children; even though there were only two initially listed. After the death of Able, we are informed of the other descendants of this couple; however, only the descendants of Seth receive a detailed accounting and description throughout the rest of the Scriptures. Once again, we note the operation of the remnant in place. Although Adam lived to be nine hundred and thirty years old, and had numerous descendants, the Bible only deals with the remnant of Seth's lineage; those who had been elected to be the bloodline through which Messiah Jesus would be born.[48]

Look again and you will see the concept of the remnant in the account of Noah and the flood.[49] It is painstakingly obvious that this man and his family were separated from the entire human race, and chosen to be the means by which Jehovah would repopulate the earth after He totally destroyed it. What a heavy responsibility was on Noah and his family. They were tasked with the regeneration of the entire world. Theirs was the responsibility to restore and rejuvenate a planet that had experienced a death sentence more severe than the one which was imposed on Pharaoh and the Egyptians. It was an angel of death sent to the first born that would influence the Egyptians to release God's

THE REMNANT CHURCH

chosen people from the bondage of slavery; in their land of captivity.[50] Yet, Jehovah believed that Noah and his family, the remnant, had the desirable quality it would take to bring life out of the devastation of the death of the entire human race caused by the great flood.

The nation of Israel was continually finding herself in a position where she was in some way operating in the role of a remnant. She was notorious for experiencing the pruning process of God. Let us begin with the call of faithful Abram. We will notice a pattern prevalent in earlier encounters of mankind with his Creator; which we will take a closer examination of its continued use. Abram was called out from among the totality of the then known world, separated from known civilization, and asked to do the unthinkable. He was asked to leave his familiar surroundings, go to an unknown place, to serve an angry God who had just thrown the whole of humanity into a tailspin. He was singled out, removed from a place of safety, and cast into a journey with an unknown destination, with only the promise of greatness; from a God who had just exacted a horrific judgment on His disobedient creation. Do you think that Abram was going to tell Him no? He was being asked to do what the whole of humanity had just failed to do; obediently serve God, and govern in the sphere where they were designated to have authority. He was being asked to accomplish this without the support systems he was accustomed to, and he was expected to succeed in doing so.

As we look at the concept of The Remnant Church, we must do so with the realization that it is a deliberate function that God allows; so that His purpose can be accomplished. In the world of the Spirit, there is no such thing as an accidental remnant. The remnant is intentionally elected by God to fulfill what the group, out of which it has been extracted, could not fulfill. When we study the situation surrounding Isaac and Ishmael, we see another example of parts not destroyed or used up. These boys were chosen to stay in place and be unchanged; even though their parents got in the way and tried to help God out. Abraham and Sarah mistakenly thought that God needed their assistance to fulfill His prophetic promise concerning them. Yet in spite of their mistake, God chose to bless both sons with descendants who would frame the course of world history; then and now. Ishmael's twelve sons would go on to produce the Arab nations; which certainly have impacted world events. While the descendants of Isaac, the child of promise, would produce the twelve tribes of Israel; who also have certainly impacted world history. Neither of these world changers have been able to be destroyed or used; even though there have been multiple attempts against each group to do exactly that. They remain the remnant elected by grace and mercy.

Jacob and Esau also represent the concept of the remnant. What we see is the one to whom the prophetic promise was spoken having to separate himself from the larger group in order to function in the role and capacity that had been reserved for him. He had to go away from his familiar surroundings to find the women who would bear his seed. The way God chose to make Jacob great necessitated him being separated from his larger group; in order to have a wilderness experience. He had to be separated so that he could be touched by an angel, and subsequently have that life-changing experience that would cause a nation to be birthed.

An exemplary example of the remnant can be found in the separation of Joseph from his brothers. In order to save the tribe of Judah, which would be the channel through which the Father would send the Messiah, Joseph had to be separated from the sons of Jacob. In order for the covenant promises made to Abraham to come to fruition, Joseph had to be positioned so that he could be the savior of his father's seed. He had to become a remnant. Yet, the deposit made by his father sustained him as he journeyed from Potiphar's house, to the prison, on his way to the throne room, and being the most influential man in Egypt. During a time of crisis, God will always raise crisis leaders. Those leaders aren't just instantaneously made. They are formed in the cauldron of trials, tribulations, and hardship. Joseph had to survive his intended destruction in order to continue to operate in the purpose for which he was created. He had to abide, and wait for the coming change in the world economy; which the Lord revealed to him as he interpreted Pharaoh's dreams.[51]

Although it may be a little hard to conceptualize at first, the group of African Edenic Hebrews that left Egypt in the "Exodus" can be considered to be a remnant. We must acknowledge that when Jehovah extracted the Hebrews out of Egypt, they had been inhabitants of that land for over four hundred years.[52] That time period is longer than the United States is old. The Hebrews had been assimilated into Egyptian society. They were a part of the patchwork of peoples that made up that nation. Please

CHAPTER TWO: WHY A REMNANT CHURCH?

remember that the world flocked to Egypt to benefit from the wisdom and anointing of the one who had been put in charge of the world's most abundant storehouse; during the time of the world's worst famine & drought of that time; that remnant was Joseph. These Hebrews were an integral part of Egyptian society and had, over the course of their stay, inter-married with the peoples of that land. They were definitely a part of the whole population of Egypt; even though they had their own living quarters. So, when God sent the death angel to kill the first born of the land, they were the leftovers that were spared that tragedy. They were the remnant that escaped God's judgment on that land, and subsequently escaped that nation and its slave masters.[53]

There was also a remnant in place as a result of the separation God allowed in the wilderness as He split the Jewish camp with venomous vipers. As God viewed the African-Edenic group of people that had come out of Egypt; that mixture of those two million plus Hebrew-Egyptian people, He saw the need for a remnant. He observed the compromise and division that crept into the camp of those people. They were recipients of His divine deliverance and miraculous support in the wilderness. He recognized the necessity of separating a group from the whole; a remnant that would remain true to their God, and the integrity of their call. As He observed the backbiting and dissent, He understood the need to call forth a group that would honor His intentions and submit to His purpose; so He allowed a division to be made by poisonous vipers. What was left over, that which remained, was allowed to be positioned to enter the Promised Land. They were allowed the opportunity to receive the inheritance. When the Father sees mess and compromise that brings shame to His name, He orchestrates the circumstances that will cause a separation to take place. He brings the sword of division, to make a distinction between that which represents His purposes, and that which does not. He extracts out of the chaos and confusion, the remnant that will exemplify order, and submission to His divine will.

> *"When the Father sees mess and compromise that brings shame to His name, He orchestrates the circumstances that will cause a separation to take place."*

The separation of the Hebrew nation into the two kingdoms of Israel and Judah is another example of the concept of the remnant in the Old Testament. We find it interesting to note that while it was the sin of the descendants of David that created the need for a remnant, and caused the separation of the kingdoms, the seed of David was also the beneficiary of the separation. King Solomon disobeyed the Lord's command and intermarried with the women of the surrounding nations.[54] God had specifically forbidden the Israelites to participate in this practice; God knew the influence women have over men. Hmmmm, Garden of Eden; maybe? God knew that the women of these nations would be able to influence the Hebrews to serve the foreign gods of those nations. He was trying to keep the Jews from participating in the idolatry they had practiced in the wilderness. This was the act that had previously caused Him to divide the camp. Solomon did not heed the warning, and as a result the Hebrew nation was divided into two kingdoms; the northern kingdom of ten tribes (Israel) and the southern kingdom of two tribes (Judah).[55]

CHAPTER TWO: WHY A REMNANT CHURCH?

Although Solomon had broken covenant, God did not exact the punishment on him, but rather on his son. It is of particular interest to note the fact that God was able to still use the tainted leftover to accomplish His purpose. Although it was the seed of David that created the need for a remnant to emerge, it was through that tainted leftover that the Messiah came.

What we observe is the heavenly Father making an adjustment to the order He had placed in the Hebrew nation. As we study the God instituted priesthood, we find that it was reserved for the tribe of Levi. The Aaronic priesthood was comprised of members of the tribe of Levi.

"And take thou unto thee Aaron thy brother, and his sons with him, from among the children of Israel, that he may minister unto me in the priest's office, even Aaron, Nadab, Abihu, Eleazar, and Ithamar, Aaron's sons. And thou shall make holy garments for Aaron thy brother for glory and beauty."
Exodus 28:1-2

Yet, our Great High Priest did not come from the lineage of Levi. He was referred to as a priest after the order of Melchizedek. Jesus came from the tribe of Judah,[56] and represented a divine shift in how God was now giving man access to Himself in Christ. No longer would men have to go through an earthly mediator to reach, and have relationship, with their Creator. Instead, now mankind could go to God for themselves; through the broken body and shed blood of Jesus, the Christ of God. In His foreknowledge, God knew that Jeroboam would succumb to idol worship and lead the northern kingdom of Israel into mass idolatry.

> *"Whereupon the king took counsel, and made two calves of gold, and said unto them, It is too much for you to go up to Jerusalem; behold thy gods O Israel, which brought thee up out of the land of Egypt. And he set one in Bethel and the other one put he in Dan."*
> *I Kings 12:28-29*

The Father also knew that the kings of Judah would eventually repent;[57] and thereby position that kingdom to fulfill her destiny, and birth the Savior who would take away the "sin" of the world. In what appeared to be a loss of integrity, God had a way of reversing the seemingly obvious outcome, and getting victorious glory out of the situation. God was able to salvage the destiny of the Jewish nation which had been polluted by the consequences which idolatry caused her to experience. He was able to prompt, among His chosen people, the repentance necessary to allow the much needed divine virtue to be deposited into that polluted remnant. This deposit of divine virtue established that polluted remnant as being fit to birth and house Messiah Jesus.

If Israel did not have the hope of there being a remnant, they not only would have despaired, but they would have thought Jehovah to be a liar and a covenant breaker. They would have never returned to serving Him. If the Jews could not see a remnant in their future, they would have never even tried to repent, and keep the Law as a means of maintaining relationship with God. If the Hebrews could not hold on to the promises made to father Abraham, as still being available to them if they would repent and return to the Ancient of Days, they would have kept worshipping the false gods of the Gentile nations surrounding them. They would not have been able to have the proper relational posture to receive the benefits of the covenant relationship God had extended to them. The whole notion that God would still be available to them if they forsook their backsliding ways, and returned to their first love, would have been as foreign to them as the idea of the Gentiles having access to Jehovah and everlasting life. It was the idea that God would somehow sustain them in their exile in a strange land, in the Diaspora, and ultimately return them to the land promised to their forefathers, that anchored them as they faced the perils of ethnic persecution.

The Old Testament remnant theology allowed them to hope against hope, that the God of Abraham would be true to His Word, and that He would not utterly forsake them. Their expectation was that He would respond in loving care to their earnest cry for deliverance. The concept of the remnant served as a catalyst to push them into a decision to return to God. As they saw the error of their ways, and the futility in serving the graven images that were powerless to move themselves; much less powerful enough to move in the affairs of men; they had hope. The hope of still having access to the one true living God, the hope of a remnant, was enough to catapult them into repentance.

The notion of there being a remnant was critical to the house of David, and God's promise concerning the lineage of David. God's promise to David was tied into God's promise to Abraham. The reality is that everyone who has ever received God's free gift of salvation is the beneficiary of the promise God made to Abraham; that all nations/families of the earth would be blessed in him.

"And I will bless them that bless thee, and curse them that curseth thee: and in thee shall all families of the earth be blessed."

Genesis 12:3

The nation of Israel, the Hebrew descendants of Abraham, strayed from the God of their forefathers. They were in danger of being cast aside from receiving the benefits and provisions of the covenants of promise. Had it not been for the promise God made to Abraham and David, there would be no hope for the Jews; or mankind. The conditions of covenant mandated obedience to the commands, and worship of God; relative to the terms of covenant. When Israel went whoring after other gods, she violated the terms of the covenant. By rights, Jehovah was no longer obligated to fulfill His part of the agreement; because Israel had failed to keep her part. The saving grace for Israel, and the world, was that God had foreknowledge of the dilemma in which mankind would find itself, so He purposed to extract a remnant out of those disobedient Jews. He had to have a group separated from those idol worshippers; in order to keep the Davidic bloodline open and available for usage.

Purposing to have a group left over, that would still be determined to maintain relational purity with Yahweh, was the only way He could send the Messiah through the descendants of Abraham and David. If there were not a remnant during the time of the divided kingdom, it would have been impossible for the seed of David to fulfill her prophetic destiny. The only way God could remain true to His Word to send a Savior, and defeat

CHAPTER TWO: WHY A REMNANT CHURCH?

the enemy, was for a remnant to remain which would be committed to the purpose for which God had originally established His chosen people.

God made a promise to crush the enemy's head, back in the Garden of Eden, which could only be fulfilled by there being a remnant of David's seed, Jesse's seed, Abraham's seed, Seth's seed, and Adam's seed. The whole idea of a remnant being in place was the only way Israel could achieve God's expectation of her to be the vessel through which He could redeem His lost creation. Not only was remnant theology significant to Israel then, but it is also significant now. Paul's discourse on the remnant in the 9th through 11th chapters of the book of Romans allows us to understand that the hope for all of Israel's salvation is predicated upon there being a remnant in place. There must be a leftover remainder to encourage the Jews to accept the Christ of God; who happens to be Jesus of Nazareth, Yeshua Ha'Mashiach.

The spiritual Gentiles are the recipients of God's mercy and grace, having been grafted into the provisions made for natural Israel. It is of paramount importance for the spiritual Gentiles to understand the role they play in relationship to Israel and her remnant. The Church must acknowledge that salvation is first and foremost of, and for, the Jew. The Holy Scriptures were written by, and for, Jews. God, in His omniscience, knew that the Jews would not receive Jesus as their Messiah. Their rejection of Him paved the way for the Gentiles to be saved. However, The Church must never get it twisted, and think that Jehovah has given up on the Jewish nation. The Church must never delude herself into thinking that God has abandoned Israel for His "new

THE REMNANT CHURCH

chosen people." She can ill-afford to adopt that philosophy, for to do so will invalidate all the New Covenant promises; which, in fact, were made to the Jews.

The Gentile Church is a tool that God will use to draw a remnant out from among the Jewish nation. This Jewish remnant, which is drawn to Christianity, will be instrumental in drawing the whole of Israel to salvation.[58] The Gentile Church will be used by God to make the Jews jealous. She will bring them to the realization that Christians are experiencing, and are in possession of, the salvation that was originally intended for God's chosen people; the Jews. As she ministers here at the end of the age, the Remnant Church that will emerge out of the compromised, deceived, conformist-Church must bear in mind that her function is to serve as the catalyst that makes the Jews jealous enough to want the brand of worship they see being given to their God, the Ancient of Days...Jehovah. In order to make them jealous, The Remnant Church cannot be guilty of offering up "strange fire."[59] Her worship and lifestyle must be exemplary and beyond reproach; it must be pure. She has to be walking the life she is talking about. Holiness must not be something the Jews have to search to find in The Remnant Church, but rather should be the apparel in which the remnant is clothed. The Remnant Church will have to appear as an organism without spot or blemish, to attract a group of people who are intent upon keeping all of the Law as the means of having relationship with Jehovah. There has to be a holy remnant to spark the Jews to receive the Messiah, and thereby fulfill their destiny.

As we examine the Book of Acts, we can explore and dis-

CHAPTER TWO: WHY A REMNANT CHURCH?

cover the makeup of the original New Testament Church. First and foremost, we must recognize that the event at which the Church was birthed was one of the major traditional festivals of the Jews. The Feast of Pentecost was celebrated seven weeks after the end of the Feast of Passover. The Jews had been celebrating Passover since 1300 B.C. It was a traditional celebration of the Jews, by the Jews, for the Jews, and for those of other ethnicities; who had been converted to the practice of Judaism. So, just as the original recipients of salvation were Jewish,[60] so were the initial recipients of the Holy Ghost on "Resurrection Day" primarily Jewish,[61] and the vast majority of those who were birthed into the Church on the Day of Pentecost were ethnic Jews. Along with Christ's disciples, these converts on the Day of Pentecost could properly be referred to as the first "Messianic Jews."

In addition to these Jewish converts to Christianity, there were also non-ethnic practitioners of Judaism who converted to Christianity on that day. There were people from Mesopotamia, Judea, Cappadocia, Asia, Phrygia, Pamphylia, Egypt, Libya, Italy, and Arabia [62] who became members of the first century remnant New Testament Church that day. So, that in what has been termed the birth of the New Testament Church, we can see the prophecy Jehovah made to father Abraham, of being a blessing to the whole world, beginning to be fulfilled. It would take quite a while for all nations to be blessed through him and his seed. Nevertheless, the emergence of an inclusive Church, out of a religion that for over two thousand years had been exclusive to the Jews, was an indicator the promises of God to faithful Abraham were coming to fruition.

As we read further in Acts, we will find Paul, an aggressive evangelist, reaching out to the other Gentile inhabitants who were not practicing Judaism. We can see the advance of the Gospel message being made among people who were not present at the Feast of Pentecost. We can see attempts being made to convert people who were actively worshipping idols and false gods. We can see the borders of the first century New Testament Church expanding across the boundaries of the nation of Israel, and extending to the farthest reaches of the Roman Empire. Neither Jew nor Gentile, bond nor free, neither male nor female, but an inclusive worldwide aggregation of believers and worshippers of the God of the Hebrews, and His Jewish Messiah; the first century remnant New Testament Church was alive and well.

A major shift happened for the early Church as a result of Constantine's vision, victory and subsequent declaration of his Christianity. The shift involved a basic change in the apostolic leadership and governance of the Church. It also reflected a change in the requisites necessary to become a member of the Body of Christ, and receive the benefits of the free gift of salvation. This shift also helped to eliminate the virtue and sacrificial lifestyle which had come into place with the emergence of the first century New Testament Remnant Church; as it emerged out of the shadows of Judaism. The Remnant Church that surfaced on the Day of Pentecost was earmarked by acts of repentance, which resulted in a sacrifice of self-pleasing behavior; in exchange for living a life that was submitted to the priority of pleasing God. As Constantine's actions gave way to a new brand of Christianity that was void of the concept of repentance, we can see one

CHAPTER TWO: WHY A REMNANT CHURCH?

of the first vestiges of compromise and deception seeping into this newly formed remnant.

Repentance was the message of John the Baptist, Jesus, and the apostolic leaders of the first century Church. It is a concept that had been espoused by Jehovah, through the prophets, all throughout the Old Testament. It is a necessary "turn" that has to take place in order to begin walking in the right direction. Before one can properly follow God, they first have to turn from going the wrong way, in their own direction, and get pointed in the right direction; this is what repentance is. With the advent of Rome's new Christianity that proposed one could be born or baptized into a relationship with the Church, a deception was being birthed, and a seduction was being enabled. If there were no need to repent and change what one is doing, who wouldn't want to be Christian. This marked the beginnings of a lowering of the standards which had been put in place by the Christ, and His apostles. This began to remove the criteria of a changed life to be the distinction by which those who belonged to "the way" could be recognized. The relaxing of these standards resulted in a form of worship that was more of a ritual, than one of a lifestyle that reflected a personal relationship with God.

> *"This shift also helped to eliminate the virtue and sacrificial lifestyle which had come into place..."*

Ultimately, Constantine's personal deception was advanced from being an edict of toleration to being a government mandated requirement in order for citizens to conduct business in the Roman Empire. What had started out being a voluntary decision to accept God's provision and His answer to the sin question had been transformed into a mandatory government regulation and law. What a deception, what a compromise, what a seduction. What a tragedy had befallen this newly formed first century New Testament Remnant Church. With this compromise we see the origins of the Holy Roman Catholic Church, and the basis and opportunity for the establishment of the Eastern Orthodox Church. These were the early deceived, conformist-Churches from which the Protestant Reformation, the mid-century Remnant Church, would emerge.

As we further explore the first century – fourth century New Testament Remnant Church, it is interesting to note that by the end of the first century there were only 1,000 Jewish Christians left in the Roman Empire.[63] Some Hebrew Christians sought refuge from persecution in the city of Maximianopolis on the plains of Megiddo, while others sought refuge in the city of Pella in the country of Jordan. Still others sought sanctuary in other cities in the Decapolis. These cities included: Gerasa (Jerash); Scyhthopolis (Beit She'an); Hippos; Gadara (Umm Qais); Pella; Philadelphia (Amman); Capitolias (Dion); Canatha (Qanawat); Raphana (Abila), and Damascus. More sought refuge in the Qumran communities and in Arabia.[64] These Judeo Christian communities were groups labeled as Ebionites, Judaizers, and Nazarenes, and represented communities in which traditional Jewish worship and form were practiced. Additionally, there were other cities where Jewish form or Jewish worship was incorporated into the new Christian way of life; with acceptance of Jesus

CHAPTER TWO: WHY A REMNANT CHURCH?

of Nazareth as Jehovah's Messiah. These people were known as Bereans, Bashanitis, and Pasagians. According to Church history, as relayed by Eusebius, there were Jewish Christian Bishops until the Bar Kokhba Revolt in or about 132-136 A.D.[65] Post Constantine, there were also Jewish Christian communities in Egypt, India, Syria, Lebanon, and Greece.[66] These communities, which did not succumb to the practices of the Holy Roman Catholic and Eastern Orthodox Church, resulted in and contributed to the formation of the Syriac Orthodox Church, Greek Orthodox Church, and Melkite Greek Catholic Church.[67] In spite of the effect of the Roman Empire stealing the governance of the Church from the hands of the Jewish apostles, there was still a Jewish influence on the practices of Christianity after the Constantine era. There was still a remnant that practiced the form in which the Church had been birthed at Pentecost. There was then, and always will be a Remnant Church.

When Jesus returns, He will be looking for a Church that resembles the one He deposited in the earth when He left. He will be searching for a body that is without spot or blemish, like the one that was fashioned when He came back in the form of the Holy Ghost, on the Day of Pentecost,

"That He might present it to Himself a glorious church, not having spot or wrinkle, or any such thing; but that it should be holy and without blemish."
Ephesians 5:27

He came back to indwell those who would dare to come out from among the old dead way of keeping the Law (Judaism).

THE REMNANT CHURCH

The first century New Testament Remnant Church was called to come into a relationship with God, through Jesus Christ. In this relationship, the God of creation would be allowed to inhabit His new temple, the bodies of the "called out ones."

"What? know ye not that your body is the temple of the Holy Ghost which is in you, which ye have of God, and ye are not your own."
I Corinthians 6:19

Our returning Savior will be in search of a Church that is walking in the power and authority that replicates that of the Church birthed on Pentecost; a Church standing as the personification of the power for which it stands in proxy. The Lion of the tribe of Judah will be looking for that body of believers who are casting out demons and defying natural science; by the working of the power of God in them.

He will be in quest of those who have given all things in common, and are committed to evangelization of their own world as a daily lifestyle.

He will be seeking those in the earth who are the quintessence of the propagation of the principles of the Kingdom of God.

He will be looking for those who are accurately representing His image in the earth.

He will be seeking those who are an active part of the proliferation of the spiritual message of no compromise, no conformity, no surrender to seducing spirits of religion.

He will be looking for The Remnant Church.

Chapter Three
The Sum Total & The Remnant

Looking at The Remnant Church, it is easy to classify her as the sum total of all things, recognizing what she represents. As far as accomplishing God's intended purpose of the Church, *driving the Jewish nation to salvation;* the reality of her completeness is an inescapable fact. Though she might only be that which is left over, she yet remains full of all of the virtue and power necessary to stand as a bulwark and tower against the pressing forces of darkness. This is true in spite of the massive falling away from the principles upon which the first century Church was founded. She may be small in her personage and number, yet she still possesses every milligram of anointing needed to break the yokes of bondage, and set the captives free. Her commitment to fulfilling purpose causes her stature and greatness to loom as a formidable foe against the hordes of satan. She stands unwavering against the deceptive winds of doctrine, as they try to blow her into the sea of compromise. Yet, she stands like the proud palm tree with her roots going deep and anchoring around that immovable stone; so as not to break under the winds of false doctrine. Instead, she sways, bends, and seems so vulnerable. Yet, her purpose and destiny are anchored in the set gift, who Himself is the Chief Apostle, Chief Prophet, Chief Evangelist, Chief Pastor and Chief Teacher—Jesus, the Christ of God.

Nothing can sway the end-times Remnant Church from walking the plumb line, as she ministers in power and authority. She is the culmination of everything the Father intended the visible Body of Christ to be in the earth; His emissary and manifested representation in the earth. She literally sums up all that God wants to do in the earth; to bring all of His prophetic promises to pass.

A sum is a total arrived at through the counting of all involved parts. It is the total accounting of everything that has been put into the formula as a component necessary to cause the whole to function. The Remnant Church represents the totality of all that God purposed for His called-out ones. She is the aggregate of what He expects the Church to look like, and function like. She is the full summation of God's design against the enemy, and the kingdom of darkness. She is the whole and total completeness of Jehovah's strategy to have a body that will function in similarity to the One sent out of eternity to destroy the works of the devil.

The Remnant Church is the overall comprehensiveness of the Father's intention to punish evil, and execute judgment against those who willfully disobey His commands, and refuse to accept His Messiah. She stands as the amassing, and lion's share, of the weaponry He has designated to decimate the forces of seduction and deception. She stands opposed to the great liar that has aligned against the masses of humanity; as mankind seeks to come into true relationship with the only true and living God. The end-times Remnant Church is the entirety of the volume of the "moves of God," in this sphere known as time; as He prepares to usher the world into eternity. She is the manifestation of the anointing of God in human flesh. She serves as an extension of the ministry of Christ in the earth.

The remnant is the weapon which the Father is prepared to utilize against the god of this world; as Jehovah finishes the war that was started in Heaven when He had to kick lucifer out. The Remnant Church represents the entire total volume of truth and the combined cumulative amount of restorative purity, needed to bring about God's salvation to the whole of Israel. She also serves to extend God's provision of salvation to as many Gentiles who will receive His solution to the sin problem, Jesus Christ, Yeshua Ha'Mashiach.

A sum total is the whole amount of its collective parts.

It is a combined group of factors that cooperatively are joined together, and shared in order to function as a whole unit.

It is an aggregate; an amassed collection that is united, cohesive, and unified.

It is a cumulative integration of all of the inclusive factors, resulting in a comprehensive, complete collective; consisting of a summary of the chief points of the otherwise disjointed collection.

It is a full high point representing the greatest maximum outcome, relative to the small parts comprised in the makeup of the spectrum of entities or integers. The sum total speaks to the apex or peak of something.

It is the zenith or highest point possible to be achieved.

It is the pinnacle or capstone; the crescendo or climax.

The sum total is the crown, the conclusion or finale. The total is the summit, the culmination, the finishing touch. Such is the Remnant Church; she is the culmination of God's plan through the ages. She is the finishing touch to all that He has destined for mankind in general, and for the Hebrew Jewish nation in particular. The end-times Remnant Church is the crescendo; the conclusion of the matter. She is the finale, the last act of God to redeem His creation; she is His crowning touch.

CHAPTER THREE: THE SUM TOTAL & THE REMNANT

She is the sum total of all things. The Remnant Church is the full summation of God's redemptive act to rescue His creation from a penalty He never intended for her to have to experience. All that God has attempted to do, to save His people from a devil's hell, is comprehensively aggregated in the end-times body of believers known as The Remnant Church.

First and foremost, we have to say that the Church is the sum total of God's plan for His people. She epitomizes the Father's plan to culminate His judgment against evil disobedience to His will, His command, and His government, by having a people that would be separated unto Himself. The Church is His crown and glory. She is a trophy with which He can taunt satan. She is the proof that there are human beings who are willing to let Him sit on the throne of their lives; as they live a life that is submitted to His dictates, and governance. The Church is the comprehensive summation of Jehovah's intention of having His creation share eternal life with Him. She is the sum total of His plan for mankind to be eternally in communion with Him. She displays His intention for communion with His creation, as was evidenced by His placement of the Tree of Life in the Garden of Eden.

The Church is the pinnacle of His love for His creation; which can be seen in that the purchase price of her redemption cost Him heaven's best; His Son. The Church exemplifies His willingness to allow a portion of Himself to leave His heavenly existence, house Himself in human flesh, and die a brutal death. He did all of this in order for man to be reunited with Him. This was a part of the "process" necessary to provide the regeneration of man's dead spirit. The "process" is called being "saved" or "born again." God allowed a portion of Himself to be separated from Himself. He left His home in glory, shrouded His divinity with our humanity; yet never lost His divine nature. Jesus allowed Himself to become the sacrificial lamb; in order to satisfy the requirement of there being a shedding of blood for the remission of sin; thereby mediating the New Covenant.

> "What the blood of bulls and goats sprinkled could not accomplish caused Him to show His great love for mankind."

The Church, God's dwelling place for those who receive Messiah Jesus, is the prime example of the height of God's good intentions for His creation. Jehovah allowed something that had never happened in all of eternity to take place; in order to restore His creation to the fellowship they had with Him before the fall of Adam. The Father allowed Himself to be separated from the Son for the first time in all of eternity. Not only did the Son leave His heavenly existence to come to earth to die for the "sin" of the world, but He also experienced a disconnection from the Father. Jesus hung on Calvary's cross, to pay the "sin debt" for all of creation; past, present, and future. The Father turned His back upon Him; for God could not look on Jesus as He bore the sin of all humanity. This is what caused Jesus to cry out, "My God, My God, why hast thou forsaken me?" The great price that the Father was willing to pay for the salvation of the world is a manifestation of the finale, and finishing touch, He needed as a statement to verify that the head of the serpent had indeed been crushed.

CHAPTER THREE: THE SUM TOTAL & THE REMNANT

Whether it is The Remnant Church, the Structural Church, the compromised deceived conformist-Church, or however you want to name it; God has always been searching for a people who would willingly be called out from among the sensual ways of the world to holiness. He always looks for a people willing to operate in a distinct way of serving a holy God. Since the proclamation in the Garden of Eden of a Messiah coming forth to bruise the head of the serpent, God has always had it in His heart to have a people that would be willing to please Him; instead of pleasing themselves. The Church is the sum total of all that God had ever designed for mankind; an eternal existence and relationship between the Creator and His creation.

The Church is the sum total of God's original intention for mankind as He intended for Adam to be His designated authority and designated representative in the earth. As we look at the Church, and the final instructions she received from Jesus as He went to the Father and prepared to return in the form of the Holy Ghost, we can see that His expectation for her was the same expectation the Father had for Adam. We can hear Him say, "If you love me, obey my commandments." Jesus plainly stated that,

"And I will ask the Father, and he will give you another Advocate, who will never leave you. He is the Holy Spirit, who leads into all truth. The world cannot receive him, because it isn't looking for him and doesn't recognize him. But you know him, because he lives with you now and later will be in you. No, I will not abandon you as orphans—I will come to you."
John 14: 15-18 NLT

As we understand the purpose that the Holy Ghost was given, it is easy to see the parallel between what the Church was tasked to do, and what Adam was tasked to do.

"And God blessed them, and God said unto them, Be fruitful, and multiply, and replenish the earth, and subdue it: and have dominion over the fish of the sea, and over the fowl of the air, and over every living thing that moveth upon the earth." Genesis 1: 28

Then Jesus came to them and said,

"All authority in heaven and on earth has been given to me. Therefore go and make disciples of all nations, baptizing them in the name of the Father and of the Son and of the Holy Spirit, and teaching them to obey everything I have commanded you. And surely I am with you always, to the very end of the age."
Matthew 28: 18-20 NIV

He said to them,

"Go into all the world and preach the gospel to all creation. Whoever believes and is baptized will be saved, but whoever does not believe will be condemned. And these signs will accompany those who believe: In my name they will drive out demons; they will speak in new tongues; they will pick up snakes with their hands, and when they drink deadly poison, it will not hurt them at all; they will place their hands on sick people, and they will get well."
Mark 16: 15-18 NIV

CHAPTER THREE: THE SUM TOTAL & THE REMNANT

When we look at these four scriptures, it should be obvious that both Adam and the body of apostles that Jesus left in charge of the first century New Testament Remnant Church were tasked with doing the same thing... reproduction. Both were commanded to replenish the earth with offspring after their own kind. They were commanded to populate the earth by multiplying, and reproducing themselves. Just as Adam and Eve were charged to be fruitful, the Church was commanded to do the same. If taking the Gospel message to the whole world is not a multiplication function, nothing else can be considered to be so. God authorized Adam to subdue the earth and have dominion over every living thing whether in the air, in the water, or in the earth. Surely that can be no greater than having dominion over demons, poison, and sickness. The extent of Adam's domain was increased to include the spiritual world also; as God charged the Church to fulfill her Adamic role.

The Church produces a resounding crescendo as she steps into her role as the designated representative and delegated authority for the God of creation. He has commissioned her to rule in His stead, until the "kingdoms of this world are offered up to the Kingdom of our God."[68] Just as Adam was chosen to be the steward over God's creation, so the Church has been chosen to be steward over the ministry Jesus has established in the earth. The Church is the caretaker of the gift of deliverance God has given to the inhabitants of the world. She is tasked to safeguard it better than Adam protected the domain he had been given charge of. Just as Adam was warned not to partake of the knowledge of evil, so the Church is charged to beware of the seducing doctrines of devils, designed to contaminate her, and cause her to fall from her position of power and influence.

The Church is the sum total and culmination of God's intention to have a human vessel to stand guard over the provisions He has established for the sustenance of His creation, and the eternal relationship He seeks to have with His creation. The Father has intricately designed an agenda that allows man to exercise his gift of "free will," yet at the same time experience the benevolence of a loving father who has a stop gap in place to insure the salvation of His creation. The Church has the full authorization of Jehovah to perpetuate His divine intention of maintaining communion with the chosen subjects of His Kingdom. By employing the provisions of Covenant, which have been established to make sure that His subjects do in fact receive their rightful inheritance, the Church stands guard over God's most prized possession: His chosen people, the seed of Abraham. The Remnant Church is God's shining example of His amassed collection of all those seemingly disjointed parts, and His ability to cause them to be united, cohesive, and unified the sum total of His power, His wisdom, and His love. The remnant!

The Remnant Church is the sum total of God's original intention for His redeemed creation after the Fall of Adam and Eve. After 'The Fall' of man, God didn't change His mind for man being His designated representative and delegated authority in the earth. The fact of the matter is that when God gathered Adam, Eve, and satan after the fruit was eaten, He could have ended that creation and started all over again. He did not rescind His command for man to multiply, be fruitful, and replenish

CHAPTER THREE: THE SUM TOTAL & THE REMNANT

the earth. He did not relieve man of his duty to subdue the earth and have dominion over it. Instead, He prophesied of the mechanism, the Messiah, that would crush the head of satan. He spoke into motion the provision He had put in place "from before the foundation of the world."[69] He still purposed for His creation to have fellowship with Him, and to still experience eternal life. He merely legislated that from now on, man's caretaking of the creation would be laborious, and woman's childbearing would be painful. Jehovah knew that after man abdicated his position of authority to satan, there would be a need for a vehicle to provide shetlter and empowerment to those emissaries who would still need to operate on His behalf. If God were to use man, after man fell from his place of innocence and authority, there had to be a way to restore man to the place he occupied before he fell. The Church represents God's way of restoration for His creation. She is the divine intervention necessary to thwart satan's plan to keep the creation separated from the Creator. The Church is God's way of placing mankind back in her rightful place of rulership over the earth. She is the unification of all the seemingly disconnected pieces from the results of the Fall, morphing into a creation demonstrating the outcome of God making Himself available to all who would

> *"Just as Adam was warned not to partake of the knowledge of evil, so the Church is charged to beware of the seducing doctrines of devils, designed to contaminate her, and cause her to fall from her position of power and influence."*

receive Him. She is the sum total of Jehovah's worshippers empowered to continue Christ's ministry of reconciliation, through the power provided by the Holy Ghost on the Day of Pentecost. She is not an afterthought, but the zenith of an all-knowing God's plan to have a people for Himself...the Church.

As we study the concept of the Remnant Church, we cannot do it without recognizing the intentions of God for Israel; relative to the concept of "the sum total." The Church is the sum total because she is the culmination of the "promise" God made to Abraham. In the precursor to the Old Covenant or Abrahamic Covenant, God promised Abraham that the whole earth would be blessed through the nation that came out of Abraham.[70] Abraham's seed produced the Hebrews, Israelites, known as the Jews. This was the ethnic group through which Jesus Christ came; Jesus was a practicing Jew. The Church is the inheritance of God. She is the fulfillment of His promise to Father Abraham; the culmination of the covenant He made with Abraham, Isaac, and Jacob. Another thing we must understand is that the Jews were not just given Canaan because they were so good. In fact, they disobeyed and disappointed God time and time again. The inhabitants of the land were so bad, that God decided to dispossess them, and use the Jewish nation as a light to point them towards the one true God. Although the Jews had a duty to rid the land of some of its wicked nations and their practices, they also had a duty to shed the light of the righteous worship of Jehovah. The Hebrews sinful ways prohibited them from fulfilling their duty and reaching the rest of their world for Jehovah. Jesus came to do what Israel failed to do; redeem the

CHAPTER THREE: THE SUM TOTAL & THE REMNANT

world.

As we define the concept of the Remnant Church, we must show a relationship between the general definition of "remnant" and the definition of the "Church." The remnant is the part of something that is left over when other parts are gone; it involves the notion of something smaller being used to accomplish that which the larger part failed to accomplish. The idea that something which is void of its other parts, parts which appeared to be necessary, is still able to function in the purpose and role for which it was created, and intended to be used is a mystery. The Church fits the definition of a remnant in many ways. She is the sum total of all of God's experiences with man since the Day of Pentecost. First of all, she is the part leftover when the overwhelming majority of earth's inhabitants refuse to accept Jesus Christ as their personal Savior, and consciously reject God's answer to the sin problem. She is the portion that remains acceptant of the idea of there being more than a higher power, but that there is rather a Creator, who is the One true and living God; Jehovah being His name. She is the remaining portion when the other parts of mankind are rushing down the wide path of destruction, towards a devil's hell. Hell is a place that is reserved for those who would rather serve their own self pleasures; as opposed to living a life surrendered to serving the Creator. The Church is a noticeably smaller group of people; they do not constitute a majority. Instead, she is much smaller numerically; yet she is so

> *"The Remnant Church is the sum total of God's original intention for His redeemed creation after the Fall of Adam and Eve."*

much stronger than the majority; due to the indwelling power of the God of creation; residing in her. Through the baptism of the Holy Ghost, being resident in the lives of her members, she has a supernatural advantage over the nonbelieving majority of humanity. While the larger majority is not able to submit itself to the Kingdom of God, this smaller portion gladly accepts the government of God in their lives, and positions themselves to carry on major spiritual warfare against the kingdom of darkness. She is able to accomplish what the majority cannot see themselves doing; embracing a God-centered life and a "selfless" agenda.

The fact that she is void of other gifts, graces and talents belonging to the majority does not impede her from functioning in her designated office; nor does it diminish her ability to fulfill her purpose. In spite of her small numerical size, she is still more than able to accomplish her God-given assignment. Although the Church is that portion which has been separated from the much larger mass of society, she is still capable of being the visible representation of the invisible God; in the earth today. She is still the conduit of His message of repentance, and a conductor of the power necessary to take a life off of the road to hell, and change it to a heavenly direction. She is able to help the "concept" of conversion become a life-changing "reality."

Yes, even though she is merely a remnant, merely a leftover, she is still able to embrace, fellowship, and help stabilize the uncountable number of those who are willing to receive the free gift of salvation through Jesus Christ our Lord. She IS the epitome, the apex, the pinnacle of all of the events that happened since the Fall of man, that have provided the opportunity for man to be ushered back into right relationship with God. The Remnant Church exists to help usher man back into his rightful position as God's designated representative and delegated authority in the earth.

While exploring the notion of The Remnant Church, it must be examined in conjunction with the after effects of the Jews who survived the initial Sanhedrin persecution; after the crucifixion and the Day of Pentecost. While the group who heard Peter's gospel message on the Day of Pentecost became the first century New Testament Remnant Church, we must recognize that a remnant also emerged out of that remnant. The first century Christians experienced a lot of persecution from the Sanhedrin, the Sadducees in particular. It is commonly believed, and held to be true, that the Sanhedrin was comprised of a mixture of Pharisees and Sadducees. The Sanhedrin was the supreme council, or court, in ancient Israel. The Sanhedrin was comprised of seventy men, plus the high priest, who served as its president. The members came from the chief priests, scribes and elders, but there is no record on how they were chosen. The Sanhedrin had its own police force which could arrest people, as they did Jesus Christ. While the Sanhedrin heard both civil and criminal cases, and could impose the death penalty, in New Testament times it did not have the authority to execute convicted criminals. That power was reserved for the Romans, which explains why Jesus was crucified—a Roman punishment— rather than stoned, according to Mosaic Law. The Sanhedrin were abolished after the Fall of Jerusalem in A.D. 70.[71]

Originally the Sanhedrin was an assembly of twenty to

twenty-three men appointed in every city in the land of Israel. The Mishnah arrives at the number twenty-three based on an exegetical derivation. A "community" must be able to vote for both conviction and exoneration. The minimum size of a "community" is ten men, therefore, one more is required to achieve a majority. However, since a simple majority cannot convict, an additional judge is required. Finally, a court should not have an even number of judges to prevent deadlocks; thus twenty three. This court dealt with only religious matters. The court convened every day except festivals and Shabbat. The final binding decision of the Sanhedrin was in 358, when the Hebrew Calendar was adopted. Unfortunately, the Roman Empire dissolved the Sanhedrin during its persecution of the Jews. The Sanhedrin was an active participant in the trial of Jesus and the stoning death of Stephen. The Sanhedrin as a body claimed powers that lesser Jewish courts did not have. As such, they were the only ones who could try the king, extend the boundaries of the Temple and Jerusalem, and were the final authority on all questions of law. Before 191 B.C. the High Priest acted as the ex officio head of the Sanhedrin, but in 191 B.C., the Sanhedrin lost confidence in the High Priest.[72]

The Sadducees were "sad, you see," because they did not believe in "resurrection from the dead," while the Pharisees did believe in resurrection. This might account as to why Nicodemeus sought to engage Jesus in a conversation about eternal life; Nicodemeus was a Pharisee. The Sadducees were a sect or group of Jews that were active in Judea during the Second Temple period, starting from the second century through the destruction of the Temple in 70 A.D. The sect was identified by Josephus with the upper social and economic echelon of Judean society. As a whole, the sect fulfilled various political, social, and religious roles, including maintaining the Temple. The Sadducees are often compared to other contemporaneous sects, including the Pharisees and the Essenes. Their sect is believed to have become extinct sometime after the destruction of Herod's Temple in Jerusalem in 70 A.D. The Sadducees rejected the Oral Law as proposed by the Pharisees. Rather, they saw the Torah as the sole source of divine authority. The written law, in its depiction of the priesthood, corroborated the power and enforced the authority of the Sadducees in Judean society. According to Josephus, the Sadducees believed that:

◊ There is no fate
◊ God does not commit evil
◊ Man has free will; "man has the free choice of good or evil"
◊ The soul is not immortal; there is no afterlife, and
◊ There are no rewards or penalties after death

The Sadducees rejected the belief in resurrection of the dead, which was a central tenet believed by Pharisees and by early Christians. The Sadducees supposedly believed in the traditional Jewish concept of Sheol for those who had died.[73]

Therefore, it should be easy to understand that in addition to the persecution of the first century Church being Sanhedrin driven, it probably originated with the Sadducees. The Sadducees were focused on stamping out "the Way," this brand of abhorrent Judaism that had the audacity to intentionally propagate the notion of a resurrection; with the promise of eternal life attached to it. They perceived the whole concept of Christianity or "the Way" as repugnant, repulsive, disgusting, and detestable. Is it any wonder that they so aggressively pursued the members of the first century Church, and vehemently put them to death? This same Sanhedrin had aggressively pursued Jesus, as He walked the sandy shores of Galilee. They were intent about stamping out His message, and had no reservation in delivering Him up to Herod for crucifixion. If they had been legally able, they would have stoned Jesus to death; according to the Law of Moses. Since the death penalty was beyond the Sanhedrin's scope of authority, Jesus ended up dying the Roman death of crucifixion. He who knew no sin became a curse for us; bringing to fruition what the Scriptures said about His death.[74]

The newly birthed first century Remnant Church was in the crosshairs of this anti-resurrection group of Jewish professionals, doctors, and clergy. They were seen as another unwanted sect that had separated itself from Orthodox Judaism. How dare they think that they could exercise a positional relationship with Jehovah that superseded the order which had been established by Father Abraham and the great prophet Moses? How dare Christ utter that He was greater than Abraham, and before Abraham was I AM! The Sanhedrin was appalled by the insolence of this poor prophet from Nazareth; because everyone knew that no prophet or good thing came out of Galilee.

CHAPTER THREE: THE SUM TOTAL & THE REMNANT

"They answered and said unto him, Art thou also of Galilee? Search, and look: for out of Galilee ariseth no prophet."
John 7:52

It is interesting to note that these Messianic Jews had become a small separated portion of a larger group. The large group had refused to believe that their Messiah would come as a lowly servant; instead of a reigning king. The two mainline prophecies concerning the Messiah depicted Him as a servant and a king. This small group became a remnant because they chose to believe that Messiah would first be a servant; then a king. The Messiah would, in fact, first be lowly, then exalted. This made sense. If the reverse were true, exalted then lowly; that would have been an embarrassment and a defeat. If it had not been in the purposes of God for the Jews to reject Jesus, in order to fulfill His prophecy concerning the seed of Abraham blessing the whole world to come to fruition, then even the Sanhedrin would have logically recognized that it made sense for the Messiah to come as a servant first. Maybe they would have accepted Jesus as their Messiah. Think about it, if you were looking for a savior, would you want him to come as a king first and then as a servant? This proposition makes no logical sense. So, from the start, this mixed remnant of Messianic Jews and converted Gentile proselytes were doomed to be the objects of massive persecution by the greatest Jewish minds of that day. They were doomed to be a casualty of the war between those who believed in the resurrection of the dead, and those who did not. Those who first dared to disassociate themselves with the synagogue, and become people of "the Way" were the targets of some of the worse self-inflicted genocide the world has ever seen. They were predestined to be a remnant.

Additionally, The Remnant Church must also be considered in terms of the aggregation of the saints who survived after first century Christianity was accepted by the Roman government, and subsequently the Church lost its apostolic flavor. There was a noticeable difference that happened to the Church when Rome accepted Christianity as the official religion of the empire. The group of Messianic Jews and proselytes which remained were survivors of a massive persecution leveled against them by the Orthodox Jews and the Roman government. They were left over after the persecution that was leveled against that first century New Testament Remnant Church. They were those left over from the massive numbers that were added to the Church on the Day of Pentecost, and afterwards; who had not perished in the persecution. The remnant was now faced with another test of survival. They had to now position themselves to maintain the fervor, flavor, and virtue of that great group of called out ones; which had been established when Jesus, the Holy Ghost baptizer, returned and indwelt His original disciples and apostles.

This new remnant was now tasked with maintaining the power and authority that had been vested in the original first century New Testament Remnant Church. They were now in a situation where they had to maintain the apostolic flavor that had marked the apostles as those who had been with Christ. The same flavor that marked the disciples who had been with Jesus. The apostolic government that had been charged to oversee the ministry Christ left in the earth, after His ascension and return to dwell in the lives of believers, had just experienced a major coup. The enemy had just doused the Church with her first experience of compromise and conformity. The nature of membership in the body of believers called out from mainstream Judaism had experienced a drastic shift. No longer were the apostolic requirements of repentance and conversion in place, and mandatory. The requirements for membership had shifted.

Repentance deals with our thoughts, actions, motives, lifestyles, social customs, family and economic ties. There should not be a single area of our lives that is unaffected by our conscious turning from self-government to God-government. Repentance is a radical change that involves putting the axe to the root. As we separate ourselves from the nature of sin, we should allow the new God-consciousness to have free reign in every area of our lives. Repentance produces a conscious awareness of our rebellion to the law of God, and our basic sin nature; which is a spirit that is disconnected from God. It produces awareness that we are governing our own life, and not living a life subject to God's ways and rules. It allows us to see that we are moving in a direction that is opposite of God's direction, and in fact are moving away from Him; not towards Him.

The accompanying results of this awareness should result in us turning from our own self-will, and self-rule, to a place where we position ourselves under the Lordship of Jesus Christ. It should cause us to submit to the government of God in our lives, and allow the Spirit of God to convict us of sin, and convince us that we should be pursuing the ways of righteousness.

Repentance is not optional. It is a command from God given to His people from their days of the kings, through the days of the prophets, through the days of the forerunner of the Christ, through the days of the Christ, through the days of the apostles, until NOW. It is God's call for man to forsake his ways, and change to the ways of God. Conversion expresses the action of the will, in turning to God. When we receive God's gift of repentance, we take the first step in the obedience of faith to be reconciled to God. Conversion involves the turning of a sinner to God. In a general sense the heathen are said to be "converted" when they abandon heathenism and embrace the Christian faith. In a more special sense, men are converted when, by the influence of divine grace in their souls, their whole life is changed, old things pass away, and all things become new.

> *"Repentance is a radical change that involves putting the axe to the root."*

The Biblical root of the word conversion conveys the idea of turning. To turn to embrace God, or to turn to Judaism from a Gentile lifestyle. It usually follows repentance, requires self-examination, and is accomplished by faith and the power of The Holy Spirit. It is commanded, necessary, and is accompanied by confession of sin and prayer. These scriptural requirements of repentance and conversion had disappeared. No longer was there a need to have the evidence of a changed lifestyle; as a requisite for membership. No longer was there a need for a sacrificial shift in priorities, and no longer an urgent need to share the "faith" with those who were not a part of "the Way." No longer was there an urgency to demonstrate a commitment to carry out "The Great Commission." The requirements for membership had shifted.

The lines in the sand had shifted, the battle plan had been watered down, and purity of the relationship with Jehovah had been compromised. After the persecution ended, tolerance became normal, and the sense of uniqueness also dissipated. No longer were there stringent requirements necessary to be identified with "the Church;" but now, a more relaxed atmosphere existed. You no longer had to change your ways, and entry into the Church was as easy as being sprinkled with water; not immersed and buried in a watery grave. Or you could be simply physically born into the Church; if your parents were members of the church. No longer did you have to be spiritually reborn; the physical elements of entry were deemed to be adequate to consider yourself a part of the church. If the truth be told, these requirements were enough to be a part of the physical church that the Roman Empire had crafted. However, they were sorely inadequate to be a part of the Universal Church; the Body of Christ.

It is of paramount importance to maintain the distinction between these two bodies as we examine the history of the Church from that point onward. Although we do recognize that the first fifteen centuries of Christianity took place under the structural churches that were created by the Western Roman Catholic Church and the Eastern Orthodox Church, we must never fail to remember that the basis and original belief systems of those organizations drastically differed from the apostolic traditions and practices upon which the first century New Testament

Remnant Church was founded. As we have stated previously, we will attempt to reiterate again. When the governance of the New Testament Church was wrestled out of the hands of her Jewish apostolic overseers, and placed into the hands of political appointees of the Roman Empire; she began her journey down the road to her dark ages. The first century New Testament Remnant Church did not begin to experience her restoration until the Protestant Reformation of 1512.

When Rome took over the governance of Christianity, yet another remnant emerged. Even though some pagan practices were introduced into the religious body known as Christians, there were still bodies of Messianic Jews and Christians, who had been proselytes of Judaism, who still continued the worship practices that had been instituted by those original believers who were immersed in the apostle's doctrine.[75] There was yet a remnant who maintained the ways of the original body of believers that had been formed on the Day of Pentecost, and other times close to that event. There was still a residue of those who adhered to the tenets of faith upon which this great Christianity was built. There always was, has been, and always will be a remnant.

As we look at The Remnant Church, it is impossible to substantiate the need for her existence without evaluating the impact the saints who survived after the Protestant Reformation had. What effect did they have on the emergence of a new way of relating to Jehovah; God of the Hebrews? We must also examine the impact the subsequent rescue of the Church from Rome and Catholicism, had on the Body of Christ. We must remember that for fifteen centuries, the majority of those who

CHAPTER THREE: THE SUM TOTAL & THE REMNANT

practiced Christianity did so under the auspices of the Western Roman Catholic Church and the Eastern Orthodox Church. All that the world knew of the religion that was formed, when some practitioners of Judaism decided to follow the prophet from Nazareth, was manifested in the morphing of those original remnant-based belief systems with what was birthed in Rome, Alexandria, and Constantinople. Christianity no longer resembled what we read of in the book of Acts, but it now had a new look and flavor. It was compromised with an infusion of practices associated with the "worship of the sun." Although Rome had embraced some of the basic tenets of the Christian faith, she had still held on to some of her own major pagan practices.

Rome had subtly blended those pagan practices into the basic Jewish tenets and worship forms of the Judeo Christian faith. As we chronicle the growth of Christianity in a pagan world, which was widely acceptant of the worship of false gods, gods other than Jehovah, the God of the Hebrews, there is a stark reality we must face. The non-Christian nations were seeing a worship form that had lost its initial Jewish flavor. They were seeing a compromised form, which in many instances paralleled, and resembled, their own worship form. They saw the inclusion of statues, which resembled their own way of representing their idols, graven images of their gods. Is it any wonder that it was so easy to evangelize the world with this pre-Protestant Reformation brand of Christianity.

Many major cultures had their own version of the Virgin Mary and the baby Jesus. For an in-depth reading on the subject, I recommend, "The Two Babylons," by Hislop.[76] It is important to note that there was a major deviation from the apostle's doctrine, upon which the Church had been founded, and more of an inclusion of some of the ways of the "sun worshippers." This was done to make those being recruited feel comfortable with their forced acceptance of Christianity. We must acknowledge that the church that resulted from the inclusion of government into religion, that hybrid, was not necessarily full of the pure virtue of the New Testament Remnant Church from which it had originated. There were deceptive ways and compromises, which were interjected into the original belief system, that resulted in a weakened form of an otherwise acknowledged extreme way of life. The inclusion of government oversight and pagan practices, into the New Testament Remnant Church, diminished the effectiveness of Christianity to produce lifechanging behavior in the lives of her practitioners. Therefore, it was necessary for a remnant to arise to rescue the organism which had started as the first century New Testament Remnant Church. She had evolved into the Western Roman Catholic and Eastern Orthodox Churches, and needed to be saved.

Therefore, a condition existed for emergence of a body that would maintain the original values of the Church. There was a need for her to come forth out of those compromised organizations, and properly represent the intentions and design of the Father; when He mandated the Son to form the "ecclesia." As a result, another Remnant Church arrived on the scene; the Pre-Protestant Reformation Remnant Church. She was mandated to fulfill the prophetic destiny of the first century New Testament

Remnant Church, and become the culmination of what was formed as the apostles and disciples followed the Master's command. She was to represent the end-result as they obeyed to move forth to disciple the nations. Worldly deception had crept into the New Testament Church. God had to separate a portion that still had the residue of the Day of Pentecost noticeably present in its spiritual DNA, because of the compromise that tainted the holiness of that first century remnant group. There had to be a remnant that could shake off the effects of the infiltration of the Roman Empire into Christianity. Hence the pre-Protestant Reformation remnant was birthed. Long before the official Protestant Reformation, there was a group of devout Roman Catholics that were crying, "Holy, Holy, Holy; Lord God Almighty; early in the morning our song shall rise to Thee."

Just as there was a group of devout, God-fearing Jews who recognized the advent of Messiah in the earth; a Roman Catholic remnant emerged. Just as when a group of devout God fearing Jews and proselytes who heard the 'sound' that came as a result of the mighty rushing wind from heaven filling the room where the apostles and disciples were gathered and praying in one accord; a Roman Catholic remnant emerged. Even as this group of God fearing Roman Catholic Christians who recognized the error of incorporating the practices of "sun worshippers" into the liturgy of those who celebrated Jesus of Nazareth as God's messiah to the world; a remnant emerged. Even so, after these Roman Catholics protested and began to reform the way Christianity was practiced, and God began to restore moves of the Spirit back into the Body of Christ, and even unto this day a remnant was and is emerging.

As the Church was being positioned to move back to her place of origin, in as much as holiness and a changed lifestyle is concerned, a remnant was emerging out of each restorative movement she experienced. Jehovah has continually been perfecting the Church, as she moves towards the end of the age. Her perfection or maturity is going to be necessary in order for her to seamlessly assimilate into the invading Army of Heaven. In order for there to be no glitches, or gaps in performance in the Army of God, a remnant had to arise out of each move of God in the Church. This was necessary so that the integrity of the first century New Testament Remnant Church could be maintained, and the essence of what she was intended to be could be ensured. Too often, the Body of Christ becomes so attached to the move of the Spirit that the Church has just experienced, that she fails to see the big picture, and just how that move contributes to the total on-going purpose of God for the Church. Invariably, we sometimes will see a whole niche, or worship form, created by a move of God as the be all and end all of the move of God. When in actuality, that move was really intended to only be a part of the total continual perfecting of the Church. In all truthfulness, the move was only intended to be the creation of a springboard for a whole new movement to further advance the purposes of God; as He moves the Church to maturity.

After the surge that resulted from the Reformation, the Church began to settle into the normalcy of being comfortable with the restorative power of God. As He moved the Church back to her rightful place of prominence, there yet arose another need for a Remnant Church. There had to be a people who were more preoccupied with having a meaningful and intimate relationship with Jehovah, and not as preoccupied with the restorative moves of God they were seeing. We have seen it over and over again; with movements as basic as speaking in tongues, to movements as bizarre as handling snakes, roaring like a lion, holy laughter, and rolling on the floor. While God may have intended these to be a part of the move of the Spirit in the Church, He certainly did not intend for us to get stuck "there," and not move on to perfection. While those movements may have been beneficial for the Body of Christ, they were only designed to be a pit stop; not her final destination. Here again, it became necessary for God to extract a portion from the benefactors of those movements that He could depend on to stay faithful and focused. There had to be those who were dedicated to the attainment of the measure of the stature of the fullness of Christ. The same measure that was found in the first century New Testament Remnant Church is the same measure that Jehovah is trying to develop in the Church; even to this time. As He extracted remnants out of those movements, He was and is purposefully moving the Church to her final destination, the End Times Remnant Church.

With all of the false doctrine being perpetrated in, or on, the Church by the god of this world, there was definitely a need for those saints who survived the carnage, and rose from the aftermath of the satanic attack, to reformulate their relationship to and worship of the God of creation. As God continued to drive the Church back to her original form and intensity; the mode in which she operated at her inception, the enemy's attack persisted. The god of this world operates by deception. He entices man to compromise his stance, in order for man to experience self-satisfaction. These were the methods he attempted to use on Jesus, when he tempted Him for those forty days and nights in the wilderness. The lust of the flesh, the lust of the eyes, and the pride of life are exactly what he used then, and now uses to try to prevent the Church from reaching her ultimate destination. As is his way, the enemy doesn't just use an outright lie that would insult the Church's spiritual intelligence. Instead, he slightly distorts the truth, in an attempt to deceive her into accepting his half-truth. Therefore, he preys on folks who are not rooted and grounded in the Word of God. He is always searching for those who are content to allow those in church leadership to tell them what God is saying, as opposed to studying His Word, and seeking the face, and heart of God for themselves.

It is incumbent upon every saint of God to STUDY the Bible, in order to understand exactly what the will and purposes of God are. Every believer has to spend quality time with the Scriptures, in order not to be duped by the half-truths of satan. It is not enough just to read the Bible; it must be studied and cross-referenced; line upon line, precept upon precept. As the Church studies the Word of God, she must do it from the perspective of understanding who wrote the Scriptures, and the audience to whom those words were written. If the Church is ever to truly understand her place in the plan of God, and in relationship to the fulfillment of apocalyptic prophecy, she must understand the

Scriptures through the Jewish filter in which they were written. Failure on her part to do so, will result in the body of Christ missing the timing of God, misappropriating ministry resources, failing to fulfill her purpose, and a total lack of accomplishing her God-ordained destiny.

The sad tragedy is that there have been countless deceptions aimed at the Church. They have been perpetrated by the enemy, and have been designed to de-intensify the energy with which the Church focuses her warfare against the kingdom of darkness, and commits to its destruction. Again, we must note that these have appeared in the form of subtle, understated, elusive propositions; as opposed to blatant outright lies. The enemy's goal is to devalue the concepts of holiness and righteousness. Some of the main deceptive doctrines which have slipped into the Church include: moderate drinking; acceptance of homosexuality as an alternate lifestyle; tolerance of tobacco usage; relaxed sexual standards; immodest dressing; salvation without repentance; hell as a condition only on earth alone, not a spiritual reality, not an after death experience; seven year tribulation period; pretribulation rapture; acceptance of games of chance; no need for the baptism of The Holy Spirit; acceptance of worldly music as a part of worship; sensual dancing; line dancing; no need for water baptism; membership vs. relationship, and replacement theology. All of the aforementioned things serve to undermine the authority of The Holy Spirit to govern our lives in

> *"It is incumbent upon every saint of God to STUDY the Bible, in order to understand exactly what the will and purposes of God are."*

a manner which demonstrates our obedience to the mandate to accurately characterize our existence. We are Jehovah's delegated authority and designated representatives in the earth. We must reflect His character.

In addition to this, these things directly impact the nature of our spiritual warfare, and the sense of urgency with which we attempt to demobilize, and incapacitate, the kingdom of darkness. There is a gigantic list of organizations and religious entities that have been associated with the term "cult." Rather than engage in an exhaustive accusatory process of naming them, we will refer you to a couple of works you can explore, and allow the Spirit of God to speak to you. We will, however, name some of the deceptive practices of these groups. Here is a list of books you should explore:

"Handbook of Today's Religions" Josh McDowell and Don Stewart, *Here's Life Publishers, Inc*

"New Age Cults & Religions Texe Marrs," *Living Truth Publisher*

"Handbook of Denominations in the United States, *Abingdon Press*

"The Hidden Danger of the Rainbow" Constance Cumbey, *Huntington House Inc.*

"Unmasking the Jezebel Spirit" John Paul Jackson, *Stream Publications*

"Cheque Mate - The Game of Princes" Jeffrey A. Baker, *Whitaker House*

These works will give you insight into the groups and deceptive philosophies against which the remnant must be on guard. There are some extremely dangerous practices that have infiltrated the Church, in the name of Christianity. Some of these practices are not only anti-Christ, but are occultist in nature and origin. These doctrines embrace fundamental practices which are designed to appeal to man's basic human need to be loved, feel needed, and sense that our lives have meaning and direction. They usually center on new interpretation of the Holy Scriptures; with the underlying notion being that they alone have the key to interpreting the Scriptures correctly. Their interpretation is usually drastically different from the tenets of orthodox Christianity, and serves to support their organizational beliefs. These organizational beliefs are also usually drastically different from those espoused by orthodox, mainstream Christianity. In addition to sometimes having sources of authority which are non-Biblical in nature, these doctrines also have been known to: reject orthodox Christianity; propagate a non-Biblical teaching denying the nature of God being a triune deity; believe in salvation by works; be characterized by the interpretive teachings of a strong founder; engage in false prophecy concerning the second coming of Christ, and have a theology that is ever changing, and constantly evolving.

> *"Jehovah has continually been perfecting the Church, as she moves towards the end of the age."*

We are not talking about the doctrines which have out right denied that Jesus was the Son of God, and merely relegated Him to being just another prophet. We are speaking of the deceptions that teach that Jesus Christ is not God in human flesh, but merely another created being. They deny the deity of Christ, stating that while He was a god; He was not Almighty God. They have revived the ancient heresy known as Arianism. These heresies also teach that Jesus Christ was a "preexistent spirit," and not the "unique Son of God;" but merely a preexistent spirit like the rest of us. These deceptive teachings also assert that The Holy Spirit is not a part of the Godhead, and is not God. They do not believe in the doctrine of the triune God (Trinity). Please note that these teachings are not relegated to one individual group, but are believed by many "supposedly" Christian organizations. These heresies also reject the notion of salvation being a free gift received by faith, but rather see it as an object to be earned by works. Furthermore, they do not believe that mankind needs to be saved from the inherent "sin nature" that was passed onto mankind due to the "original sin" of our father, Adam. While yet others state that there is "no need, or requirement" for salvation or repentance; all of these are being passed off as Christian doctrines.

    They also do not subscribe to the existence of a burning hell; an everlasting place of punishment and torment. The denial of this Biblical fact removes the fear of not obeying the commands of God, and removes any consequences for not receiving Jesus Christ as one's Savior and Lord. Many of these seducing doctrines do not recognize the canonized version of the Holy Bible as the inerrant, indisputable Word of God. They contend that it is incomplete, and that it is merely the works of mortal man; as opposed to The Holy Spirit inspired Word of God, penned by mortal men. This heresy gives reason to doubt the words found

CHAPTER THREE: THE SUM TOTAL & THE REMNANT

within the pages of the Holy Bible; thereby undermining and questioning the veracity, authenticity, and authority of the Bible. Since faith is the unquestioning trust and confidence in the Word we have heard from God, this doctrine has the potential to weaken our faith. All of this is to say nothing for the hundreds of supposedly Christian organizations that have been established where the Bible is not the final source of authority and more credence is given to the organizations publications; or the writings of their founder.

> *"An untold number of organizations with belief systems originating in the occult have seeped into Christian churches."*

An untold number of organizations with belief systems originating in the occult have seeped into Christian churches. Secret organizations and societies, that secretly are immersed in luciferian worship, have been allowed to practice their rites inside of Church buildings, and hold offices; even the office of Pastor. God have mercy on the Church, for she has allowed a host of occult practices to penetrate her gates. Practices such as: fortune telling, hypnotism, magic shows, tea leaf reading, horoscope parties, card parties, séances, Harry Potter books and movies, are as common as Bible study, choir rehearsal, and Sunday school. All of these practices are happening within the walls of some local assemblies.

In addition to some of the common cult practices that have been allowed to flourish under the banner of Christianity, there has been a frightening explosion of New Age religions within the corridors of our Christian society. The ranks of the

New Age are growing exponentially, and they are even promoting themselves now as "The New Age Religion." There is a preponderance of organizations from Adelphi to the Worldwide Church of God; that are steeped in the New Age philosophy of worshipping whatever god, or higher power, you choose. Groups like Christian Science, Church of Divine Man, Life Spring, Transcendental Meditation, Unity Church, and a vast number of others are permitted to peacefully coexist within the context of our Judeo-Christian democracy.

It is the scathing searing of these doctrines and heresies that the End Times Remnant Church must be careful of, and guarded against. She cannot allow her principles and standards to be polluted by these seductive, compromising dogmas. The remnant must rise above the fray, and not permit her standards of holiness, and consecration to Jehovah, to be tainted by all of these deceptive doctrines of devils; that the enemy is hurling at the Church. The set of guidelines established by Jesus and the apostles, must be the same set of guidelines in operation as Messiah Jesus returns for His bride; the Church. The End Times Remnant Church must mirror the virtue of the first century New Testament Remnant Church, to be identifiable as the Church the Lord is looking for, as He returns trying to find "faithfulness." Let the remnant arise! The Remnant Church is intended to be the sum total of all things that God is, to operate in the power and holiness that He deems necessary to attract non-believing Israel and Gentiles, and to wage war against the kingdom of darkness. She must guard herself against the deceptive doctrines the enemy tries to use to inject compromise and conformity into the essence

CHAPTER THREE: THE SUM TOTAL & THE REMNANT

of who the Church really is.

Chapter Four
A Different Gospel

"I marvel that ye are so soon removed from him that called you into the grace of Christ unto another gospel: which is not another; but there be some that trouble you, and would pervert the gospel of Christ. But though we, or an angel from heaven, preach any other gospel unto you than that which we have preached unto you, let him be accursed. As we said before, so say I now again, If any man preach any other gospel unto you than that ye have received, let him be accursed."
Galatians 1:6-9

    The original Gospel message, which is Old Testament driven, is more than the synoptic books of Matthew, Mark, Luke, and John. It goes beyond the smooth, rhythmic, harmonious songs we hear on our ITunes, internet radio, or streaming from our Android phones. It goes to the core of the promise Jehovah made to Adam and Eve in the Garden of Eden; when they ate the forbidden fruit. He promised He would put hatred between the seed of the woman and the seed of the serpent.[77] Also, that Satan's head would be bruised as a result of that enmity. He promised to provide His creation deliverance and salvation from the bondage into which the serpent had caused them to fall; when they disobeyed God. Yahweh prophesied of the coming of the Messiah.

The genuine message of the "Gospel" concerning Jesus Christ of Nazareth is that:

» Prophecy has been fulfilled
» Jesus was born of a virgin
» Jesus lived a sinless life
» Jesus died a substitutionary death, on the cross, for the sin of the world; past, present, and future
» He was crucified and buried
» He descended into hell and led the captives in Abraham's bosom free
» On the third day He arose from the dead
» He ascended into heaven and is seated at the right hand of God, the Father
» And now commands men everywhere to repent, be baptized, and receive the gift of the Holy Ghost[78]

As we attempt to define the Gospel message, we must be sure to include all of its components; relative to what the Bible

CHAPTER FOUR: A DIFFERENT GOSPEL

says the Gospel message is. This is necessary so as to determine the accuracy of its message, the user's expectation of what the gospel can do, and its ability to carry out God's intended purpose for what the Gospel message is. It is amazing to see how many definitions people have for this single word; the Gospel. The definition of exactly what the Gospel is often varies according to the person defining it.

The agnostic defines it differently from the atheist. The professing Christian may define it differently than the practicing Christian. Even among practicing Christians, different definitions may exist. However, the salient point which must be dealt with is that there IS definitely a correct definition. The Scripture that states there is a way that seems right to a man, but the end thereof is the way of death[79] deals with more than accepting Jesus as Savior. If man misses the message of the Gospel and fails to respond correctly, it is possible for him to be eternally separated from God; which is exactly what death is. Death is separation from life. God is life, and to be eternally separated from Him is eternal death; likewise to be with Him for all eternity is eternal life. All too often, the Gospel is merely thought to be, and referred to as, "the message about God." Although it is a message about God, it has many more components that must be acknowledged, and adhered to, in order to receive the benefit of accepting the Gospel as the life changing vehicle it is intended to be.

Before we look at the Old Testament driven definition of the gospel message, we want to look at the various ways people define the word "Gospel." The results of a recent poll I conducted show that some people thought that the Gospel is the first four books of the canonized Bible: the Gospel according to St. Matthew; the Gospel according to St. Mark; the Gospel according to St. Luke; and the Gospel according to St. John. Others thought that the Gospel is a universal value system to be followed; much like the Golden Rule. Still others felt that the Gospel is a way of being just towards all men; and an indication that we want to be like Jesus. Some said that the Gospel message is that, "All is forgiven." While others seemed to think that the Gospel message is a guideline to live your life by. It was interesting to hear that some felt that the Gospel message is what was given to show that God loves us, and is the story of how Jesus was sacrificed for mankind. One person said that the Gospel message is that, "Jesus died for our sins," while another felt that the Gospel is the message that, "God is great and God is good." The final person stated that the true Gospel message is, "The good news that Jesus has died, Jesus is risen from the grave, and that Jesus will come again."

As we can see, there are many opinions as to just what the Gospel is. Depending on what one feels that message is will directly impact the type of relationship they attempt to establish with Jehovah. The stark reality is that the Gospel is the central core of what the Bible is all about. It is a promise that has its origin in the Old Testament, and it's fulfillment in the New Testament. As stated earlier, as we discuss the Old and New Testaments of the Bible, we are actually talking about the Old and New Covenants that God has established as the basis of His relationship with mankind. Blood Covenant is the context in which God extends a mutual and binding agreement to man. It is the manner in which man can have relationship with his Creator. The first blood covenant was entered in the Garden of Eden; as Jehovah sacrificed animals to provide coats of skin to cover Adam and Eve's nakedness. This was the form of relationship God had with man, and continued to have with him until He formalized His covenant; after the destruction of the Tower of Babel. He formalized a blood covenant with Abram. Jehovah extended what became known as the Old Covenant to Abraham and his descendants. Not only was this extended to his bloodline, but also included those not of his ethnicity, who yet embraced the God of Abraham, and the form of worship He required.

The New Covenant was extended to the bloodline of Abraham, and the non-ethnic practitioners of Judaism, who would accept and receive Jesus of Nazareth as the Christ; Jehovah's promised Messiah. In the Old Testament the message is that Messiah is coming. In the New Testament the message is that Messiah is here. Hence, the Gospel message is an announcement that what was prophesied of in the Old Testament has come to fruition; thereby establishing a New Testament. Although the New Covenant is a superior covenant, it was not intended to invalidate the Old Covenant; it was intended to fulfill the promises made in the Old Covenant. Therein lies it's superiority, for it eliminated the need for an annual sacrifice for the sins of man; by providing a once and for all time sacrifice for the sin nature of man.

> *"The gospel message is that prophecy has been fulfilled; and the Messianic age has been ushered in."*

So then exactly what is the Gospel message? We can

correctly say that it is the good news. Good news of what and to whom, might be the retort? It is a proclamation, announcing, and giving notice to the world that Jesus Christ is Lord! The gospel message is that prophecy has been fulfilled; and the Messianic age has been ushered in. It loudly proclaims that Jesus Christ was incarnated in the flesh and lived a sinless life. He died on the cross as a substitutionary sacrifice for our sin nature, as prophesied; and was buried. He stayed in the grave for three days and after that was resurrected from the dead; and appeared to many witnesses. He was appointed by Jehovah, and reigns as Lord over His Kingdom. He now calls all mankind everywhere to repent, believe, be baptized, and receive the free gift of the Holy Spirit. This is the Gospel message.

Beginning in *Genesis 3:15*, and all throughout the Old Testament, the Father promised an answer to the problem that was caused when Adam and Eve listened to the deceptive lies of the evil one. Jehovah guaranteed that He would provide a way of escape from the compromised condition in which mankind found itself; and the subsequent disconnect that resulted when the forbidden fruit was eaten. Lucifer was able to seduce the original overseers of God's creation into a place of disqualification from being Jehovah's delegated authority and designated representative. Nevertheless, God was determined to rectify the situation. The Ancient of Days was intent upon reestablishing the relationship with His creation that had been broken in the Garden. He promised that He would restore the connection man had with Him by crushing the enemy's head. The Father had a provision that would rejoin the severed relationship by the shedding of His divine blood; that provision was Jesus of Nazareth. The good news is that God did not lie. In fact, He has kept His word, has kept His promise, and has sent His Messiah to pay the sin debt.

As we study the Old Testament, we read of a people, the Hebrews, who lived in hope of a Messiah coming to deliver them from bondage, exile, oppression, and war. While this is in fact what Jehovah had promised to provide, He was more concerned with this happening in the spiritual realm; thereby securing the spiritual freedom of His people. God's relationship with man has always been in the spirit. Man did not become a living being until he was first infused with the Spirit of God. This is where man's relationship with God is; and always has been. God wanted to restore the relationship which was broken by the disobedience which took place in the Garden of Eden. In Eden, perfect and complete harmony with His creation was destroyed. Satan was able to cause a breach in the relationship between the Creator and His creation. The great deceiver was able to cause a disconnection between God and man. There had once been a unified oneness and unobstructed communion that God had with Adam and Eve. It was an ideal father-child relationship; totally open and honest. That unobstructed relationship was now tainted by the knowledge of evil. What was once a fluid, continuous dialogue between God and man was now broken and challenged. The innocence and holiness of Adam can be seen in his super intelligence and ability to agree with the mind of Jehovah. This was demonstrated in Adam's ability to communicate with Jehovah, and name the animals that God had created.

We must acknowledge that with every promise God made to the people who maintained a proper relationship with Him, there was always a subsequent group of people looking for that promise to be fulfilled. The history of the Jews is the story of a people looking for their God to deliver them from their trials and tribulations in this world. The tragedy is that the Hebrews did not understand that their primary deliverance was not in the physical realm; but rather, in the spiritual sphere. This alludes to why Jesus told His executioners that His kingdom was not of this world, for if it were, His army would have been rescuing Him. As we return to examine the Old Testament, we find Israel in a continual state of looking for her Messiah. They believed God was telling the truth when He promised that the scepter would never leave the house of David.

So, from the time Jehovah took them into the promised land of Canaan, until the time of their exile, Israel had their eyes fixed with expectancy looking for the advent of their king. Nowhere in the Old Covenant, after the initial promise was made to Abraham, do we find a time when the nation of Israel was not focused on the coming of Messiah. They were continuously looking for a "Deliverer." The descendants of Abraham, Isaac, and Jacob were expecting God to keep His word and bless all of the nations of the earth through the Savior that would come through their bloodline. They expected Him: to be virgin-born; to be sinless; to be the sacrifice for sin; to die on a tree; and to only stay dead for three days. These were all of the things which were prophesied about the Messiah; and the Jews believed that all of these things were going to come to pass. This is the promise contained in the Gospel. This is what the Jews were looking for.

The New Testament reveals the fulfillment of all that was prophesied about Messiah Jesus in the Old Testament. The New Testament manifestation of the fulfillment of the original Gospel message can be seen in the following statements about Jesus of Nazareth; the Christ. He:

- Was born of the seed of a woman
- Came from the seed of Abraham, Isaac, and Jacob
- Came from the tribe of Judah
- Is an heir to the throne of David
- Was born to a virgin in Bethlehem
- Would flee into Egypt
- Was preceded by a forerunner
- Was declared to be the Son of God
- Had a Galilean ministry
- Was a prophet
- Was sent to heal the brokenhearted
- Was rejected by His own people; the Jews
- Was a priest after the order of Melchizedek
- Had a triumphal entry on a donkey
- Was betrayed by a friend and sold for thirty pieces of silver
- Was accused by false witnesses and silent to the accusations
- Was spat upon, smitten, scorned and mocked
- Hated without reason
- Was crucified with malefactors and was pierced through His hands, feet, and side
- Was given vinegar and gall
- Had soldiers gamble for His garments

THE REMNANT CHURCH

- » Had no bones broken
- » Prayed for His enemies
- » Was buried with the rich
- » Was resurrected and ascended to the right hand of God in heaven

The fact is that God took human form, and dwelt among men. This is what the name Emmanuel means; God with us. God dwelling among His creation was one of the most significant occurrences to happen in the annals of man's history. This event will not be paralleled, exceeded, or overshadowed by any other event until Jesus comes back the second time; to receive His Church unto Himself. The advent of Jesus coming into our time and space was so significant to the Jews; that according to Jewish eschatology the time of His habitation among mankind was referred to as, "the last days." The knowledge of this fact is of paramount importance, as the Gentiles who belong to the Messianic Jewish Church are involved in the study of "last things." We will be lulled into a false sense of reality, and a distorted sense of security, if we don't acknowledge this truth. We are not living at the beginning of the last days; we are living at the end of them.

As we study the apocalyptic prophecies written to the Jewish nation, we are trying to gauge where we are according to God's timetable. Unless we realize that the "last days" began over 2000 years ago, our sense of urgency and level of ministry will be compromised. We will be deluded into thinking that we have a lot of time before Jesus returns; when in reality time IS short;

really shorter than we think. So many major prophecies have already been fulfilled, and so many events have been unleashed in the heavenlies, that the final stage is set for the reinstitution of live animal sacrifice in Israel. Once this begins, the Abomination of Desolation, mentioned in the book of Daniel, can happen any day. Reader please let this sink in. Israel is finally back in their inheritance; Canaan. Red Heifer! There is already a cadre of priests in place, who have been trained in the rites of live animal sacrifices since the 80s. The stage is truly set for the chain of events to unfurl that would culminate with the second coming of Messiah Jesus, Yeshua Ha'Mashiach.

All through the New Testament, Jesus was continually alluding to the fact that He was the promised Messiah. His cousin John the Baptist recognized Him for who He was. John's response was, "Behold the Lamb of God that taketh away the sin of the world." The Father's voice echoed to the crowd who had come out to receive John's baptism of repentance. As God affirmed who Jesus was, the heavens opened up, and the Holy Ghost descended as a dove and draped Himself over Jesus. As the Spirit fell on Jesus, it was much like what happens to a sheet when you throw it over a chair. The sheet takes the form of the chair upon which it is draped. That is what happened in Jordan's River, the Spirit took the form of the person upon whom He was draped...Jesus.

The Greek word used in the Scripture describing Jesus' baptism in the Holy Ghost is "epie." It means, "superimposed" as a relation of distribution, over, having charge of." The voice of Jehovah bellowed from heaven for all the bystanders to plainly hear, "THIS IS my beloved Son, in whom I am well pleased." One of Jesus' main missions was to convince His disciples that He was the promised Messiah. Even when John the Baptist's disciples approached Jesus and asked him, "Art thou the one that should come, or should we look for another?" Jesus' response was designed to alleviate any and all doubt about Him being the promised Messiah. It is significant to note, and we keep reiterating, that Jesus was the "promised" Messiah. There were many men named Jesus in that day, and it would have been easy enough to say that there was no big thing about Jesus being born; just another Jesus in the neighborhood. The single fact that made the birth of Jesus of Nazareth significant was that everything about His birth FULFILLED PROPHECY. By Him fulfilling all that was spoken of His coming, He verified that He was the promised Savior; and that Jehovah had kept His word. The New Testament is abounding with proof of His Messiahship. He constantly validated who He was by the signs and wonders that were wrought by His hands, and by the command of His voice. So much so, that the crowds even asked, "will Messiah do more than this when He appears?"

As we consider the simplicity of the Gospel message, as taught by the post-ascension apostles and disciples, it can be summarized with the following verse of scripture...Repent and be baptized in the name of the Jesus Christ for the remission of your sins, and ye shall receive the gift of the Holy Ghost.[80] When we examine the Gospel message, we find that the Lord of the Kingdom gave a command which is an integral part of the Gospel. In that proclamation and command, we find the very prerequisite for the conversion process. He spoke this as He came out of the tempting in the wilderness; to begin His ministry. As He began His ministry, Jesus gave a clarion command for people to repent and receive the new form of relationship that Jehovah was establishing in the earth. Jesus cried. "Repent for the Kingdom of God is at hand." What was He really saying? Why was there a prerequisite call for repentance before receiving the Kingdom of God? The Kingdom of God is the government of God in man's life, because of the finished work of Jesus Christ, accomplished by the power of the Holy Spirit.

Was there any difference between what He was asking folks to do, and what Jehovah had asked of Israel in the Old Covenant? The fact that the first thing the King of the Kingdom asked folks to do, was repent is a major insight into what God thought was necessary in order for people to be able to accept His governance of their lives. To repent involves a drastic change that impacts root behavior. It does not simply mean changing the outward appearance of a thing, but it involves a process that separates a thing from the source of its sustenance; or from the thing that sustains it, and causes it to grow. Repentance involves a total one hundred and eighty degree about face; and a change of direction that sends a person in a direction that is a polar opposite from the path on which they had been previously traveling. In other words, in order for a person to live a life that is totally submitted to God, it must be marked by their commitment to be governed by God instead of their own fleshly appetites. There must first be an axe laid to the roots of self-government, self-actualization, and self-fulfillment in order to submit to the governance of God in one's life.

The basic idea is that before one can be converted; there first must be a change of direction in their life. It is hard to go in a new direction if you have not first stopped going in the old direction. Conversion or salvation without repentance is actually a misunderstanding of what the process is supposed to look like. Jesus preached repentance and the first century New Testament Remnant Church apostles preached repentance...it is the first thing that has to happen before one can start a new life. The source that feeds the old life must be put to death. Repentance represents a type of death. As Peter stood to address the crowd at Pentecost, he delivered the message that pricked their hearts and caused them to ask what they needed to do in response to being convicted; and being made known of their needful position for salvation. Peter's answer was repent, be converted, be baptized, and receive the gift of the Holy Ghost.

This was the imperative command of the Gospel message after Jesus ascended to the Father, and returned in the form of the Holy Spirit. This was the message given to the crowd who were to become the first members of the Messianic-Gentile first century New Testament Remnant Church. It is yet the imperative command of the Gospel message today. The first century Gospel message included all of the components which spoke to the prophetic fulfillment of the coming of Messiah, His virgin birth, His sinless life, His substitutionary death upon a tree; His three days in the grave, and His triumphant resurrection. The command and challenge today is the same as it was then; accept these truths and receive eternal life by following the ordered steps to procure it. Even as Peter took the Gospel message to the house of Cornelius, the message did not change.[81] God sent Peter to the city of Caesarea; which was chosen as the first city to have Gentile believers of Jesus Christ and a non-Jewish church. Caesarea was the largest and one of the most important port cities on the Mediterranean in Palestine; and the capital of the Roman province in Judaea. When Peter went back to Jerusalem, the circumcised believing Jews upbraided him for keeping company with the uncircumcised Gentiles. As Peter explained his response to the command of God, and the results, the saints of Jerusalem held their peace; glorified God; and concluded that the Gentiles had been granted the gift of repentance unto life.[82]

Everywhere the apostles and disciples went, they proclaimed the prophetic arrival of God's promised Messiah, and the fact that He fulfilled everything that was spoken concerning Him. Their challenge to the hearers was always the same; repent, change your old ways, and get on board with the new way of having a relationship with God. Their message was consistent. If the Remnant Church that emerges out of the conformed, deceived, compromised Church is ever to accomplish her God-given assignment, she must declare the same consistent message that was delivered by her first century model and example.

Now let's turn our attention to the Gospel message taught to the Gentile Church by the Apostle Paul. As we explore that message Paul taught to the Gentile converts, over whom he had been made overseer, it is easy to see that his message didn't deviate from the message given by Peter; and the other apostolic overseers. He consistently stressed the Messiah's fulfillment of the prophecies concerning Him; His sinless life; His death, burial, and resurrection; and His call to salvation. There is only one Gospel message for all people, and for every age. It was never intended to be changed. It is the power of God unto salvation, to the Jew first; and then to everyone else that believes.

Paul aggressively preached the same message as that which was given to that group of Jews and proselytes on the Day of Pentecost. He taught an uncompromising Gospel based on the grace of God, not the works of man. He preached a Gospel that acknowledged the Ancient of Days as the only one and living true God; and man's need for repentance as a requisite to salvation. God sent Barnabas to find Saul (whose name was changed to Paul) so that they could help Peter establish the saints and Church in the city of Antioch; the city where the believers in Jesus Christ were first called Christians. After spending a year there, they returned to Jerusalem.[83] When they returned to Antioch, Jehovah consecrated them as apostles to the Gentiles and sent them to Seleucia, Cyprus, Salamis, Paphos, Pamphylia, Pisidia, Iconium, and Lycaonia. They instructed the Gentiles to turn from the vanities of offering sacrifices to false gods, and instead to worship the living God; who created everything.[84]

The message delivered by the Post-Reformation Remnant Church required specific modifications, due to the spiritual environment in which that message had to be delivered. As we study the acts of the Holy Ghost, and the first century New Testament Remnant Church, we witness a presentation of the Gospel message that had repentance as a part of the core foundation upon which the presentation was made. It was not a presentation that took for granted that the hearers inherently knew that the concept of repentance was a prerequisite for conversion, and salvation. There were no assumptions made that the hearers were knowledgeable enough to know that they had to lay an axe to their root behaviors; and perceptions that had heretofore controlled their behavior. Nor was it a presentation that presupposed that the hearers would know that they could not merely change the name of the god that they worshipped, and still practice their old ways of worship. It was a presentation which explicitly made plain the notion that a conversion to this way of life mandated evident changes in mental attitudes and physical behaviors. It clearly stated that there must be obvious, visual evidence of a changed lifestyle and agenda.

The first century Remnant Church required a noticeable difference in behavior, evidenced by a form of worship that acknowledged Jesus of Nazareth as the Christ of Jehovah God. There was a requirement to change the way of having a relationship with Jehovah from one in which keeping the law met the standard requirements for acceptance. The shift was from considering one's works enough to maintain relationship with the Father, to exercising faith in the Lord Jesus Christ; as being the Messiah sent forth by Jehovah, the Ancient of Days. While the worship form of the Messianic Jews and Gentile proselytes didn't change; the way they had access to the God of Israel did. Jesus did not become the object of their worship; He became the way with which they now had access to the object of their worship, Jehovah.

This addresses, perhaps, one of the most serious deceptions

THE REMNANT CHURCH

that the enemy has introduced into the Church. Through the seduction of the Western Roman Catholic and Eastern Orthodox Churches, Christianity was introduced to a misplaced object of worship, Mary. Subsequent to that seduction, the Post Reformation Remnant Church substituted Jesus as the object of worship. While Jesus is worthy to be praised, the ultimate object of our worship should be our heavenly Father; Jehovah is His name. Now we are sure that right now, many people are crying heresy, heresy. Study the Scriptures carefully, and you will see that Jehovah, God of the Hebrews has always been the God we are supposed to worship. Jesus is the door by which we have access to God. Jesus went through painstaking measures to make sure that His disciples plainly understood His purpose in relation to the Father. He taught them to go to God through Him. He taught them that He did not testify of Himself; but of His Father who is in heaven. The Holy Ghost points us to Jesus; Jesus points us to Jehovah. God the Father, spirit; God the Son, spirit; God the Holy Ghost, spirit; all God, all Spirit. THIS is the mystery of the triune God; the Trinity.

So, as we look at the Post Protestant Reformation Remnant Church, two things that need to be addressed are: a notable absence of repentance as a foundation of the Gospel message; and the substitution of Jesus as our ultimate object of worship. While we understand that these statements may be troublesome to your theology, it is imperative for us to examine these concepts to correct some erroneous teachings found in the Post Reformation Remnant Church. These teachings are not only dangerous to the Church's correct form of worship, but they impact the way people receive salvation; and ultimately walk out their Christian life. As we note the early Church fathers teachings, we find a definite presence of repentance as a part of the conversion process. It was termed salvific repentance; and was considered to have a cause and effect impact upon conversion. Salvific denotes having the intention to bring about salvation or redemption. There are basically three views of salvific repentance. These include: turning from or being willing to turn from one's sins; changing one's mind about Jesus Christ; and repentance is not a condition of eternal salvation at all. However, a turning from sins as a condition of eternal salvation is a view consistent with faith as a mandatory condition of salvation. A willingness to turn from sin and changing one's mind about Jesus Christ are also essential for salvation.[85] Jesus' initial message after coming out of being tempted forty days and nights by Satan was, "Repent for the Kingdom of God is at hand."[86]

However, in contemporary times, there has been a blatantly apparent absence of the concept of repentance in the Gospel message. It is not uncommon to hear preachers tell their listeners that all they have to do is believe in Jesus and they will be saved. People are told that if they believe in the hearts and confess with their mouth, that they will be saved. Although this sounds Scriptural, it is not the "total message." Careful examination of the Gospel message, as given by Jesus, the apostles, and the disciples, ALWAYS included mention of the concept of repentance. Even when the word was not explicitly used, its definition was always present as being associated with salvation.

If all people had to do was believe in Jesus, then the devil would be saved. The Scripture tells us that the devils believe, and tremble. Thou believest that there is one God; thou doest well: the devils also believe, and tremble. James 2:19

The devil trembles....this is more than a lot of folks do in their conversion process. A lot of people experience a "so-called" conversion that is absent of any drama. Anytime you change from one kingdom to another, it should never be a passé event. This is not saying that it has to be an emotional circus, but anytime someone defects from one government to another, there should be something that earmarks it as more than a "business as usual" event. There is nothing "casual" about repentance; it is a "drastic" change. It is a major about face; and change in direction. It is similar to "slamming on the brakes," coming to a complete stop, and reversing your direction. Repentance should leave some skid marks on the road of your life. There should be evidence that an extreme change has taken place in your life.

Repentance is not optional. Repentance deals with roots (character); thoughts, actions, motives, lifestyles, social customs, family and economic ties. Repentance is the work of the Holy Spirit producing a conscious awareness of rebellion and lawlessness as man's basic, or root sin. It results in turning from self-will to the Lordship of Jesus Christ. Repentance calls us out of a life of sin and rebellion into a life of holiness and submission to God. God's purpose in repentance is to prepare us to learn new ways. By God's initiative, the Holy Spirit calls us to repentance, and imparts to us the necessary faith to accept Jesus Christ as Lord and Savior. Conversion expresses the action of the 'will', or volition, in turning to God. Repentance and faith are two sides of the same coin; both of which are integral parts of the Gospel message.

There have been many restoration movements by the Spirit of God, as he added virtue back into the Church; while He continues to move her back to her place of prominence; and the authority she possessed in the first century. There have been numerous restoration movements in the Church and these movements have had tremendous impact on the contents of the Gospel message. These historic movements include the Protestant Movement, the Holiness Movement, the Pentecostal Movement, the Latter Rain Movement, the Charismatic Movement, and the Prophetic Apostolic Movement.[87] All of these movements had an effect on the content of the Gospel message that was being presented during the time God was reestablishing those missing parts back into the Church. However, the core of the message has and always should be the same. The components we listed earlier in this chapter are essential parts of the message, and can never be compromised. While it may be necessary for additional explanations to bring clarity to the current move of the Spirit in the Body of Christ, the basic tenets of the Gospel must never be compromised; or taken away from. To subtract these basic tenets jeopardizes the integrity of the message, diminishes its effectiveness, and sets the possibility of rendering the message ineffectual; and not capable of delivering its intended results. The sanctity of the Gospel message is of paramount importance; and the original components must always be present. Anything short of the original components is definitely a different Gospel; and must be viewed as such. Although we recognize that sometimes clarity is needed to explain the current move of God; anything that diminishes, alters, or compromises the initial basic tenets of the Gospel is dangerous, it should be closely examined; and ultimately rejected. No form of clarification should be allowed to alter the original Gospel message; and should only be allowed to clarify the current move of God taking place in the Church. Absolutely no form of clarity should ever be permitted to replace any of the original tenets of the Gospel message; the integrity of those original tenets must always remain in place.

As we explore the concept and basis of the "love gospel," it becomes apparent that the Remnant Church has to maintain vigilance; and contend for the faith that was delivered to us by our forefathers. The "love gospel" is perhaps one of the most dangerous gospels around, due to the semi-correct message it sends. This aberration of truth sends the message that God is a loving God and would never commit such a violent and loveless act as condemning someone to hell. The "love gospel" is guilty of overlooking sound Biblical doctrine in order to accept a lot of other "faiths" as Christian faith. It leads the Church down a path where she becomes tolerant of unrepented lifestyles and endorses a form of "Christian Humanism"; rather than maintaining loyalty to true Biblical instruction. This "other gospel" places the major emphasis on "love" and "unity" as the foundational tenets of the message. This "love gospel" also serves as a basis for the Ecumenical Movement, which is aggressively leading the world towards a one world religion; here at the end of time.

This gospel is guilty of being a contributor to opening the

door for seducing and compromising doctrines to seep into the Church. In order to accomplish the sought after unity, allowances are made to the Holy Scriptures; they are compromised. In response to those who want to use the Bible as the standard for evaluating the lives of those who profess to be Christians, proponents of this erroneous doctrine cry out, "Don't judge; you are causing division." This is only one of the many false, compromised, watered down teachings that are prevalent in the Church today. There are just too many gospels being preached today that do not require any repentance, or commitment. They are teachings which fail to recognize the Lordship of Jesus Christ.

Additionally, many of the contemporary translations of the Scriptures serve to reinforce these erroneous teachings; some so blatant as to be specifically modified to endorse the foundational beliefs of a denomination. The "love gospel" is just one of many that perverts the word of God, and twists it to suit its own agenda. Unfortunately, sound doctrine is ignored, and the Scriptures are manipulated to justify unity; and to tolerate doctrinal error for the sake of maintaining the peace. According to them, the gospel is not supposed to cause division. This is totally contrary to what Messiah Jesus said. In fact, He said that He came to bring a sword of division.

"Think not that I am come to send peace on earth: I came not to send peace, but a sword."
Matthew 10: 34

Again, this doctrine discourages us from trying the spirits, proving all things, and examining ourselves and others, to determine if we are true to the faith; and the original message.

While the Church recognizes that there are going to be people who follow Jesus that don't belong to our local church or denomination, she must also be able to identify all who come in Jesus' name; and are proliferating the "true Gospel." Sound Biblical doctrine and the integrity of the original Gospel message are of the highest importance. She is commanded not to water down, sugar-coat, pervert, or deny the faith that was handed down to us by our apostolic fathers. The Body of Christ is to defend its inviolability, and maintain its veracity at all costs. The Remnant Church can ill-afford to have the purity of the Scriptures denigrated, maligned, or compromised. It would be impossible to distinguish who is disseminating the "true Gospel" if the Church is guilty of doing the same things that the erroneous gospels are doing. Proponents of any gospel that are twisting the Bible to support their lifestyle, or lack thereof, must cease that behavior. Otherwise, they will stand in judgment for the error of their doctrine.

However, make no doubt about it, that as defenders of the faith, the Remnant Church is definitely charged to judge between sound doctrine and error. She is not supposed to just blindly accept anything that comes down the pike; that sounds close to the truth of the original message. The Remnant Church must be able and willing to reject any false doctrines that do not line up with the original message of the Word of God. One noticeable fallacy of the "love gospel" is that it promotes unity over truth, and subsequently accepts the seducing spirits and doctrines of devils that are so aggressively infiltrating the Church.

CHAPTER FOUR: A DIFFERENT GOSPEL

The Remnant Church also has to do her due diligence to safeguard the thinking of the Body of Christ; in order to ensure that she did not fall prey to the "prosperity, or name it & claim it" gospel.

"Beloved, above all things, I desire that you would prosper and be in health, even as your soul doeth prosper"
III John 1: 2

This is a conditional promise; a cause and effect statement. Our physical prosperity is in direct proportional relationship to our spiritual prosperity. If we are not succeeding in the development of our spiritual, mental, emotional, and volitional well-being, why should we expect to succeed in our physical well-being? First the spiritual, then the natural, right? This is not the premise upon which the "prosperity gospel" is based. This other gospel teaches its constituents that all they have to do is name it and claim it. This gospel teaches that financial blessing is the will of God for all Christians, and that faith, positive confession, and donations to Christian ministries will increase one's material wealth.

This health and wealth gospel is guilty of disseminating, or helping to postulate, the notion that if you are not acquiring material wealth, then you are not being blessed by God. This other gospel is guilty of perpetrating the notion that one's acquisition of material wealth and health is the measure of how God is, or is not, blessing you. It further endorses the idea that if humans have faith in God, He will grant them His promises of health, prosperity, and security. It also leads one to believe that if one confesses these promises to be true, it will be perceived by God as an act of faith; to which Jehovah will honor and respond. This other gospel emphasizes that God wants His people to be happy; so He has given endorsement to the idea of personal empowerment. It often presents the doctrine by teaching about financial responsibility, and our obligation to prove God by giving. Additionally, it proposes that our reconciliation with God includes the alleviation of the curses of disease, sickness, and poverty. While it IS definitely our faith in God's ability that delivers us from sickness, disease, and poverty, this gospel ignores some blatant truths taught in the Bible. Some sickness exists for the sole purpose of God getting a person's attention. Others exist so that God can get glory out of delivering that person from the grasps of those ailments. While Jesus Himself stated that the poor would always be with us.

"For ye have the poor always with you; but me ye have not always."
Matthew 26: 11

The "prosperity gospel" first came into prominence in the United States during the 1950's. Its original origins are linked to the New Thought movement of the 1800's. During the 1980's, the doctrine became very popular and prominent among televangelists, and was endorsed by many in the Word of Faith Movement. Ministers such as E.W. Kenyon, Oral Roberts, Robert Tilton, T.L. Osborn, Kenneth Hagin, Fred Price, A.A. Allen, Creflo Dollar, and Kenneth Copeland, have been cited as proponents of this doctrine. During the late 90's and into 2000, it was adopted by many of the popular leaders in the Charismatic Movement. Many Christian missionaries have also ascribed to this notion. Often, the churches that endorse and teach this doctrine are non-denominational, independent assemblies. There have been many Pentecostal, Charismatic, as well as mainstream Christian leaders who have denounced prosperity theology as heresy. They claim that it promotes idolatry, is contrary to Scripture, and is irresponsible in its assumption of basing the blessing of God on material acquisition. Indeed, it teaches that you need prosperity in your material life, as opposed to the reality that the place where you really need prosperity is in your spiritual life.

This different gospel teaches that diamonds, rubies, gold, platinum, and a plethora of other material riches are the rewards that come to those who have sufficient faith; and donate sufficient funds into the ministries of those who espouse this "prosperity gospel." This dangerous teaching promises that if people have enough faith in God and donate generously, that God will reward their giving by returning what they've sown back to them thirty, sixty, and one hundred fold. This prosperity theology is peculiarly an American theology; but it is catching on worldwide. Pastors and ministers all over the world are wholeheartedly presenting this message; which offers false hope, false promises, presents a failed message with results which often do not materialize, and is in fact a "false gospel."

The "prosperity gospel" commonly comes packaged in "Word of Faith" theology; which was developed early in the 20th century. It is often referred to as the "Name It and Claim It" gospel. The proponents of this message assure the people of God that Jehovah promises to make them wealthy and healthy IF they will possess and demonstrate adequate faith. The sad truth is that they present the Gospel as a message that is primarily about material acquisitions and earthly rewards. This twisted form of the Gospel message teaches obedience, giving, and faith as a way to get things from God. It presents these requisites for normal Christian living as things to be used with the ulterior motive of tricking God into doing something nice for us. The "prosperity gospel" uses faith and doing good things as leverage to be used as a means of acquiring material blessings from God. It makes God a deity who is obligated to bless His people with material rewards if they possess the right amount of faith; and use it to claim their blessings.

> *"Holiness is the standard for Christian living."*

One has to ask oneself, "What about the millions of believers who live in countries with impoverished economies?" What about the indigent of the world? Does this mean that they are not among God's "blessed" people? Of course the answer is a resounding NO; but this reality does not align itself with the message of the "prosperity gospel." Unfortunately, the message of this "different gospel" is false, unbiblical, and full of failed promises. It wants the Church to believe that God has guaranteed His people physical health and material abundance. However, what Christians are promised is: forgiveness of sin; the free gift everlasting life; the riches of being a joint heir with Jesus Christ; and the assurance of splendor while dwelling in eternity in the presence of the living God of creation, Jehovah; the Ancient of Days. In the end, if the "prosperity gospel" could and did deliver everything it promised; it would still come up short; and be amazingly inadequate. The true Gospel offers forgiveness of sin, escape from eternal damnation in hell and the lake of fire, and eternity lived with God. No amount of earthly riches and health could ever compare, or compete, with those great blessings.

Another false gospel that the Remnant Church has to be on guard against is the morally deficient gospel of 'carnal Christianity'. It is an equally dangerous "other gospel" that is definitely different from the one preached and taught by the first century New Testament Remnant Church. This convoluted gospel leaves an emptiness in the hearer's ears concerning God's grace, and His requirements for a "holy life." This erroneous teaching has many souls deceived, and the conflicting appearance produces Christians who have not submitted themselves to the Lordship of Jesus Christ. God expressly warns us that we should not sow unto the flesh; but rather we should sow unto the Spirit. This hideous false gospel from the pit of hell produces an attitude in people that advocates the idea that, "I'm just a carnal Christian, so a little sin won't hurt." It endorses the idea that man can always depend on God's grace to cover his or her wanton practice of sinning. It fosters a false sense of reality that seems to cosign the notion that God's grace will cover all my sin. God's word plainly teaches us that if we sow unto the flesh, it will cause the flesh to give us a harvest of corruption.

People are erroneously being taught that once they have been justified in Christ, once they have been granted forgiveness of their sin, holy living is not required to receive the promises of God. They are led to believe that they are going to heaven any old how, and that they can live any old way. People are being deceived into thinking that their eternal soul will retain its status of deliverance from the penalty of hell; regardless as to what kind of daily lifestyle they lead. These souls are really in danger of experiencing hell's fire. The Bible clearly says that without holiness, no man will or can see God. Holiness is the standard for Christian living. Jehovah commands us, "Be ye holy as I am holy....be ye holy, as the one who has called you is holy." Our hearts desire should be for the truth of God's Word. The Remnant Church should be yearning to promote a word that appeals to our spirit; not to our fleshly desires; and emotions. She should be disseminating the message that will cut off the flesh and lay it bare before Jehovah in confession and repentance.

This "other gospel" of carnal Christianity does not encourage believers to question their commitment to Christ. Instead, they are told that they have believed, and that is all that is necessary for them to do. They are deceivingly told that all is well with their soul, but the reality is that it's holiness or hell. Holiness must characterize our lives; because God has not called us into uncleanness, but unto holiness. The Scripture states that God has chosen us in Christ, before the foundation of the world, that we should be holy and without blame before Him in love.

"According as He hath chosen us in Him before the foundation of the world, that we should be holy and without blame before Him in love."
Ephesians 1: 4

We are not to fashion ourselves according to our former lusts, but as He which has called us is holy, so we ourselves ought to be holy.[88] The painstaking truth that Christians have to acknowledge, and ask themselves, is if a Christian who continually sows to their flesh was ever truly saved?

There should always be Holy Spirit conviction and repentance in salvation. There must be a hatred of sin, and a turning from it. If a person is continuing to practice the things they did before they were saved, one must question whether or not there was really any 'deliverance' in the first place. Or was it just an emotional response to feeling guilty; and not wanting to go to hell. If a person continues to walk in the ways of unrighteousness, and satisfying the appetites of the flesh, it can be considered as an indication that there has not been an eradication of the sin nature. It demonstrates that the person is still a slave to sin; not a slave to righteousness. Sin is no longer supposed to rule and reign in our mortal bodies. According to the true Gospel message, there is supposed to be 'newness' in us; a new nature, a new way of life; a new master. The Holy Spirit should be at work in us telling us that carnality is not alright, and that perfecting holiness in the sight of God and man is not optional. It is a mandate. The long and short of it is that if we want to reap everlasting life from the Spirit; we have to sow unto the Spirit. This different gospel is one-sided, and makes no demands, or requirements of us. It is predicated on the notion of God giving, giving, and giving; and us receiving, receiving, and receiving. This whole idea totally ignores the basis of covenant, which is the context in which God offers relationship to mankind. Covenant is a "mutual" and binding agreement between two or more parties. This different gospel of carnality absolves man from maintaining the mutual, reciprocal basis of covenant.

An important notion that cannot go undetected is that the other gospel of carnal Christianity espouses a philosophy that cosigns the idea that the lust of the eyes, the lust of the flesh, and the pride of life are not necessarily all bad. Even if they are representative of this satanic world system, and its ungodly influence on people, they don't necessarily make you ungodly.

They say that God wants His people to enjoy the things this world has to offer. This carnal Christianity gospel stands in direct opposition to the purposes of God. The reason that old things pass away and all things become new is so that the nature, which heretofore gave ready compliance and obedience to the carnal body appetite of the flesh, can come subject to the dictates and commands of Jehovah; the Great I AM. The remnant must truly offer their bodies as a living sacrifice, holy and acceptable to God; as opposed to giving into fleshly appetites.

The true Gospel encourages the believer not to use the Word of God as a means to justify sin. One need not see how close they can walk to the ways of the world; and still be classified a child of God. The true Gospel nudges the believer to find the Scripture that will warn them against sin; and instruct them how to flee to Christ to escape sin. The real Gospel challenges the Christian to see how close they can walk to God in Christ; by the power of the Holy Ghost. This is the challenge to the believer, versus seeing how close he can walk to the world, and sin; and

CHAPTER FOUR: A DIFFERENT GOSPEL

still be considered to be saved. The false carnality gospel does not encourage its constituents to mortify their fleshly members, and the deeds of the flesh. It fails to insist that they put off: fornication, uncleanness, inordinate affection, evil concupiscence, covetousness, idolatry, anger, wrath, malice, blasphemy, filthy communication, and lying. Instead this false gospel tolerates these things, and says that you have made a decision for Christ; and God understands your humanity causes you to sin. Again, this perverted message doesn't challenge people to perfect, or practice, holiness. It excuses them by saying God knows the spirit is willing but the flesh is weak. It fails to reinforce the fact that Christians are called to be self-denying children of God; who say 'no' to the ways of the world, deny ungodliness and worldly lusts.

The real Gospel teaches us that we have put off the old man, with its worldly lusts, and have put on Christ; and a Christ-like new nature...old things are passed away. This carnal gospel simply does not instruct the believer that the will of Jehovah for their life is sanctification; plain and simple. It falls short in explaining that God really does want His people to be set apart from sin, by allowing the progressive work of the Holy Spirit to impact their hearts and lives. The Father's goal is to subsequently drive the Church to a place of constantly seeking to please God by sowing unto the Spirit. As opposed to the real Gospel, the false carnal gospel does not propagate the notion that the grace of God has appeared to all men, and He instructs us to reject and renounce all ungodliness and worldly passionate desires. Furthermore, it fails to instruct us to live sober, temperate, self-controlled lives in an upright, devout manner. It is missing the component that challenges us to live spiritually-whole lives, which allow the Spirit of God to have the reign over us in this present evil, and untoward generation.

This false carnal Christianity gospel does not break the power of sin, but rather tolerates it. It does not perpetuate the reality of a new heart and a new nature. It promotes an insurance policy against hell, rather than an aggressive presentation of a

> *"Any gospel that doesn't teach repentance as a mandatory prerequisite for salvation is undoubtedly a different gospel. "*

life characterized by holiness of thought, and holiness of deed. Contrary to what this false gospel teaches, one has to do more than say yes to the four spiritual laws and believe that Jesus Christ did exist. It takes more than simply believing that one is saved and is saved forever; no matter what one does. It is definitely a "false gospel" that allows one to stay in their sin and sow unto the flesh; and yet assures its followers that eternal life is within their grasp.

This other gospel is guilty of misleading people into thinking that there is another way into heaven aside from the narrow way spoken of in *Matthew 7: 13-14*.

"Enter ye in at the strait gate: for wide is the gate, and broad is the way that leadeth to destruction, and many there be which go in thereat: Because strait is the gate and narrow is the way; which leadeth unto life, few there be that find it."

CHAPTER FOUR: A DIFFERENT GOSPEL

Anytime a gospel is preached that doesn't make any demands on you, one which is not opposed to you pleasing your flesh, and makes it seem that the way of salvation is an easy road; you have to be cautious of succumbing to that message. If it doesn't challenge you to change your lifestyle to reflect one that is committed to holiness as the standard way of living, something is very wrong. This false gospel tries to put new wine in old wineskins. It doesn't admonish one to put the old life to death before receiving the new life. Instead, it tries to incorporate the things and attitudes of the world into "doing it for Christ." It says come receive the new life, and the old lifestyle will eventually assimilate into the new life; or ultimately take care of its own demise.

The message of the true Gospel instructs us to put the old lifestyle to death. We are mandated to hate the world system, and the old ways of the world. We must die to the world and all of its allurements. We must be crucified with Christ. We cannot afford to compromise with sin; but rather abhor it, flee from it, and do our best to obliterate it in our lives. Any gospel that doesn't teach these things is definitely a different gospel. Any gospel that doesn't teach repentance as a mandatory prerequisite for salvation is undoubtedly a different gospel. Without true repentance, it is hard for the justification and sanctification processes to take place. In order for these two processes to begin, there has to be a putting to death of sin in the life of the believer. God has to be able to view us just as though we have never sinned, and then set us apart to be used for His holy purposes. The only way this can happen is when we turn from practicing sin, and pleasing ourselves as our primary focus; and subsequently turn to pleasing God.

The bottom line is that the false gospel of carnal Christianity fails to stress that there can be no compromise with sin. Holiness stresses that all sin must be forsaken, renounced, repented of, and hated. Nor does the carnal gospel teach that the believer must die to the world, and the love of worldly things. It fails to instruct the believer to forsake pursuing their own pleasure in deference to pursuing the things that please God. The true Gospel teaches us that we cannot defend, excuse, or cover sin. Nor can we seek to make "terms" with God when it comes to issues of sin. In fact, the Holy Ghost will convict us of sin in our lives, simultaneously convince us that it is wrong and needs to be turned from; and forsaken. In reality, there is no middle ground or gray area between carnality and holiness. There is no room to make provision for the lust of the eyes, the lust of the flesh, and the pride of life.

If we have been crucified with Christ, buried in the watery grave of baptism, and raised in the newness of life as a citizen in the Kingdom of God; there is no room for compromise. You have died to having sin as your master; therefore it should be a natural consequence not to allow sin to reign in your mortal body. This is a conscious decision that must be made. If you are influenced by a gospel that tells you that you have a choice in the matter; it should come as no surprise that there are so many Christians who choose to live marginal Christian lives. They have no problem doing those things that please the flesh; especially since the false gospel of carnality tells them that this is acceptable behavior. This false gospel does not teach deliverance from the realm of sin and translation into the Kingdom of God's grace. It fails to teach that there is deliverance from the power and dominion of sin.

It also fails to reinforce the concept of "positional relationship," and the idea that our citizenship is not of this world; it is based in heaven. We are fellow citizens with the saints and of the household of God. There has really been a complete change in our position; we ARE seated in heavenly places in Christ Jesus. The true Gospel reiterates the fact that we are no longer under the dominion of sin; it no longer controls our destiny. This stands in direct opposition to what the false gospel of carnal Christianity propagates. This different gospel also does not communicate the reality that salvation produces a life that is free from the 'power' of sin. This false gospel does not teach deliverance from the sin that holds, binds, and reigns over us. It doesn't communicate that God eternally delivers us, and makes us more than conquerors through Jesus Christ our Lord. It fails to teach that His purpose is to break the reign of sin in our lives. It simply does not allow us to know that the Gospel is supposed to destroy sin and its entire works; and all that belongs to the realm of sin.

It is definitely a compromised message; a different gospel; if it endorses a Christian life where it is ok to habitually "practice" sin. It is not alright to abide or live in sin, and any message that co-signs this as a lifestyle is a deception straight from the pits of hell. It is a false and different gospel that teaches there is no problem walking in accordance to the course of this world.

One cannot continue to lead the same old Godless and Christless life, with no change in behavior and opinions. The gospel that allows this to be status quo is extremely different from what Christ taught. Converts to this different gospel have a form of godliness, but their lives deny the power thereof. They have been swayed by a message that is alluring to the flesh, as opposed to the spirit. Their lives are reflective of a message that lacks the principle of self-denial. They continue to be blasphemers, disobedient to their parents, unthankful, unholy, trucebreakers, boastful, high-minded, false accusers, greedy, covetous, savage with their tongue, proud, and undependable.

This different gospel endorses a lifestyle that is prone to sensual pleasures and vain amusements. Fleshly, self-indulgent, lewd, sexual, promiscuous, immoral, and unrestrained lustful activities are all too familiar to recipients of the false gospel of carnal Christianity. This message from hell produces converts that have a noticeable unconcern for holy and righteous living. They are content to live nominal and marginal Christian lives. This is because this form of Christianity makes no demands on one to live a life that demonstrates that there has been a deliverance from the bondage of sin; and the practice thereof. It only provides a mask for sin, yet allows people to still participate in sinful ways. It allows people to think they have been delivered without experiencing an actual renunciation of the world, and the ways of the world. It deceives them into thinking that there can be salvation without repentance. It allows them to think that they do not have to bear up under the weight of the cross, carry it, and willingly put themselves upon it...and DIE. This type of gospel, along with the others mentioned in this chapter, is unacceptable. The Remnant Church must emerge and distance herself from these false gospels.

Chapter Five
The Great Falling Away

*"Let no man deceive you by any means: for that day shall not come, xcept there come a falling away first,
and that man of sin be revealed, the son of perdition."*
II Thessalonians 2:3

*"Now the Spirit speaketh expressly, that in the latter times some shall depart from the faith,
giving heed to seducing spirits, and doctrines of devils;"*
I Timothy 4:1

All throughout the Bible, and even up until today, we have been able to observe different times of falling away by believers of Jehovah and the Lord Jesus Christ. As time winds up and we stand on the precipice of eternity, there is yet a major falling away that will happen. It will be one that supersedes the previous falling aways; one that will set the stage for the return of Christ for His Church. There will be such a drastic and enormous departure from the foundations of the faith, that it will even cause the remnant to question their belief system. They will begin to question whether they did actually hear God speak, and understand what He said. This last falling away will be so recognizable, that the lack of the Spirit of God moving in and among the mass of persons claiming to be Christians will be easily detected by those outside of the ark of safety; those who are not born again. This last falling away will represent such a major departure from the ways of the first century Remnant Church, that this compromised form of Christianity will be totally acceptable by those who don't recognize the righteousness of Jehovah, and His holiness. It will cause the formation of a counterfeit Church, and of an unholy alliance between the god of this world and those claiming to be children of God.

This falling way will facilitate the incorporation and assimilation of the compromised pseudo-Christian ethics of this world's system into a body of believers, who will ultimately be tainted. They will be crippled, and callous to the holy mandates of the Ancient of Days. This will happen as the Church rapidly runs headlong down the road to ecumenism, and prepares to lose herself in the quagmire of deceptive compromised teachings. She will embrace teachings that lack the integrity upon which the Church was founded. We will see the simultaneous attempts of

CHAPTER FIVE: THE GREAT FALLING AWAY

this deceived group to form a one world religion, a one world government, and a one world economy. The great falling away will be a part of the series of events which signal the beginning of the end. It will help set the stage for a form of Christianity that denies the power of God to break the power of sin in the lives of the people. It will foster the formation of a Church that doesn't mind the fact that it has a reputation for continually existing under the mantle of "having an on-going power shortage."

This falling away will be a signal to the enemy that he has accomplished a great victory over the Church of the Lord Jesus Christ. It will testify to the enemy's accomplished purpose of deceiving the Church into thinking that it's no problem living a life that is not dedicated to the principles of holiness, sanctification, and self-denial. It will allow Lucifer to boast that he has successfully infiltrated the ranks of the righteous, and convinced those belonging to this group to think like he thinks; in terms of self-pleasure and self satisfaction. Additionally, this falling away will open the door for the revealing of the man of perdition. While there have been many hypotheses as to just who this man of perdition is, suffice it to say that whoever or whatever he is, he represents a critical point in the countdown to eternity; and the Last Day.

According to Jewish eschatology, the "Last Day" refers to the day that Jesus executes His judgment on the earth, and simultaneously gathers the dead in Christ and those who are alive and do remain. The term is repeatedly used by Jesus in the sixth chapter of John, to indicate the day of resurrection and judgment. Although it is related to the "last days" and "last time" to denote the Messianic age; it is definitely different from 'the last days'. In *John 7: 37*, "the last day, the great day of the feast" refers to the eighth day of the feast of Tabernacles. According to *Leviticus 23: 36*, this "closing day" was observed as a Sabbath.[89]

In John's Gospel there is also the thought that God will take care of his own in those troubled times. Jesus repeatedly said concerning those the Father "has given" him that he will "raise them up at the last day." John is the only New Testament writer to use the expression "the last day." It is used as an expression that points to Jesus' activity right at the end of time. It also makes it clear that Jesus' care for his own extends right through the sphere of time to the ushering in of the final state of affairs. On the negative side, the person who rejects Jesus and His teaching will find that Jesus' teaching "will condemn him at the last day." The spirit of evil will continue to the end; this is clear, as many passages testify. There are different views, and difficulties of being sure what parts of Jesus' discourse on the Mount of Olives in the 24th chapter of Matthew refer to the destruction of Jerusalem; and what parts refer to the end of the world. He makes it clear that, while His followers will hear of "wars and revolutions" which must happen, "the end will not come right away." Believers will encounter troubles throughout this world's history, and this will persist right to the very end.

Very important is the fact that the final, great day will see the triumph of God. This is foreshadowed in the Old Testament, for example, in the great passage in which Job says, "I know that my Redeemer lives, and that in the end He will stand upon the earth; and after my skin has been destroyed, yet in my flesh I will see God" (*Job 19:25-26*). There are problems in this passage, but plainly there is the clear expectation of God's final triumph. Before Jesus was born the angel told Mary that the child she was to bear "will reign over the house of Jacob forever; his kingdom will never end" (*Luke 1: 33*). In this great passage on the resurrection, Paul says that Christ will come with "those who belong to him. Then the end will come, when he hands over the kingdom to God the Father after he has destroyed all dominion, authority and power" (*I Corinthians 15: 24*). The apostle goes on to speak of the raising of the dead in a different form, one in which they will be "imperishable" (*v. 52*). Again and again the New Testament brings out the truth that when Jesus returns all evil will be defeated and the redeemed will know the fullness of everlasting life.

For the New Testament writers, the coming of Jesus Christ into the world to bring about our salvation was the decisive happening in the entire history of the world. This occurance set in motion the train of events that would bring about the salvation of sinners. It would eventually reveal God's kingdom, as Revelation makes so clear. This did not mean that all evil would immediately disappear; both the New Testament writings and Christian experience make it plain that evil continues. The important thing from the Christian point of view is that the saving work of Christ has altered everything. Sin has been decisively defeated and believers have already entered into salvation. However long or short a time it will be before the end of this world as we measure time, we are living in the last times as the New Testament writers understand it.[90]

The second coming of Christ is referred to as "the last day." Therefore we must understand that everything that is associated with His second advent happens at the same time..."the Last Day." This is also referred to as "the Day of the Lord." *I Thessalonians 5:1-6; II Peter 3: 9-14.*[91] There are a few things that are crystal clear concerning the second coming of Christ. Consider that He will return visibly with a mighty shout; there will be an unmistakable cry from an angel; there will be a trumpet fanfare such as never been heard; believers in Christ who are dead will rise from their graves; and believers who are alive will be lifted into the clouds and meet Christ.[92]

Let's take a look at the term son of perdition; as it is commonly associated with the second coming of Christ. He is also described as the one who will be revealed before the Day of the Lord comes; and is directly associated with a great falling away...a great apostasy. This term, son of perdition, is only used twice in New Testament scriptures. Once by Jesus in *John 17: 12*, as a direct reference to Judas Iscariot; who betrayed Messiah Jesus. It's used another time by Paul in *II Thessalonians 2: 3*, as a direct reference to the man of sin. Both references can be said to symbolize the one doomed to destruction. Both references can also be construed to be demonical title. Some theologians consider the beast that goes into perdition in *Revelation 17: 8, Revelation 17: 11* to be references to the son of perdition.[93] It is not uncommon for a lot of believers to use this term in reference to the anti-Christ. When a person is called "son of perdition," the connotation is that of a person in an unredeemable state, someone who is already damned while he is still alive. Forgiveness is not in the plan for them, but they are indeed doom to destruction; God's plan for them is eternal damnation.[94] The great falling away spoken of in Thessalonians is directly linked to this son of perdition being revealed.

Without a complete understanding of the spiritual and mental impact of the Abomination of Desolation, it is impossible to comprehend the fallout among the faithful believers who finally realize what time it is spiritually. The majority of believers only have enough faith to take them to the door of the Great Tribulation. Not many people even think that the Church will actually have to go through the Great Tribulation. The Remnant Church will have to step up to be a stabilizing force in the lives of the disillusioned believers who find themselves having to go through the Great Tribulation. When the spiritual eyes of those who witness the Abomination of Desolation[95] are opened and they still find themselves here, and not raptured, they will definitely lose faith and succumb to despair and discouragement.

There is a time coming in the earth when the beasts spoken of in the book of Revelation will manifest and be revealed.[96] They will make war with the saints and prevail.[97] They will make a treaty with the nation of Israel.[98] They will desecrate the daily sacrifice being offered in the third Temple, located in Jerusalem.[99] They will set up an image of the first beast in that Temple and require all of mankind to worship that image and accept the mark of the beast. Without having that mark people will not be able to buy or sell.[100]

According to Jesus, this Abomination of Desolation marks the 'beginning' of the Great Tribulation period.[101] Jesus comes back 'after' these things,[102] but the lack of preparedness on the part of the Church and by the Church will cause the hearts of many to grow faint, lose hope, and fall away from the faith; the gospel of Jesus Christ. Then it will be imperative for the Remnant Church to stand in the gap, intercede for the believers, and provide the explanation and teaching that will help stabilize the Church. She will have to experience, and recover from, the numerical loss, and falling away from Christianity; of those who had hoped to escape these days via the rapture.

As we examine the phenomena of this great falling away, it must be noted that this singular event will stand out from every other falling away that has taken place in the past history of mankind. It will represent such a significant departure by such a large group of people, that the magnitude of the departure of believers from the foundational tenets of Christianity will rock the Church; and impact the nations. The tidal wave effect of the departure of these Christians will produce widespread panic among the conservative religious community. Cries of heresy, and accusations of being seduced into cult-like activity, will emanate from every corner of the faithful remnant. These things must needs be for the agenda of Jehovah to come to fruition. Formerly faithful believers will abandon the principle tenets of fundamental Christianity in exchange for a less demanding gospel, which de-emphasizes self-sacrifice. The stage will be set for an increasingly more relaxed set of morals and mores; all of which will contribute to a sensual, carnal Christian experience. What transpires in the Church represents a mass exodus from the principles of holiness; upon which the first century New Testament Remnant Church was founded. The subsequent result will be a Church steeped in self-gratification versus God gratification. It will produce a body of so-called Christians who give in to their fleshly, sensual body appetites, as opposed to dying to the slave master of sin; and living a life devoted to pleasing Jehovah God. This event will be perceived as a mass exodus from the exclusionary doctrine of New Testament Christianity, and an endorsement of the popular philosophy that all paths lead to God. The belief that there are multiple access routes to salvation, and that it doesn't take all of that holy-roller lifestyle to maintain a relationship with God will run rampant. Among those who are not rooted and grounded in the Scriptures, this belief will be widespread. It will also be viewed as a surrender to the notion that the pleasures of this world are not really all that bad. Folks will be deceived into thinking that all one has to do is to mouth their conversion to Christianity. They will be convinced that their lifestyle does not have to reflect an abandonment of sinful behavior; in exchange for a holy lifestyle submitted to Jehovah God and His dictates.

> *"This great falling away will serve as a catalyst, and fuel for the satanic agenda of inclusion."*

This mass departure from the righteous tenets of the first century New Testament Remnant Church will set the stage for a mass acceptance and endorsement of the ecumenical movement. It will send the message that the priority really should be a peaceful coexistence among the world's different religions; even though Jesus stated that everyone who was not for Him was actually against Him. This great falling away will serve as a catalyst, and fuel for the satanic agenda of inclusion. It will serve to muddy the waters as to what is the true and right way of worshipping Jehovah; the God of all creation. It will serve as a signal to the evil one that it is time to reveal who he is, what his nature is, and his presence in the various organizations, and systems in the world. This falling away will serve to further alienate the true believers, who are intent about the purposes of God being fulfilled in the earth, from those who merely name the name of Christ. It will separate those who are more interested in preserving their own agenda; from those who are totally sold out to the purposes of God.

This single act will launch a series of events that will lead us to the very brink of the edge of time and eternity. It will launch the release of the demons that will drive the events leading up to the false pact the 'beast' makes with the nation of Israel. Among believers, this event is typically referred to as the time when the anti-Christ is revealed. As stated in our previous work, the Bible never names a single figure archetype entity as the anti-Christ, it always, and only, refers to the "spirit of anti-Christ" which was released into the earth ages ago. However, in the Revelation, the Bible explicitly refers to "the beast," "the false prophet," and "the great dragon," we should learn how to, and begin to, do the same. Once the beast and his agenda are revealed, the slope to Armageddon will be steep and slippery. The hordes of hell are anxiously waiting for the Church to get fed up with trying to please Jehovah, and make the transition to wanting to please themselves; and feed their body appetites. They are waiting for the massive demise of the principles of holiness and self-sacrifice

CHAPTER FIVE: THE GREAT FALLING AWAY

as the standard operating procedures of the Church. They can hardly wait until the saints say "time out for all this self-denial"; I want to feel good. If the enemy can get the Church to operate in her feelings (soulish realm) instead of operating in the Word of God (spiritual realm), then the enemy will have influenced the Church to buy into Satan's "I, me, my" syndrome. Instead of it being all about the Kingdom of God, it becomes all about the Kingdom of self.

This last falling away is one of the most significant things to happen before the second coming of Christ. When such a large number of the body of Christ chooses to leave the lifestyle which is earmarked by the noticeably holy behavior, the floodgate is opened up for demonic oppression. Then, all of the Christians who have a form of godliness, but deny the power thereof, will feel totally free to publicly masquerade their carnal ways. They will do this without a shred of embarrassment or remorse. There will be no shame in the public exhibition of questionably moral behavior being passed off as acceptable Christian behavior. The demons who oppress the people of God will no longer be undercover in their display of who they are, and what they represent. The godlessness of the age will be totally unmasked, and unabashedly put on display. This will be perceived as an example of how understanding God is, although inaccurate. They will reason that it shows how forgiving God is concerning the humanity of His creation. The presentation of this train of thought, in and of itself, is a major deception. This falling away will serve to create a massive deception regarding the ways of holiness, and the necessity of it being a part of the

Christian experience. It will legitimize a Christian lifestyle that falls way below the standard of holiness associated with the first century New Testament Remnant Church.

During our study of the record of Christ's physical time on the earth, and in the earth as the Holy Ghost, we will find several mentions of a falling away. Consider the Master's words captured and shared by the apostle John, the beloved disciple. They are recorded in John 6:51-68:

51 "I am the living bread that came down from heaven. Anyone who eats this bread will live forever; and this bread, which I will offer so the world may live, is my flesh."
52 Then the people began arguing with each other about what he meant. "How can this man give us his flesh to eat?" they asked.
53 So Jesus said again, "I tell you the truth, unless you eat the flesh of the Son of Man and drink his blood, you cannot have eternal life within you.
54 But anyone who eats my flesh and drinks my blood has eternal life, and I will raise that person at the last day.
55 For my flesh is true food, and my blood is true drink.
56 Anyone who eats my flesh and drinks my blood remains in me, and I in him.
57 I live because of the living Father who sent me; in the same way, anyone who feeds on me will live because of me.
58 I am the true bread that came down from heaven. Anyone who eats this bread will not die as your ancestors did (even though they ate the manna) but will live forever."
59 He said these things while he was teaching in the synagogue in Capernaum.
60 Many of his disciples said, "This is very hard to understand. How can anyone accept it?"
61 Jesus was aware that his disciples were complaining, so he said to them,

CHAPTER FIVE: THE GREAT FALLING AWAY

"Does this offend you?
62 Then what will you think if you see the Son of Man ascend to heaven again?
63 The Spirit alone gives eternal life. Human effort accomplishes nothing. And the very words I have spoken to you are spirit and life.
64 But some of you do not believe me." (For Jesus knew from the beginning which ones didn't believe, and he knew who would betray him.)
65 Then he said, "That is why I said that people can't come to me unless the Father gives them to me."
66 At this point many of his disciples turned away and deserted him.
67 Then Jesus turned to the Twelve and asked, "Are you also going to leave?"
68 Simon Peter replied, "Lord, to whom would we go? You have the words that give eternal life"

This particular segment of the sixth chapter of John serves to illustrate that the concept of falling away is an idea that no one is exempt of being impacted by; not even Jesus Himself. This chapter tells the story of just how shallow humanity can be sometimes. In this account, we see how a certain group of Jews had been eyewitnesses to the miracle working power of God, through Jesus, the Christ. They had borne witness of His power as He healed the man at the Pool of Bethesda. They also saw Him perform other miracles on the diseased people of that region. Additionally, they witnessed in amazement as He fed five thousand men and an enormous amount of women and children as well. This feeding was done with just five barley loaves and two fish. Even more astonishing was the fact that after feeding such a multitude, the disciples were able to collect twelve baskets of leftovers, remnants. However this group of Jews failed to see the significance of His disciples being able to collect twelve baskets of remnants out of the original source of seven elements. Yet many fall away.

The number twelve is a perfect number and it signifies perfection of government or governmental perfection. It is associated with the concept of "ruling" and "governing." It is a product of three times four; the perfectly Divine (heavenly) and the earthly, that which is material and organic. With spiritual perception, it can be recognized as denoting organization, production, and increase. There are numerous twelves in the Bible. Twelve: patriarchs; sons of Israel; sons of Ishmael; persons that were anointed; Apostles; foundations in the heavenly Jerusalem; gates; pearls; angels; legions of angels; thousand sealed from the twelve tribes of Israel; and years of age for Jesus to make His first public comments.[103] The significance of governmental perfection (number 12) emerging out of spiritual perfection (number 7) eluded these Disciples of Christ. They failed to see the perfect Lamb of God establishing a new way of ruling in the affairs of men. They failed to see the perfect remnant arising out of the perfect original.

Yet, in spite of being eyewitnesses to the majestic miracle working power of the living God of creation, they baulked at Jesus' encouragement to be partakers of Him. This goes to show that even as God revealed the greatness of who He was to those folks, in spite of their visual and auditory reception of the workings of Jehovah; they still did not really understand who He was. Nor did they understand what He said; and the implications associated with His message. Despite being in the presence of the Magnanimous One, their mortal minds still did not process the greatness of who He was. They failed to appreciate the importance of being in Him, and Him being in them. How easy it was for them to reject His invitation, and instead pass it off as something that was weird and far-fetched. They sat in the number of the people who saw the healing. They were recipients of the fish and the loaves. Yet, their spiritual understanding was darkened so that they did not comprehend the magnitude of what Jesus was saying.

Sometimes, it is too easy to be in the presence of God, and yet not benefit from the message being given. Sometimes there is an inability to receive and digest the life changing power of the message. Subsequently, when Jesus invited them to partake of His body and blood, being a direct reference of His body which was to be broken by the crucifixion process; they had no idea to what He was referring. Likewise, when He invited them to partake of His blood, they didn't know that He was talking about the blood that He would shed for the healing of the nations. They were in the presence of the live-giver who would deliver eternal life to them; yet they knew not the time of their visitation. So, unfortunately, they were a part of the group whose rejection of Yeshua Ha'Mashiach made it possible for the Gentiles to have access to the God of Abraham, Isaac, and Jacob. Their spiritual ignorance facilitated the avenue for Jehovah to fulfill His promise to Father Abraham (not that God needed an avenue to do this) that he would be the father of many nations. Their falling away helped provide a way of the Gentile's salvation.

So, here they were, in the presence of the Bread of Life,

recipients of a firsthand invitation to eat from the physical manifestation of the New Testament version of the Tree of Life. They were given access to the same type of eternal life which had been in the Garden of Eden. Yet their stupid button was stuck on ON; and they had passed up this golden opportunity. They flatly refused access to eternal life because they could not understand the message, the messenger, nor accept the implications of the message. So, what did they do? They fell away, walked away, shrunk back, and deserted the Lord's Messiah. They jumped ship, abandoned the captain of life, walked away from their post; and spiritually went AWOL. They allowed their inability to internalize the message, and readily receive the benefit of it, to offend them. In essence, their spiritual hearing became closed; or at the least, blocked. They walked away from eternal life. What a wasted opportunity.

This falling away by some of Jesus' earliest disciples opened the door for some of His later followers to also depart from the way, the truth, and the light. So, the precedent was set for disciples of the Christ to desert the chosen one of Israel; at least visibly at first. The enemy of Jehovah was able to blind the spiritual understanding of those who had been first hand observers of the grace and mercy of the Savior. Lucifer was successful in dulling the spiritual senses of those who had been eyewitnesses to the miracles, healings, and deliverance of Jesus Christ; as He went about doing the works of the Father. As He fulfilled *Isaiah 61*, those who were privileged enough to be first hand witnesses of Emmanuel, God among us, were not strong enough to hold onto the knowledge of the experience; and walked away. Obviously, they did not understand what Jesus meant when He said that the Son of Man must be delivered into the hands of sinful men; to be tortured and killed.

"Saying the Son of Man must be delivered into the hands of sinful men; and be crucified and the third day rise again."
Luke 24:7

So, it is no wonder that we see the falling away that accompanied the crucifixion of Christ. There were literally thousands who followed Jesus after the mass feedings of five thousand men and four thousand men; not to mention the women and children. Yet, when we see the disciples numbered at the upper room in the book of Acts; we only find one hundred and twenty of the faithful waiting on the "promise of the Father."[104] Not to say all of those thousands fell away; however it seems like there should have been a lot more than only one hundred and twenty waiting on the baptism of the Holy Ghost. Apparently, a lot of those followers did not have enough spiritual acumen to understand that Christ's kingdom was not of this world. They failed to understand His first mission into our time was not as the reigning king; but rather as the suffering servant. It was easy for them to walk away from Golgotha with the notion that He must not have been the One for whom they were waiting.

It was in a state of confusion that they descended Calvary's hill; with thoughts of betrayal, abandonment, and disillusionment. How sad it must have been to have their hopes dashed, and their expectations deflated. Yet this was not due to Jesus' inability to keep His word or fulfill His promise. Their sunken state was due to a lack of their own discernment of what Jesus represented during His tenure with them. Their disillusionment was directly associated with their lack of perception, and an inability to correctly spiritually perceive the significance of what Jesus was teaching. They failed to properly translate the message that was given to them. Such was the case after the crucifixion. There were large groups of people that walked away from Jerusalem feeling that they had wasted their time, displaced their hopes, and believed the hype of a pseudo-prophet from Galilee. They felt justified in saying no to the Jewish adage and question, "Can any good thing come out of Galilee?"

> *"Sometimes the saints lose their ability to maintain a visible image which reflects that they are associated with the Christ. "*

Subsequently, there was a mass departure, a gigantic exodus of people who had been mesmerized by the teachings of Jesus, enthralled by His healing abilities, and captivated by His propensity for the miraculous. They abandoned ship quicker than roaches running for cover; when the lights are turned on. They quickly and quietly blended back into the throngs of masses who practiced Judaism; and resumed their regular Sabbath worship at the synagogues; and at the Temple. They quickly forgot all that their eyes had seen, and their ears had heard. They easily dismissed the memory of what it had been like to be in the presence of God living among men. They did not remember the glory of His presence. They forgot the movement of the Holy Spirit of God among them as He ministered. It was too

CHAPTER FIVE: THE GREAT FALLING AWAY

easy for the trauma of the crucifixion to paralyze their spiritual senses and incapacitate them. The trauma of His gruesome death left them in a spiritual fetal position; unable to press onward and fulfill the Great Commission. Many were spiritually debilitated, and unable to carry out the last commandment given to them by the Christ of God. Oh, the perils of falling away from God! Yet, a remnant remained.

That remnant had to suffer through the perils of the persecution. We speak of the falling away that took place after the Jews and the Roman government began their persecution of the first century New Testament Remnant Church. However, we are not necessarily talking about the followers of Christ abandoning their belief that Jesus of Nazareth was in fact the Messiah prophesied of in the Old Testament. We are not intimating that they forsook the newly established Christian faith. Nor are we stating that they denied the prophet from Galilee as the Lord's Messiah; we're not saying that at all. What we are talking about is their choice to go into hiding, to become invisible; and to not be the visible representation in the earth of the invisible God of creation. Too often as we speak of 'falling away', we have a tendency to equate that with walking away from the practices of the faith. While that may be true in some instances, it is not always necessarily the case. Sometimes the saints lose their ability to maintain a visible image which reflects that they are associated with the Christ.

Sometimes our Christ-like physical witness, reflected in our demeanor and personage, is absent. There are times when the physical image and persona of God's people just does not reflect the fact that they belong to Jehovah; and have been cleansed by the blood of the Lamb. There are instances that members of the Body of Christ just do not reflect the image of God; this represents a falling away of sorts. Since the Church is intended to be the light set upon the hill, whose light cannot be hid, she should always be recognizable, and distinguished from the secular world in which she finds herself; yet maintain her position that she is not a part of the secular world.

As we examine the first century New Testament Remnant Church, we find a body of believers running for their literal lives. We see this group of visible vibrant members of "The Way" consciously deciding to fall away from visibility, to fly below the radar, in order to preserve their existence. There are many different views of their decision. Some say that in abdicating their visibility, they impeded the salvation of those non-believers who were looking for someone to lead them to Christ. Still others say that going into the Catacombs was the only way to survive the persecution and insure that there could even be a 21st century New Testament Remnant Church. We are not here to judge their actions; only to observe that it did happen. Since God knows all things, and since His will shall always be accomplished; it must have been in His permissive will for that body of believers to fall away. Obviously, He was confident in their commitment to the faith; and did not confuse their visible falling away with a positional change in their relationship with Him.

Having said that, let us go on to examine what part purpose', or 'motive', plays in a person's decision to fall away. Are there times when circumstances justify how we present

CHAPTER FIVE: THE GREAT FALLING AWAY

ourselves? Without a doubt, there are. We just have to make sure our motive is a positive healthy one. We must ensure that our falling away is in no way indicative of a loss of trust in the Lord; and His ability to be the Sovereign Lord over every aspect of our lives. Our falling away must be for the strategic purposes of aligning ourselves for battle; versus a demonstration of our lack of preparation; and being ill-equipped to fight in the war. While there may be times when it is necessary for the New Testament Remnant Church to reposition herself in order to insure longevity and viability, there should never be a time when her falling away has anything to do with an abandonment of the faith. Nor should it be absolutely indicative of a shrinking away from the absolute undeniable truth of the Gospel message.

Our falling away must be indicative of a conscious choice to "shut in or shut away," in order to attain a more intimate relationship with our God. It must be a deliberate decision to factor out all obstacles that would impede our ability to hear a 'clear' word from God. It must be an intentional withdrawal from all stimuli that would distract us from pressing into the bosom of Jehovah. It should demonstrate our attempt to know the mind of God concerning our personal relationship, personal ministry, and corporate attachment to the Body of Christ. It is only in this type of falling away that we allow Jehovah to develop His specific strategy for us as a soldier in His army. It is in this context that we are to hear His commands for our position in the battle plan to decimate the army of Satan. Hence, it is the context of this type of falling away that we come up with the word 'retreat'. When we use this term, it is not so much to communicate a withdrawal from the battle, as much as it is to express the idea of going undercover to strategize on how to more effectively wage the war. Such is the case when we go on a retreat. We are attempting to draw ourselves into a more intimate position with our Heavenly Father.

It should also be evident to notice that their time of falling away provided the Post-Persecution New Testament Remnant Church the opportunity to spiritually grow, to become spiritually infused with the power of God. It also gave her the opportunity to be restored. It assisted the remnant, and helped her to preserve her physical numbers; and not be obliterated. If the current New Testament Remnant Church is to experience any falling away at all; it should be as it was for the persecuted first century New Testament Remnant Church. Said falling away should facilitate a time of spiritual growth, restoration, and sustaining size; versus a decrease in physical size. The by-product of this falling away should be a spiritual and numerical explosion; as a result of the revival of purpose and determination that has taken place within the walls of that incubation period.

If one were to try to accurately convey the real meaning of post-persecution falling away, it would have to be compared to Moses' experience on the back side of the desert. It would have to be described as a temporary withdrawal from the public's sight in order to experience a time of ultra-intimacy with the Lord. It could, in fact, be described as a necessary journey in order to ultimately arrive at a correct positional relationship with God. It should serve to make us suitable for Him to channel His agenda through us; and use us for His glory. To be correctly stated in

CHAPTER FIVE: THE GREAT FALLING AWAY

this case, instead of being characterized as a "falling away," it can more accurately be described as a "falling toward."

There must be a time in every believer's life, when they separate themselves from all of the other voices and distractions. Every now and then everyone needs a time when the Lord, and the Lord alone, has their undivided attention. A time when only He has their ear; a time of refreshing. As we draw near to the end of time, it is imperative for the 21st century New Testament Church to 'fall forward' into revival, retreat, and strategic planning in order to design the strategy to victoriously counteract the end-time attack Lucifer has unleashed upon humanity. That strategy needs to be designed and implemented.

Consequently, the Protestant Reformation provides another opportunity for us to discuss yet another form of 'falling away.' It gives us a chance to take another glance at some of the conditions, situations, and attitudes that contributed to the formation and development of the Remnant Church. It is of the utmost importance for us to understand that before the Protestant Reformation of the early 1500s, the whole form of the Christian experience, in the practice of organized religion, was completed under the framework known as the Roman Catholic Church, and the Eastern Orthodox Church. These were the organizations that became known as the progenitors of Christianity. Although there were still small Messianic Jewish congregations scattered throughout the then known world; the majority of Christianity was propagated by the Roman Catholic and Eastern Orthodox Churches. They were the ambassadors who were actively evangelizing the pagan world with the message of the Christ. They were the models, and representatives, of the religion that the world had come to know as Christianity. They were the structures the world looked to, as the reflection of those principles ascribed to Christianity. The only major physical organizations that the world could look to, as the followers of Jesus of Nazareth, was this assembly of leaders and congregants; known as the Church of Rome and the Eastern Orthodox Church.

The dogmas and doctrines of these organizations served as the tenets to which believers in Jesus Christ followed, and to which they swore their allegiance. These assemblies had been the embodiment of what had come to be known as followers of the Messiah for over fifteen hundred years. They were deemed the designated authorities and delegated representatives of Jehovah God, for all of the inhabitants of the earth. They were the only models to which those who sought to follow Jesus could look. If anyone claimed to belong to Jehovah, through the shed blood of His Son, their membership was either affixed to the Roman Catholic Church or the Eastern Orthodox Church; they were the only game in town.

When God allowed the Protestant Reformers to see some of the fallacies of those organizations, is it any wonder that those who accepted their message made a mass exodus from that form of worship. Luther (Lutherans), Wesley (Presbyterians), Knox (Episcopalians) and other devout Catholics such as Calvin, Melanchthon, Zwingli, Waldo, Wycliffe, Huss, and Savonarola began to expose some of the fundamentally paganism practices evident in Catholicism. The Spirit of God began to shed light

CHAPTER FIVE: THE GREAT FALLING AWAY

on these things. Subsequently, devout Catholics, who yearned for genuine relationship with God, were left with no choice other than to abandon this religion. They realized that their religion had allowed these pagan practices to become acceptable dogma within the tenets of her faith.

Although the holy Roman Catholic Church branded them as heretics, these faithful believers in the Lord Jesus Christ chose to maintain loyalty to the illumination they had received; and decided to accept the new alternative. They stood steadfast on the illumination which Jehovah had provided for those who truly wanted to serve Him. They chose to 'fall away' from the only forms of organized Christianity in the then known world. They became pilgrims, the cadre of a movement that would revolutionize religion like nothing the world had ever seen.

This new network of believers provided the framework for a new configuration of faith, as it pertained to the virgin birth; and the role of Jesus Christ as the real mediator between God and man. They chose to separate from the mainstream of religious thought. They voluntarily alienated themselves from the only recognizable monikers of Christendom; in an otherwise Islamic and pagan world. They retreated and shut in, in order to create a new infrastructure for religious thought, which was in true alignment with the principles of 'the faith'; which were passed on to us by our first century apostolic fathers. Their obedience to Jehovah set the stage for the advent of some of the most relevant movements of the Spirit of God upon His Church. These movements have paved the way for Yahweh's pivotal restoration process for the New Testament Church; as

He re-establishes her back to the form of power and vibrancy she possessed in her first century origination.

It is necessary for us to examine some of the major reasons for the Protestant Reformation, and the subsequent 'falling away' of hundreds of thousands of devout Catholic believers in Christianity. These factors are central to our conversation, and the notion of a Remnant Church. Whereas John the Baptist, Jesus the Christ, the Apostles, and Disciples all taught repentance as being central to the forgiveness of Jehovah and subsequent salvation, the Catholic church replaced that concept with the notion of 'penance'. When penance replaced repentance, it introduced the idea that one could remove or atone for the punishment due for their sins merely by giving gifts to the church. In addition to giving gifts, doing good works, killing the flesh by inflicting punishment on the flesh, and self-denial were also acceptable means of payment. The principle of justification through faith in Jesus Christ was replaced with the notion that one could be justified before God simply by doing good works. The concept of 'purgatory' was introduced as a place where Christians who had not achieved perfection would go after death to undergo purifying suffering. Gifts and services rendered to the church, and prayers could decrease or eliminate a soul's time in purgatory. The sale and worship of holy relics, plus the extensive use of statues of people as objects of worship was also an accepted practice. During this period, the greed of ambitious political princes and rulers was running rampant. Special Indulgence by Pope Leo X was granted to John Tetzel to sell certificates throughout Germany to raise money to finish the

CHAPTER FIVE: THE GREAT FALLING AWAY

building of St. Peter's Church in Rome. These certificates, signed by the Pope, purported to bestow the pardon of all sins without repentance, penance, confession, or absolution by a priest. This indulgence was promised to the holders of these certificates and more amazingly to people both living and dead, for whom they were purchased. These certificates were said to have the power to take care of sins that were actually committed and intended.[105]

> *"By turning their backs on what had become the accepted norm of worship, they placed themselves in the crosshairs of public opinion, and skepticism."*

What we witnessed in the Protestant Reformation was in fact, a 'falling away' of epic proportions. Hundreds of thousands of Christians left the sanctuary of the only vestige of Christendom the world had known up to that point. They made a conscious decision to withdraw their membership from the only source of Christianity in the then known world. Their choice to voluntarily excommunicate themselves from the Catholic & Orthodox Church was much like the Jews who chose to be baptized by John the Baptist in the Jordan River. When those Jews entered the water to be baptized by John, there were Pharisees and Sadducees taking record of them; and taking that report back to the synagogue. When Jews received John's baptism of repentance, they were voluntarily forsaking their old way of trying to maintain relationship with Jehovah through their Jewish lineage, and affiliation with the Jewish religion. It was an open declaration of accepting the 'new way' that John was preaching about; and usually resulted in them being expelled from the synagogue.

What we must understand is that the synagogue was the epicenter of the Jew's life. Not only was it the religious center, but it was the core basis for the Jew's political life, social life, legal life; it was their identification with the nation of Israel. When a Jew was excommunicated from the temple, they were virtually cut off from the nation of Israel. They were like a person without a country. When one decided to step into the Jordan to be baptized by John, it was an ultra-significant decision; one that would affect every aspect of a person's life. In other words, this major, life-changing resolution was a step that would result in a person 'falling away' from everything they had come to know as 'normal everyday life'. It was one of the weightiest choices a person could make. It was a deliberate action which would result in religious, social, and political isolation. These were some of the same consequences that lay in store for those reformers who chose to 'fall away' from the Roman Catholic Church. They experienced some of the same rejection received by those Jews who chose to receive John's baptism of repentance in Jesus' day.

We today, who are the products of that 'falling away', consider the Reformation as the grandiose occurrence that spawned the formation of the current major Protestant denominations. We sometimes fail to recognize the trauma that was experienced by those who were the initiators of this event. Not only were they ostracized by the religious leaders of that day, but they also were targeted by the political realm; since religion and politics were almost synonymous. The reformers who chose to fall away from the old system of religion voluntarily set themselves up

CHAPTER FIVE: THE GREAT FALLING AWAY

for persecution, ridicule, and isolation. By turning their backs on what had become the accepted norm of worship, they placed themselves in the cross-hairs of public opinion, and skepticism. They became targets for public contempt and criticism. Although we see them as heroes of the faith, their contemporaries labelled them as arrogant rebels and heretics. There was no ticker tape parade for them. The Church did not erect statues in their honor; or make proclamations classifying them as champions of the faith. As the Bible depicts Jesus as having no comeliness or anything that would make Him desirous, so it was with these Reformers. Their falling away from Catholicism actually caused them to be viewed as adversaries of the Church; and antagonists of Christianity.

It is important to realize that while our motives may be correct and just, when we separate from the accepted mode of Christian worship, it is in the scope of possibility that we will conceivably be viewed as heretical. How dare we deviate from that which has been rubber-stamped as correct, in deference to a Spirit-led call for a return to the faith that was passed on to us from our Jewish-apostolic Church fathers. We can expect to be labelled as adversaries of the Church; and antagonists of Christianity. Should this deter us from becoming the end-times Remnant Church that God is calling forth from the contemporary compromised, deceived, conformist Structural Church? God forbid!!! It should serve as a catalyst for us to whole-heartedly seek to fulfill the purpose for which Jehovah has called, ordained, and sanctioned this auspicious assembly of believers. Know for a surety that the remnant will catapult the

Church into a deeper, more intimate relationship with Yahweh and Yeshua Ha'Mashiach.

As we remember the tragedies and misgivings associated with the Praise The Lord Club (PTL), Jimmy Swaggart, Ernest Ainsley, and the Discipleship movement, it is unmistakably apparent that the failure of these ministries led to major loss among the ranks of Christian believers. The number of believers who backslid or totally gave up on God are hard to enumerate. Yet, a remnant remains. There are those who are sold out to the purposes of God, and understand that the enemy of God will always come to kill, steal, and destroy what God is growing in the earth.... A Remnant Church! We definitely understand that the 'great falling away' prophetically spoken of; preceding the 'Last Day' and the end of time, is not a good thing. Yet, we are also mindful that every falling away is not necessarily a bad thing.

As we examine some of the recent disgraces in the Church, we find ministries and movements that previously had a significant positive impact on the Body of Christ becoming responsible for a great falling away among the faithful. There have been ministers and ministries, which had risen to become faith-filled household words among Christian believers; entities that had captured the attention of hundreds of thousands of people. Yet, these very same charismatic persons and movements have engaged in actions and practices which have driven untold thousands from their ministries; and unfortunately even from the Christian faith.

Taking note of their personal indiscretions, and inerrant ministry practices, we can see their humanity at work; and the

CHAPTER FIVE: THE GREAT FALLING AWAY

resultant impact it has had on the faith of those who had put their trust in them. It is not necessary to name all of these individuals or organizations. Those of us in the Church are painfully aware of them. Those readers who are outside of the Church do not need to be given objects that might divert their focus away from Christ. It also goes without saying that even some of those outside the Body of Christ were privy to those persons falling from grace. Many used the demise of those ministries as fodder to justify non-belief in Christ, or Christian ministries. Yet the truth remains that those who fell from grace were people, organizations, and movements that had a positive start. Sadly, they hit a bump in the road that rendered them ineffective; and ultimately counterproductive.

The object lesson to be learned from these tragedies is that while someone or something might have an extremely positive beginning, there must be consistency and purity of purpose to keep them from becoming an entity that causes a mass 'falling away'. There are spiritual principles and accountability, which must be maintained in order to preserve the holy purpose for which those people, organizations, and movements were established. A good start is truly commendable, but an excellent finish is the desired end result. While we can graciously grant that the learning curve is a reason for mistakes being made, the failure to improve and reach completeness, utilizing the process of repentance, is unacceptable. Grace and mercy are provisions God has made for us, as we strive for perfection. However, if we fail to utilize these gifts, and the repentance process, we are held accountable for our failure to mature into our God-given purpose and destiny.

The awareness that our Christian lives are being lived under the scrutiny and microscope of the unsaved world should serve as a motivation to make sure our personal indiscretions do not lead to anyone falling away from the Christian faith or lifestyle.

Another lesson to be learned is the danger of allowing people to put one's ministry or personage on a pedestal. There is an inherent consequence of allowing people to perceive a ministry or person as an entity to be glorified; in essence, one that steals the glory from God. It is extremely hazardous to allow ourselves, or ministry, to become an object of worship. If that ministry or person fails to maintain a holy Godly standard, their fall and resulting loss of trust in God, among those who had faith in those entities, could possibly be irreversible. The negative outcome, generated by that failure, is certain to produce a significant falling away. The focus of ministry must always be to glorify God, and His greatness; as opposed to the greatness of the ministry. In reality, the ministry is not even ours, it is His. All true ministries are an extension of the ministry of Jesus Christ. His is the only ministry in the earth. Every other ministry is an outgrowth of His; a branch growing out of the root.

> *"The sad reality of fallen leadership is the subsequent effect it produces in the lives of the followers."*

The previous and current moral improprieties of contemporary Christian leaders results in a duplication of behavior among the congregation. The result is a "loosening" of morals, sexual standards, and financial boundaries. Without a further naming of fallen ministers and ministries, suffice it to

CHAPTER FIVE: THE GREAT FALLING AWAY

say that the 'cause of Christ' has suffered major damage. When leadership displays improprieties because of a lack of discipline and mind renewal, a falling away is inevitable. Yet, this absence of holiness is sometimes evident among those responsible for feeding the flock of God. The sad reality of fallen leadership is the subsequent effect it produces in the lives of the followers. Those who have looked upon these ministers and ministries as sources of inspiration and example, now find themselves drowning in the quagmire of disbelief, disillusionment, and doubt. They find themselves in a place of not knowing where to look for direction. They find it difficult to recover from the trauma of 'fallen trusted leadership', and struggle to regain the level of faith they previously held.

In the face of such overwhelming disappointment, the human mind looks for a coping mechanism to counteract the dejection and despair their leader's improprieties have produced. In an attempt to justify their leaders 'humanness', a large portion of the followers accept it; and regrettably replicate the behavior of the persons in charge. There are too many examples of congregations and organizations where moral and ethical lack of decorum has been exposed, and condemned. Yet, because it has not been dealt with to the fullest extent of spiritual law and punishment, it has been duplicated by onlookers. These onlookers take the lack of prosecution as an indication that the indecent behavior is somewhat tolerable by the religious powers that be. As a result of this, one can notice a decline in the moral fiber of our congregations, a "loosening" of ethics and sexual standards, and a disappearance of principled boundaries.

Promiscuous dress, and seductive dance movements, have been allowed into our worship services. Additionally, homosexuality, adultery, and fornication have been welcomed into the leadership of some congregations and denominations. The domino effect of falling away from moral purity, and the concept of holiness, among Church leaders has resulted in a downward spiral in the moral environment currently found in the Body of Christ. One finds everything from prostitutes to pedophiles operating freely in positions of authority; from the pulpit and through the entire body of the church. One sees open lewdness and abuse on display among the congregation; because it has received the message that sexual improprieties can be forgiven and tolerated. This is not acceptable. What kind of message does the Church send her children, and the world of non-believers, if she allows these ungodly routines to persist? The Remnant Church must rise in opposition to these practices; she simply cannot allow this sort of misbehavior to continue.

Again, it is not this author's intention to point fingers, yet one must take a critical look at the 'discipleship movement' since it has so much to bear on the conversation concerning the Remnant Church. In all actuality, 'discipleship' is the model that was left for the Church to follow. It was the model Messiah Jesus used as He singled the 'apostles' out from among the thousands of followers He had; and poured into them. These men were given the benefit of observing Jesus up close and personal. They ate with Him, slept alongside Him, and watched Him as He performed all facets of ministry. They had the privilege of being fed by Him; much like the mother eagle feeds her chicks.

CHAPTER FIVE: THE GREAT FALLING AWAY

They were given private, individualized, intensive attention. Discipleship was the method the Lord used to prepare the men with whom He would entrust the governance of the Church; the one He would establish by His death, burial, and resurrection. It was also the method the apostles used as they sought to root and ground those three thousand believers who were converted on the Day of Pentecost. We find the record that bears witness to this in Acts 2: 41-42:

"Then they that gladly received his word were baptized: and the same day there were added unto them about three thousand souls. And they continued steadfastly in the apostles' doctrine and fellowship, and in breaking of bread, and in prayers."

Accordingly, it is fair to say that the Church we now see in the earth today, Catholics, Protestants, and Orthodox, are all a product of the process known as 'discipleship.' Without this extremely important process, it is safe to say that there would not have been such an identical impartation and dissemination of the doctrines espoused by the Christ; as He walked the sandy shores of Galilee. Discipleship was the model Jesus chose to train His apostles. It was the process the apostles chose to establish the new converts to Christianity. It should be the process we use today to fulfill the command of the Great Commission to 'make disciples of the nations.' It is the method the Savior chose to expand the base of believers who had chosen to be obedient to His dictates.

During the late 1970's and early 1980's, there was

a movement in the Church known as the 'discipleship movement'. This movement has been commonly associated with the Charismatic and Full Gospel movements. While it achieved widespread usage, it was also widely contested by mainstream Christianity; both Evangelical and Pentecostal camps. There were even some voices that denounced it, and labelled it "cultism." Conceptually, discipleship was and is a sound model. It is an excellent way to establish new converts. At the same time, it ensures that the more mature believers are receiving the instruction needed to advance their spiritual knowledge base. It facilitates the expansion of the experiential knowledge of Christianity. It provides an opportunity for the disciple to be exposed to 'transparent' leadership. Additionally, it simultaneously positions them to receive immediate answers to their questions; both spiritual and secular. Discipleship also provides immediate feedback regarding the formation of their developmental practices; as they attempt to operate in the principles they are being taught. It gives the disciple, both old and new, occasions to observe their teacher, trainer, or mentor, as those instructors operate in the very functions and capacities they are trying to introduce to said disciple.

The problem that gave 'discipleship' a bad reputation in the Christian community was not an inherent flaw in the model. It was not a deficiency in the composition of the idea, but rather an error linked to the proclivity of men to misjudge human character. The major issue that caused so many problems with the successful implementation of the model was not a hidden matter. The main difficulty dealt with the stark reality that many of the persons who were placed in positions of authority were ill-prepared to operate in those capacities.

In addition to placing novices in positions that should have been reserved for more seasoned Christians, there was a widespread practice of placing people in power that had no previous management, or leadership experience. The results were devastating. Not only did those ill-prepared leaders give directives that were not spiritually sound, but many 'lorded' their positional authority over those they were supposed to nurture. Instead of guiding the sheep, they drove the sheep. Instead of leading them to green pastures, those shepherds led them to parched fields of crabgrass. Instead of being led to streams where the still water flowed, they were led to streams that flowed so rapidly, the sheep choked while trying to refresh themselves.

The result was that the Church was unable to benefit from the Christ-given model that was intended for the proliferation of the Gospel message. This was a message that was powerful enough to keep a person from going to hell. The Church 'fell away' from the method which was established to provide exponential growth of the Body of Christ. She withdrew from the method that was designed to instill and ensure the integrity of the disciple that was being produced. The lack of judgment on the part of those leaders, responsible for placing those under-shepherds in position, proved to undermine the purposes of God. Instead of producing high-quality Christian converts who reflected the image of Christ; Christians were formed who reflected the character of those ill-equipped under-shepherds. The Church missed out on the opportunity to provide a continuity of development in the converts, and assist them to come to the unity of the faith. She lost the opportunity to develop them unto a perfect man, unto a measure of the fullness of the stature of Christ. She fell away from the 'best practices' and the protocol that had proven to be a successful method of reproduction.

As the contemporary New Testament Christian Church continued to become more compromised and deficient of power, it made it easy for the beliefs and practices of the New Age Movement to creep into the Body of Christ. This movement, which is the forerunner of the advent of the beasts spoken of in Revelation, is one of the most dangerous movements to exert ungodly influence in the earth. Not only are they a threat to mankind in general, but they represent a specific nemesis to the compromised Church and the Remnant Church. They are a wily antagonist of Jehovah, an adversary of Christ, and an archenemy of the Holy Ghost.

What is the New Age Movement? How do we define it? What is its relevance and impact upon the Church and the notion of a falling away? Why is it even discussed in conjunction with the Church? These are pertinent questions that need to be answered as we discuss the concept of a Remnant Church. There is, in fact, a direct correlation between these two groups. It is impossible to discuss end-times ministry without addressing the reality of the New Age Movement; and the impact it has had on Christendom. In an attempt to give a general overview of the New Age Movement, we will share some information from a variety of other sources.

Exactly what is the New Age Movement? This question

CHAPTER FIVE: THE GREAT FALLING AWAY

resonates in the minds of hundreds of thousands of people. According to excerpts from an Internet article written by Christian Apologetics and Research Ministry, here are some explanations. While the New Age Movement has many subdivisions, it is generally a collection of Eastern-Influenced metaphysical thought systems. It is a conglomeration of theologies, hopes, and expectations that are held together by teachings of salvation, correct thinking, and correct knowledge. It is thought to be a theology of sorts, with an emphasis on moral relativism, universal tolerance, and feel-goodism. Almost like if it feels right, just do it. According to New Age thinking, man is the central figure in everything. He is viewed as divine, as co-creator, and as the hope for future peace and harmony. If there is a quote that can be thought to be representative of this movement, it might be this, "I am only affected by my thoughts. This is the only thing needed to let salvation come to all the world. For in this single thought is everyone released at last from fear."[106]

    The writers of the article felt that the unfortunate thing for members of the New Age Movement was the fear from which they wanted to be released might very well be the fear that hides in the mind of every unregenerate sinner. It is the fear of damnation to hell, conviction of sin, and it is even, sometimes, the fear of Christianity and Christians. Although the New Age Movement is supposed to be tolerant of almost any theological position, it is adamantly opposed to the narrow-mindedness of Christianity because it teaches that Jesus is the only way and that there are moral absolutes. The concept of there being only one true and living God, Jehovah; and His Son Jesus, is not an acceptable belief system to the New Age Movement.[107]

Again, the authors of that article offer this information. The term New Age purportedly refers to the Aquarian Age or the Age of Aquarius. According to New Age followers, this age is dawning. The Fifth Dimension singing group sang about it back in the 1970's. Constance Cumbey wrote about it in the 1980's in her book 'The Hidden Dangers of the Rainbow'. It is supposed to bring in an age of peace and enlightenment; and reunite man with God. The New Age Movement believes that man is presently considered separated from God because of a lack of understanding and knowledge concerning the true nature of God and reality; and not because of sin. This is totally opposite of what the Holy Scriptures teach. What it really boils down to is that the New Age Movement is basically a religious system that has two basic beliefs. They can be described as Evolutionary Godhood and Global Unity. Evolutionary Godhood is the next step in spiritual evolution. However, the New Age Movement propagates evolution of both the body and spirit. They believe that man is continually evolving and developing, and will soon leap forward into new spiritual horizons.

The following is a laundry list of some of the principles, concepts, and practices New Age followers believe in. They believe in astral projection. This is training your soul to leave your body and travel around to different places. They believe you can contact spirits so they may speak through you and guide you. New Agers use crystals to purify their body's and mind's energy systems. Additionally, they believe in visualization, where you use mental imagery to imagine yourself as an animal. They do believe in

CHAPTER FIVE: THE GREAT FALLING AWAY

the presence of a divine being and being healed of sickness. In addition to all of these things, they believe that mankind will soon see itself as god; calling this the 'Christ Principle'. The New Age Movement teaches that man's basic nature is good and divine. It teaches that man has divine qualities since man is divine by nature. Since New Agers consider themselves divine, they believe they can create their own reality, can create, and they also believe in reincarnation.

The other major element of the New Age Movement is the concept known as Global Unity. This concept consists of three major divisions: (a) Man with Man, (b) Man with Nature, and (c) Man with God. The New Age Movement teaches that we will all learn our proper relationship with one another, achieve harmony, achieve mutual love and acceptance through the realization of this proper knowledge; and acceptance of it. Within this hoped-for harmony, economic unity will be attained. Included in the framework of Global Unity is the idea of a single world leader. This leader will guide the whole world into a single harmonious economic reality; by using New Age principles. Additionally, this world leader will unite the world into spiritual unity through the introduction and establishment of a one-world religion.

Another teaching of the New Age Movement centers on the notion that God is all, and all is God. Therefore, nature is a part of God. As such, man must get in tune with nature, learn to nurture it, and be nurtured by it. By doing this, all people can unite. In truth, New Age philosophy attempts to merge with the philosophies that put man and nature on the same level; an equal level. It purports that man is no more or less different, nor important, than our relatives; the animals, birds, or fish. Subsequently, we must understand them, learn from them, and live in harmony with them. New Agers call the earth Gaia, and believe that Gaia is to be revered and respected. Some in the New Age Movement even worship the earth and nature. As a result of New Agers believing that man is divine by nature, they believe all people, once they see themselves as such, will be helped in their unity of purpose, love, and development. Once this occurs, they believe that the goal to fully realize our own goodness will be accomplished and attained.[108]

These are some of the ways that New Agers view God. They say He/It is impersonal, omnipresent, and benevolent. Therefore He/It will not condemn anyone. The New Age god is impersonal. An impersonal god will not reveal himself, nor will he have specific requirements as to morality, belief, and behavior. The majesty and personhood of the true God must be lowered, because the New Ager seeks to elevate himself to godhood. This has to happen because the universe is not big enough for the one true God, but it is big enough for a bunch of little ones. The New Age Movement also teaches that there are no moral absolutes. Therefore, they claim to have a spiritual tolerance for all "truth systems." They call this concept 'harmonization'. It should be noted that while the New Age Movement does espouse honesty, integrity, love, peace, and other Judeo-Christian principles, it does not want to practice these on God's terms. They want to exhibit these on man's terms versus submitting to the governance of the true and living God.[109]

According to Wikipedia, the New Age Movement is, 'a

CHAPTER FIVE: THE GREAT FALLING AWAY

movement that spread through the occult and metaphysical religious communities in the 1970s and 80s'. It looked forward to a 'New Age' of love and light and offered a foretaste of the coming era through personal transformation and healing. The movement's strongest supporters were followers of modern esotericism, a religious perspective that is based on the acquisition of mystical knowledge, and that has been popular in the West since the second century, especially in the form of Gnosticism. Ancient Gnosticism was succeeded by various esoteric movements through the centuries, including Rosicrucianism in the 17th century and Freemasonry, theosophy, and ritual magic in the 19th and 20th centuries.

The Encyclopedia Britannica helps to shed light on the origins of the New Age Movement, and the birth of the movement in American society; and the people who pioneered the Movement. Helen Petrovna Blavatsky, cofounder of the Theosophical Society, announced a coming New Age. She did this during the late 19th century. She believed that theosophists, who embrace Buddhist and Brahmanic notions such as reincarnation, should assist in the evolution of the human race. They would do this by preparing the race to cooperate with one of the Ascended Masters of the Great White Brotherhood whose arrival was imminent. She believed that members of this mystical brotherhood actually guided the destiny of the planet; since they were really the world's hidden leaders. Her ideas contributed to the expectation of a New Age among practitioners of spiritualism and believers in astrology. These people were anticipating the coming of the new Aquarian Age as a promised period of brotherhood and enlightenment.

During the 1940's Alice A. Bailey made her contributions to the Movement. She was the founder of the Arcane School, which was an organization that disseminated spiritual teachings. She suggested that a new messiah, the Master Maitreya, would appear in the last quarter of the 20th century. Bailey also established a program to bring people together to meditate in groups of three. It was called "Triangles." Participants in the program believed they received divine energy by meditating; which they shared with those around them. Thus, this meditation raised the general level of spiritual awareness. After Bailey's death, former members of her organization created a host of new independent theosophical groups. The hopes for a New Age flourished within these groups. These groups claimed the ability to transmit spiritual energy to the world. Allegedly, they could also receive channeled messages from preternatural beings; particularly Ascended Masters of the Great White Brotherhood. The Findhorn Foundation, located in Scotland, believed that its supposed contact with a variety of nature spirits produced spectacular agricultural feats and amazing crops; despite the poor soil and climate conditions prevalent at the group's settlement location.

David Spangler was an American theosophist who moved to the Findhorn Foundation in 1970. There, he developed the fundamental idea of the New Age Movement. He believed that the release of new waves of spiritual energy, signaled by certain astrological changes, had initiated the coming of the New Age. Those changes, the movement of the earth into a new cycle, known as the Age of Aquarius, was the dawn of a new age. He

CHAPTER FIVE: THE GREAT FALLING AWAY

then suggested that people use this new energy to make manifest the New Age. Spangler's view was diametrically opposed to Bailey's view. Bailey and her followers believed that the New Age would arrive independent of human efforts, or actions. Spangler's viewpoint, however, demanded an active response from proponents of it, and shifted the responsibility for the coming of the New Age to those who believed in it; and were anticipating its appearance.

Upon his return to the United States in the mid 1970's, Spangler became the major architect of the New Age Movement. In 1976, he presented his ideas in a set of popular books; beginning with 'Revelation: The Birth of a New Age'. He attracted many leaders from older occult organizations and metaphysical organizations to this rapidly growing movement. The simultaneous collapse of the psychedelic movement provided new supporters to the New Age Movement. One such supporter was noted psychologist Richard Alpert. He was an advocate of the use of hallucinogenic drugs to achieve mystical experiences. Having found enlightenment in India, Alpert returned to the West as Baba Ram Dass. His enlightenment caused him to disavow the drug experience and become an advocate for the more traditional spiritual disciplines. At the same time, periodicals began to be published to disseminate information, and also create a sense of community within the decentralized movement. Over time, and with the growth of the movement, bookstores began to open that specialized in the sale of New Age books, videos, and meditation aids.

Another development in the Movement was the integration

of traditional occult practices. The inclusion of such things as astrology, yoga, tarot card reading, mediumship, and meditation techniques were being blended into the acceptable New Age teachings and practices. The combination of Eastern mysticism and Western rationalism to understand psychological health and spiritual well-being is known as Transpersonal Psychology. This type of psychology, along with other new academic disciplines that study states of consciousness, encouraged the belief that consciousness-altering practices, such as Zen Meditation, could be practiced apart from the original contexts in which they were originated. Furthermore, there were many other techniques used to help New Agers achieve personal transformation. The use of these techniques and practices was designed to help bring about 'planetary healing' and 'societal transformation'. The New Age Movement also spoke to people who had not been able to find help through traditional medicine and psychotherapy. Special attention was paid to those who were either sick or wounded psychologically. New Agers also promoted spiritual healing. The Movement aligned itself with the Holistic Health Movement. These doctors and medical practitioners advocated alternative and natural healing practices such as acupuncture, natural food diets, massage, and chiropractic treatment.

However, it was evident by the end of the 1980's that the New Age Movement had lost its momentum. Although it was primarily considered a religious movement, it was derided for its acceptance of unscientific ideas and practices; especially its advocacy of using crystals and the practice of channeling. In spite of this, the New Age Movement did prove itself to be one of the Western Hemisphere's most significant religious phenomena in the 20th century. In addition to improving the image of the older esoteric religious groups, it allowed many of the New Age community's largest groups to find a place in the pluralistic culture of the Western Hemisphere. Although its vision of massive social transformation was not fully achieved, and ultimately died, the movement was still able to attract thousands of new adherents to one branch, or another, of the Western esoteric-metaphysical tradition. By the late 1980's three to five million Americans either identified themselves as New Agers or accepted the practices and beliefs of the New Age Movement. The continuing presence of New Age thought in the post New Age era can be easily seen in the number of New Age organizations, periodicals, and bookstores that continue to be found in nearly every major city and urban center.[110]

From a Judeo-Christian perspective, there are many inherent dangers in the New Age Movement. We would like to submit the following for your consideration. The movement cultivates the notion of one's own divine existence or potential. Their holistic interpretation of the universe prohibits a belief in a dualistic good and evil. It teaches that negative events are not a result of evil, but rather are lessons designed to teach an individual; and enable them to advance spiritually. The New Age Movement rejects the Christian emphasis on sin and guilt. It believes that these generate fear and negativity, which in turn hinders spiritual evolution. New Agers criticize, blaming and judging others for their actions or inactions. They believe that if an individual adopts these negative attitudes, it harms their own spiritual evolution. Another danger of this movement is that it encourages repeated recitation of mantras and statements carrying positive messages; the Scriptures refer to this type of practice as vain repetition. New Age philosophy also encourages visualization of a white light. Additionally, they believe in reincarnation as a part of humanity's progressive spiritual evolution. The movement promotes karma as a law of cause and effect; which assures cosmic balance. New Agers claim that the part of the human soul that carries the personality perishes with the death of the body. Simultaneously, the Higher Self, which connects with divinity, survives in order to be reborn in another body. It is believed that the Higher Self chooses the body and circumstances into which it will be born. This is done in order to use it as a vessel through which to learn new lessons; and thus, advance its own spiritual evolution. Finally, the New Age Movement aims to create a spirituality without borders, boundaries, or confining dogmas; that is pluralistic and inclusive. All of these concepts are dangerous and contradictory to the principles upon which Christianity is based. These must be adamantly opposed by The Remnant Church.

The core tenets of the New Age Movement have caused millions of people to reject the basic tenets of Christianity, which acknowledge Jehovah God as the only 'divine' entity in the universe. This movement denies the existence of heaven and hell, and the reality of the consequence of one's actions; resulting in the form of eternal judgment. It also rejects the notion of sin and guilt; and believes that man is inherently good. Thus this movement does not believe in an inherent sin nature in man,

CHAPTER FIVE: THE GREAT FALLING AWAY

which needs to be born-again in order to be re-connected to God. This movement also rejects the notion that there is only one access to God, through the shed blood of Jesus Christ. Consequently, the movement has been responsible for literally millions of people falling away from accepting the Gospel of Jesus Christ. Instead they chose rather to believe that they themselves are divine, and not in need of salvation. Although the popularity of this movement may be diminished in our contemporary society, the effect of its influence on world government and economy is regrettably apparent as we watch world events unfold before us.

The 21st century New Testament Remnant Church must decry the institution of the New World Order which the New Age Movement has conceived, nurtured, birthed, and continues to directly or indirectly propagate. She must stand as a watchman on the wall to sound the alert of the deception and danger this New World Order poses. The Remnant Church must be aware of the "falling away" from Christian values that the New World Order endorses. She must also be cognizant of the role in which the New World Order functions; as a forerunner of the Beasts of Revelation. The Remnant must "cry loud, and spare not." Although, up to this point, a lot of mention has not been made concerning the institution of the New World Order, more attention will be given to this subject in following chapters.

Chapter Six
Characteristics of Remnant Israel

"Not as though the word of God hath taken none effect. For they are not all Israel, which are of Israel: neither, because they are the seed of Abraham, are they all children: but, In Isaac shall thy seed be called That is, They which are the children of the flesh these are not the children of God: but the children of the promise are counted for the seed."
Romans 9:6-8

As stated earlier, the biblical concept of the remnant has always been associated with the nation and people of Israel. So, as we explore the Remnant Church, it makes sense for us to look at examples of remnant; as it pertains to Israel. In this chapter, we will lean heavily on information provided in the commentary and study notes of the "New Living Translation" of the Bible and Wikipedia. We will take an exhaustive examination of the journey of Israel as she came out of Egyptian bondage. We will explore the different forms of remnant seen in her state of affairs from then until now. *Exodus 32* allows us to explore the state of affairs of remnant Israel as they arrived at the mountain that, for them, represented the seat of the government of God; Mt. Sinai. The children of Israel had sojourned through the wilderness and finally arrived at Sinai. They had experienced the mighty hand of God as He delivered them via supernatural wonders, and judgments against the Egyptians. Yet in spite of it all, when their physical leader was out of sight, when they could not engage the physical image in whom they had placed their confidence and loyalty, they immediately lost faith. They resorted back to trusting what they could see. They lost confidence in God's ability to supernaturally deliver and sustain them. They felt that they needed a physical representation of the invisible God; something tangible that they could see, and feel.

The people were not willing to wait, and see what God had been saying to Moses. The people wanted to shape God into their own liking; into whatever image they desired. The people thought that the divine realm and the visible world are contiguous with each other. They were guilty of trying to mold God to fit their expectations. This showed that while Moses was absent, there was a spiritual decline in the remaining leadership; and in the people. The people were running wild, out of control, and had cast off restraint. Anarchy reigns among the people who refuse to obey and worship the Lord. The people had been robbed of all ethical alertness and moral discernment. The people felt the need for 'protective guidance', but were unwilling to wait on God to provide it. Their fear, disrespect for, and unbelief in God's delegated authority and designated leadership motivated them to try to meet their own needs. They failed to maintain fellowship with Jehovah God; and depend on Him to be the source through which their needs would be met. God cannot work in us whenever we elevate anyone or anything above Him.

After four hundred years of Egyptian bondage, some of the pagan practices with which they were familiar, still exerted a strong influence on their thinking. This resulted in a tendency to erroneously find comfort in pagan practices, and yet they still believed that they had a working relationship with the God of Creation. After being called to a higher level of relationship, their sensory deprivations caused them to resort back to that which they were most familiar. The symbolisms and idols of Egypt caused them to forsake the reality and power of Jehovah being in their midst. In a time of panic or impatience, the people succumbed to a polytheistic pagan world view. They allowed their recent intimate experience with Jehovah to be tainted by a spirit of self-gratification and self-indulgence. The pagan world view had blinded them to the undeniable real life experience of being led by the 'living God'. Lucifer was able to seduce them into a deceptive desire of being led forward by the false gods they had embraced from their Egyptian captivity.

Syncretistic worship is the attempt, or tendency to combine

or reconcile different philosophical or religious beliefs. It is the fusion of two or more originally different inflectional forms into a single form. This is what Israel was guilty of. As a result, Israel had willfully, and defiantly broken covenant. This is what God's chosen people were experiencing. When the ringleaders, the Levites who had led the people in worshipping the golden calf, did not respond by choosing to be on the Lord's side; Moses had them killed.

What was the state of affairs of the remnant during the situations after the camp was divided? Why had the Lord allowed Moses' enemies to be bitten by snakes, and the ground to open up and swallow his enemies? *Numbers 16* recounts the rebellion of Korah and his associates Abiram and Dathan. Korah desired more than the high duties that he already had; providing service in the Tabernacle...he wanted the priesthood. He used deception to advance his claim. Korah and his associates may have seen the advantages of the priesthood while they were in captivity. This was evidenced by the Egyptian priest's great wealth, political influence, and their control of others. They actually referred to Egypt as a land flowing with milk and honey.[111] They let themselves be deceived into thinking that what was in reality "their prison" was by some strange way of reasoning 'a paradise'; not a prison. Although Korah already had significant, worthwhile abilities and responsibilities, he ended up losing everything because of his inappropriate ambition and greed.

Two hundred and fifty Levites, leaders of Israel who had their own complaints, joined him. They claimed that Moses had gone 'too far' in taking, or assuming, spiritual leadership

CHAPTER SIX: CHARACTERISTICS OF REMNANT ISRAEL

of the people. Which in fact was a role that in reality, had been given to him by Jehovah. They used the deceptive claim that 'the whole community' was holy, so there was no reason for Moses and Aaron to set themselves above the rest of Israel as spiritual leaders. Dathan and Abiram accused Moses of not fulfilling his pledge to lead Israel to 'the promised land'. These rebels were jealous of Moses and envious of Aaron. This rebellion called for the necessity to distinguish the difference between the Levites and the Aaronic priests. This was also a clear 'power struggle' against God's authority; and His chosen leadership. The rebel's complaint was not with Moses and Aaron; it was actually with the Lord. Grumbling, complaining, and murmuring against Jehovah and His chosen leadership are negative attitudes that cause rebellion. These attitudes erode faith in God; and encourages thoughts of giving up and turning back. Dissatisfaction and skepticism are paths that lead to open rebellion against God, and separation from His divine guidance.

Moses wanted the people to know that the wrath of God that, was about to be revealed to those rebels of God's designated representative and delegated authority, was not going to be something that happened by coincidence. They needed to know that what was about to happen, this judgment, was going to be a 'new' 'apparent' sign of His anger; and displeasure with these rebels. His unprecedented display of wrath against their insubordination was also a way to vindicate Moses' position of leadership. Moses' intercession saved the entire people from destruction; because of their opposition to God. The Lord answered Moses' plea of intercession for the nation by warning them to remove themselves from close proximity to Korah. God wanted the innocent bystanders to move away from Korah's tent; so they would not be included in the wrath and punishment He was about to send Korah's way. Korah's sons were wise enough not to join their father's rebellion.

The two hundred and fifty men who wanted to be priests, and challenged Moses' authority by fire and incense, were ironically destroyed by fire sent from the Lord; perhaps lightning. Since they were seeking a position that had not been granted to them by God, the instruction was for them to 'act like' priests by burning incense. God would decide who the legitimate priests actually were. The censers of the deceased impostors were hammered into a covering for the altar of the Lord. This was done as a memorial of the folly of self-proclaimed priesthood. It was also a warning not to strive for positions of authority that have not been sanctioned by the Lord. The cover for the altar (censers from the want-to-be priests) was to serve as a perpetual reminder that Jehovah had chosen Aaron and his descendants for the priesthood. In spite of God's display of displeasure for questioning, or challenging, His leadership, the whole community of Israel still grumbled against Moses and accused him of killing the Lord's people. As a result God sent a plague that killed fourteen thousand and seven hundred people.

As we read the 21st chapter of Numbers, we see that the people became impatient with the direction God had given Moses to not engage Edom; and once again rebelled. They forgot that their victory over Arad was granted by the Lord, in response to their solemn pledge to obey Him. Their impatience caused

CHAPTER SIX: CHARACTERISTICS OF REMNANT ISRAEL

them to: blaspheme God, reject His chosen leader, and despise His miraculous provision of manna. Rejecting the heavenly bread, or manna, was tantamount to rejecting God's grace. Israel once again showed their lack of obedience and commitment to honor their pledge to Jehovah. Israel complained because they were not faithful to God. They refused to obey God's law; and they forgot the Lord's miracles towards them. Jehovah had to afflict them with a plague of poisonous serpents. In response to the people's confession of their sin, Jehovah provided a way of deliverance from the intended punishment of that sin; that He had determined to release on them.

There were parallels between Israel's return from Babylon and the exodus from Egypt. The following are some of the parallels: other nations provided resources for the journey; they were to build a dwelling place for the presence of the Lord; the reinstitution of the Law; the challenge of the local residents, or enemies; and the temptation to intermarry the non-Jew pagans.

Major cataclysmic events always set the stage for a falling away from the faith, and the creation of a remnant. God had punished Judah's persistent wickedness by sending the Babylonians to: destroy the city; demolish the Temple; and take thousands into a seventy year exile. When the people's attitudes and desires changed, God ended their punishment. He gave them the chance to return home, and be restored.

Look at the state of affairs of the covenant community, and the remnant, that was created after the Israelites were released from their Babylonian exile. The book of Ezra helps us understand some of the mental, emotional, and psychological attitudes prevalent among those who had been impacted by the exile to Babylon. This book also reinforces the fact that God provides for and protects those who trust Him; and faithfully obey His word. It was twenty three years, 538 BC - 515 BC, before rebuilding the Temple was complete. It was forty one years, 486 BC - 445 BC, before the rebuilding of Jerusalem's wall was complete. The Temple and the Wall of Jerusalem were built over the course of ninety three years and five Persian kings.

Cyrus, the Persian king, defeated the Babylonians, and allowed the Jewish people to return to their homeland; which was a four-month trip. One of the Persian practices was to return exiled people to their homeland, expecting them to be thankful, obey the Persians; and pay their taxes to the Persians. The first exiles were released with the instructions to rebuild the place where the presence of Jehovah resided. After all of their years of captivity the arrogant nation, that had lost their devotion to Jehovah, was humbled. Israel had a remnant that

> *"God is sovereign, even when rulers and nations don't recognize His authority."*

was eager to: return home; be restored; and accept the commission to rebuild a dwelling place for the presence of the Lord to reside, the Temple. Jehovah moved on the hearts of the leaders, family heads, priests, and Levites to give them a 'great desire' to return to Jerusalem to rebuild the Temple.

The returning exiles were able to overcome the discouragement of their captivity, and hold onto the hope they had in God's promise to return them to their own homeland. Cyrus' permission for the Jews to return to Jerusalem

CHAPTER SIX: CHARACTERISTICS OF REMNANT ISRAEL

demonstrated how God's 'covenant community' was restored from exile to the 'covenant land', as a theocratic community. This happened even while Israel was continuing to be governed under Gentile, pagan rulership. God is sovereign, even when rulers and nations don't recognize His authority. Jehovah can use 'world powers' to judge His people. Just as well. He can use world powers to restore His people to their 'covenant designated place of dwelling, or existence', to help fulfill their destiny and purpose. God's recurrent action in Israel's history proved to the post-exilic community that they represented the continuation of God's redemptive plan for Israel. The returning exiles were experiencing the sovereign hand of God at work; in perfect keeping with His plan at His appointed time.

Only a very few Levites, seventy-four, responded to King Cyrus' directive. Most of the people who returned to Jerusalem were from the tribes of Judah and Benjamin. Ezra brought thirty-eight more Levites with him when he came to Jerusalem. There was an eighty year gap between Zerubbabel leading the first group of exiles to Jerusalem; and Ezra bringing the second group. Many Jews did not want to leave the comforts of Babylon, to build the house of the Lord. It was much easier for them to make a financial contribution to the effort, rather than make that four month trek to Jerusalem. Many Jews in captivity had accumulated great wealth, and did not want to return to Jerusalem to have to start all over. They preferred wealth and security to the 'sacrifice' that God's work would require. King Cyrus encouraged the Jews who decided to stay in Babylon to financially help their countrymen who were returning to Jerusalem. Additionally, the captivity may have made some people unsure of their heritage, and doubt their purpose in the earth. Thus this made them unwilling to share in the vision and mission to rebuild the place of habitation for the presence of the Lord. Nearly fifty thousand people made the first trip to Jerusalem to rebuild the Temple with Zerubbabel. Approximately eleven thousand Israelites who returned from the Babylonian exile did not belong to the southern tribes of Judah or Benjamin.

When they returned they found that Jerusalem was now a desolate city inhabited by foreigners.[112] The priests, the Levites, the singers, the gatekeepers, the Temple servants, and some of the common people settled in villages near Jerusalem. The rest of the people returned to their own towns throughout Israel. After the people of the Northern Kingdom of Israel were exiled in 722 BC, some moved into Jerusalem. Additionally, some local residents were foreigners from abroad who were resettled there by the Assyrian king, Esarhaddon.

The returning Jews found other foreigners had settled in their land, who wanted to worship with the Hebrews; claiming they worshipped the same God. The occupants who resided in Jerusalem during Judah's exile saw the returning Israelites as a threat to dispossess them of the city and land. They immediately wanted to undermine the returning exiles allegiance to Jehovah. In actuality, they wanted to combine pagan and Jewish ideas and practices into a spiritually compromised form of worship. Idolatry had been the chief cause of Judah's Babylonian captivity. When the Samaritans, and other occupants of Jerusalem, made the false claim that they also worshipped Jehovah in a pure way,

CHAPTER SIX: CHARACTERISTICS OF REMNANT ISRAEL

absent of pagan rituals, the returning exiles immediately rejected the occupant's offer to help them in the rebuilding project. The returning Israelites rejected these occupants' superstitious form of worshipping Jehovah, and their form of mixed religious practices. They also rejected the offer of cooperation from the current occupants of Jerusalem. They saw it as an attempt to compromise the spiritual purity of their restoration process. Consequently, these Samaritans ultimately built a rival temple on Mt. Gerizim.

The woman saith unto Him, Sir, I perceive that thou art a prophet. Our fathers worshipped in this mountain, and ye say, that in Jerusalem is the place where men ought to worship.
John 4:19-20

The returning Hebrews position was that, "We must avoid accepting pagan practices, as it will pollute our 'religious' purity and endanger the future of our covenant community, and spiritual nation. This is the inherent danger of spiritual and natural intermarriage." As a result of intermarriage with the pagans that had settled in Jerusalem, it became necessary to completely separate from those pagans; in order to avoid adopting pagan religious beliefs. They also believed that since they were seeking to be restored to their covenant relationship with Jehovah, it made it necessary to require an absolute and total separation from paganism in their hearts. Even if the separation did not immediately manifest one hundred percent in their actions, they felt that they must have at the center of their purpose the intention for that manifestation to be the ultimate outcome. One hundred percent separation, total devotion to God in our intentions, thoughts, and deeds has to be the ultimate goal. When the Jewish community refused to allow these foreigners to join them, it resulted in many years of conflict, which caused delay in rebuilding the Temple. There will always be adversaries and opposition to God's work and purpose in your life. We must not falter or withdraw; but stay faithful, focused, active, patient, and steadfast. God ordained restoration often evokes fierce opposition from bystanders and onlookers.

Upon returning to Jerusalem, the first thing that was reconstructed was the Altar of the Lord. This showed the people's enthusiasm to faithfully worship God at every opportunity; even with the Temple, the walls, and the city in disrepair. In addition to celebrating the Feasts, and giving the traditional offerings, the people also brought "voluntary offerings." The Altar of the Lord symbolized God's presence and protection. It also demonstrated their national purpose and commitment to serve Jehovah alone; Him only. Sacrificing to God demonstrated that the people were: seeking God's guidance; rededicating themselves to Him; and attempting to reestablish their covenant relationship with Him. The Temple was built before the wall because if spiritual protection is not in place political, or military, protection has no chance of succeeding. Spiritual before natural, political, and military was the norm. God had always been the nation's protector. The returning exiles knew that the strongest stones could not protect them if Jehovah was not with them. They chose to build the Temple before they built anything else. The beauty of the Temple was not as important to God as the attitude

CHAPTER SIX: CHARACTERISTICS OF REMNANT ISRAEL

of the builders and worshippers.

Cyrus' proclamation permitted the returning remnant to work "together" on the huge task of rebuilding the Temple in a desolate city, with broken down walls, and inhabited by foreigners. Some of the covenant community did the actual building, while others operated the supply lines. Both were important roles. In a significant venture, teamwork is mandatory; some people are required to function in supporting roles, while others must operate in the background. It must be in the Remnant Church. Each role is vital in order for the task to be accomplished. The workforce that rebuilt the Temple was made up of everyone; it was accomplished by unity. Putting the Levites in charge ensured that the work was going to be done according to Jehovah's specifications. The same must be true in the Remnant Church. The spiritual leaders of the Church must take the lead in bringing the Church back to Jehovah's requirement of holiness. The things that were missing from the Temple as the rebuilding process began were: the Ark of the Covenant; the splendor, riches, and accouterments from the days of David and Solomon. The huge size of the original Temple; and the Shekinah glory of the Ancient of Days, the Most High God Jehovah were also absent. Those elders that wept aloud were either disappointed that the foundation of the Temple wasn't as wonderful as the old one had been, or they were deeply moved with joy to see that the Temple of the Lord was being restored. The money that had been gathered by David to build Solomon's Temple was a thousand times more than what was gathered to rebuild the second temple.[113] Some people wept as they remembered the splendor and glory of the first temple; compared to what was going to be built by the returnees.[114]

Jehovah sent the prophets to encourage the people, which resulted in completion of the Temple in only four years; after a sixteen year layoff. There was a sixteen-year gap in rebuilding the Temple because of the remnant's negative reflections, and because enemies were allowed to infiltrate and influence the workforce. Discouragement and fear are two of the greatest obstacles to completing God's work. Discouragement eats away at our motivation, and fear paralyzes us so that we don't act at all. The Jews dealt with the pressure, and attempted intimidation, by recognizing that they were workers for God. When you feel surrounded, outnumbered, overpowered, out-classed by difficult situations, remember that God's power is not limited to, or by, your resources. If we contemplate the reactions and criticisms of hostile, anti-covenant people, we will be paralyzed with fear. Realizing that Jehovah is our leader will help us live to please Him; versus attempting to please those who oppose His work. The Remnant Church cannot allow our preoccupation with our own interests to sidetrack us from placing the rebuilding of God's Temple as our primary priority. We must continue to rebuild God's church, and the principles of holiness. God's word must be the basis for our faith and actions in order to fulfill our obligation to finish God's work; per His instruction to us.

There were some very important lessons Israel learned as a result of their exile. They now realized that the principle of preparation is vital if any project is to be completed correctly, and well. They learned that everything that happened resulted from

CHAPTER SIX: CHARACTERISTICS OF REMNANT ISRAEL

God's sovereign control over Israel's history. Also that God's people must be pure, and separate from sinfulness in the world. They accepted the fact that following God's word is of primary importance. Additionally, intercessory prayer invites God's compassion and power. The Jewish remnant had learned that the compromise of the purity of their faith would not produce positive results. This exiled covenant community had also learned that Jehovah doesn't offer special protection to people who ignore Him. They learned the importance of obeying God 'from the heart', and not merely out of habit. It is attention to these 'learned lessons' that will help the compromised, deceived, conformist Church transition into the Remnant Church.

God showed His mercy and compassionately restored His people. The entire nation of Israel was repatriated through a representative remnant. The restoration of the covenant community was complete; even though political independence had not yet been attained. Restoration can often require continual chastening, rebuke, renewal and reformation. In order to grow spiritually, our commitment to God must be reviewed, renewed, and often rededicated. We must establish a spiritual foundation for our rebuilding efforts. Sometimes 'God's ownership' of a project is only recognized after our best efforts have failed. When God gives us important jobs to do, it is not because He needs our help; but it is because He trusts us. True worship involves, and requires, devotion to Jehovah God; and to Him alone.

> *"God's people must be pure, and separate from sinfulness in the world."*

Just as Israel had to experience the continual 'pressure'

of the restoration process, so the Church must have the same pressure applied to her; if she is to emerge as the Remnant Church. At this point, it is extremely important for us to examine the historical events that happened in the Holy Land, as they had a direct impact on the physical looks of the people in that region. One cannot explore the concept of the Remnant Church apart from it being in conjunction with the history of Israel; the two are inseparable. According to Wikipedia, there were multiple major changes in the state of affairs of remnant Israel after the conquest of the Holy Land by the Germanic tribes. Although the war effort of the Germanic tribes were directed against the Roman Empire, since the Jews were subjects of the Roman Empire during the time of the conquest, the Israelites were directly affected by the outcome of the conquest. These changes not only impacted the culture of the covenant community, but they also altered the physical look of the covenant community. Prior to the invasion of the Holy Land by the Germanic tribes (sons of Japheth) of the north, the complexion and hue of the inhabitants of Palestine bore evidence that civilization had started in the fertile crescent between the Nile Valley in Egypt, and the Tigris-Euphrates Valley in Iran and Iraq. The Jewish people of the region were of a darker hue, reflecting their African-Edenic origins, and living a life under the effect of the sun's heat; as is typical of living near the equator.

We must understand the physical characteristics of the Jewish people before the Germanic invasion of the region. Paul, the apostle, was being led into a castle by a chief captain.[115] Paul spoke to the chief in Greek, asking permission to speak with him.

CHAPTER SIX: CHARACTERISTICS OF REMNANT ISRAEL

The chief captain was surprised that Paul could speak Greek and asks Paul, "Are not you that Egyptian?" Paul responded, "I am a man of Israel." In order for this chief captain to mistake an Israelite for a black-skinned Egyptian, Paul had to look like an Egyptian, as scripture tells us the whole nation of Israel did. This is why the angel of the Lord told Joseph to arise and take the young child Jesus, and his mother Mary, and flee into Egypt.

"And when they were departed, behold the angel of the Lord appeared to Joseph in a dream, saying, Arise, and take the young child and His mother, and flee into Egypt, and be thou there until I bring thee word: for Herod will seek the young child to destroy Him."
Matthew 2:13

He was told to stay there until he received further instruction, because Herod would seek the young child to destroy him. The reason Joseph, Mary and Jesus were told to flee into Egypt, an African nation, was not for military protection. During this time, Egypt was a Roman province under Roman control. They fled into Egypt because Egypt was still a 'black' country, populated by a majority of black-skinned Egyptian people. Joseph, Mary and Jesus would have been just another black-skinned family among many. Remember, they fled into Egypt to hide from Herod; who was seeking to kill Jesus. If Jesus and the rest of the Hebrews looked like those typical pictures of Christ we see, it would have been hard for him to hide in Egypt, and not be noticed. It would have been hard for Jesus to hide among the Egyptians, if he looked like the traditional painting of Jesus. Jesus could not have been white skinned.

According to Dr. Gene Rice, since the Hebrews and Egyptians looked alike; it would have been impossible to identify any. The ancient Egyptians of biblical times, descendants of Noah's son Ham, called themselves and their land 'Khemet.' Ham means black, hot, and burnt. Khemet means the land of the blacks. The Bible calls Egypt the land of Ham in various places of the Psalm. Psalm 78: 51; Psalm 105: 23 and Psalm 105: 27 to be specific. The Scriptures substantiate the fact that the Egyptians of antiquity were a black-skinned people. In Amos 9: 7, Israel is being compared to the children of the Ethiopians. The Ethiopians are a black-skinned people. Would it make any sense to call a white-skinned people the children of a black-skinned people? No. The prophet compares Israel to a black-skinned people because the Jews of antiquity were a black-skinned people.[116]

It is common knowledge that the Ethiopians were intrinsically associated with the Hebrews, as evidenced in the account of the Ethiopian Eunuch; recorded in Acts 8: 26-36. In those days, only Hebrews came to Jerusalem to worship; because this is where the Temple of Jehovah was located. Additionally, this Ethiopian Hebrew had Hebrew scriptures in his possession; which were still considered sacred and germane to the Hebrew/Jewish people. This Ethiopian man was a Hebrew that lived in Ethiopia; an Ethiopian Hebrew. This Hebrew was not called an Ethiopian just because he lived in Ethiopia, but because he looked like a black-skinned Ethiopian; who were a little darker hued than the Egyptians. Their darkness was due to their closer proximity to the equator than the Egyptians. Yet, these residents

CHAPTER SIX: CHARACTERISTICS OF REMNANT ISRAEL

of Africa, along with their Hebrew occupants of Palestine, were a black-skinned people.[117]

Although present day Jews are mainly a white-skinned people, this is due to the Germanic tribes of the north conquering the Holy Land. These were the descendants of Noah's light-skinned son, Japheth. Subsequently, the spoils of war included rape and pillage; resulting in the lightening of the peoples of that region. We will discuss this in a later chapter. Many of the people who are called Jews today are white-skinned people who come from Europe. They make up the majority of the people living in Israel today. Yet, we are hard-pressed to find any scripture that likens Israel to any white-skinned nations. Historians and scholars both agree that the majority of the people of antiquity were a dark-skinned people. This is basically due to the geographical locale of the places in scripture being in an area of extreme exposure to the rays of the sun.

Acts 13:1 speaks of Simeon and Lucius of the Church at Antioch. One person that was called Niger, another person that was from Cyrene. Both of these are references to black-skinned people. Niger is a Latin word that means black, and Cyrene is a city located in Libya; North Africa. The Hebrews/Jews were a black-skinned people. Remember that Paul himself was mistaken for a black-skinned Egyptian. All of the prophets, teachers, and characters we read about in scripture were dark-skinned people. The Cambridge Encyclopedia testifies to the physical appearance of the Hebrews in its listing about the coin of Roman Emperor, Justinian. His coin has the image of Justinian on one side, with straight hair and the image of Jesus on the other side; with woolly kinky hair and Negroid features. All the preceding information is sufficient proof of the hue of the Hebrew people of antiquity.

Dr. Charles S. Finch III, M.D., in his book, "Echoes of the Old Darkland," allows us to know that albinos in Africa are subject to fatal grotesque, disfiguring cancers due to unprotected, light skin; due to a lack of Melanin. Melanin is the substance that gives skin a dark brown or black pigment by absorbing ultra violet radiation. It scatters the ions which are produced, thereby protecting the skin from cancer. It is a sinuous gland that is prevalent in people of color. Conversely it is a gland that calcified in the descendants of Japheth, as they moved further away from the equator, Fertile Crescent; thus, further explaining the lightening of their tribes. Since Abraham, the father of the Hebrew-Israelite nation, came from Ur, he had to have been a very dark, black-skinned person. The Hebrews of antiquity were just one black-skinned people among many black-skinned nations. These black-skinned nations had skin tones that ranged from light brown to the darkest black hue; some even called purple.

Even though the Hebrews of antiquity did mix with other nations, because they were a black-skinned people, their genes would have carried the dominant trait. Lamentations 5: 10 states that Israel's skin was black like an oven because of the terrible famine. Professor Rudolph Windsor in his book, "From Babylon to Timbuktu," tells us that the complexion of the Chaldeans, the people of Abraham's ethnicity, was jet black. He states that the root word of Ur, which is orr, means fire oven. These facts are significant for people of color in that they give persons of African descent an opportunity to discover consistent,

CHAPTER SIX: CHARACTERISTICS OF REMNANT ISRAEL

favorable mentioning of their forefathers in the Holy Scriptures. Additionally, it allows people of color to read the Bible in a manner that is free of a Eurocentric point of view. This provides a basis for racial reconciliation, and the opportunity to help dispel the discrimination and oft times segregation which can result from improper interpretation of the scriptures.

Dr. Gene Rice, Professor of the Old Testament offers a substantial amount of information depicting the presence of Blacks in the Hebrew Bible or Old Testament. The following are some of the persons he has cited as prominent blacks in the Scriptures:

» Nimrod, son of Cush – Genesis 10: 8-12
» Hagar, Sarah's Egyptian maid; mother of Ishmael, Abraham's oldest son – Genesis 16; 21: 8-21
» Asenath, Joseph's wife; mother of Ephraim and Manasseh – Genesis 41: 45, 51-52; 46: 20
» Moses Cushite wife Zipporah – Numbers 12: 1; Exodus 2: 21-23
» Jethro, Moses father-in-law – Exodus 8: 13-27
» Phinehas, grandson of Moses brother Aaron – Exodus 6: 25
» Unnamed Cushite soldier in David's army – II Samuel 18: 21, 31
» Solomon's Egyptian wife – I Kings 3: 1; 11: 1
» The Queen of Sheba – I Kings 10: 1-13
» Zerah, the Ethiopian – II Chronicles 14: 9-15
» Ethiopian ambassadors representing Pharaoh Shabaka – Isaiah 18: 1-2
» The Ethiopian Tirhakah – II Kings 19: 9; Isaiah 37: 9

- » The prophet Zephaniah – Zephaniah 1:1
- » Jehudi ben Nathaniah ben Shlemiah ben Cushi – Jeremiah 36: 14, 21, 23
- » Ebed-melech the Ethiopian – Jeremiah 38: 7-13[118]

Alexander the Great subscribed to the notion of interracial marriage; he wanted all of his subjects to have Greek blood flowing through their veins.

> *"The ancient people of the New Testament were not Europeans..."*

The ancients had no problem with black people. Additionally, many Jews of the first century lived in regions where Africans freely intermingled with other ethnic groups. Hence, it is easy to understand that the African presence in the Bible is not just limited to the Old Testament; but the black presence can also be found in the New Testament.

We can note that in Matthew we find Joseph, Mary, and Jesus fleeing into Egypt to escape the death sword of King Herod. Hosea 11:1 testifies to the Messiah being called out of Egypt. Egypt has always been a part of Africa. The holy family went there to hide because it was easy for them to blend in and not be noticed. They did not stand out because the Egyptians and Hebrews were the same people; they looked alike. Only the way they wore their beards differentiated them. Please remember that the Hebrews were slaves in Egypt for over 430 years. During this time, they intermarried with the Egyptians. Although the sons of Jacob/Israel went into Egypt as a little over seventy souls, they came out over two million strong; African-Edenic peoples. Africans migrated out of biblical Egypt and Ethiopia for

CHAPTER SIX: CHARACTERISTICS OF REMNANT ISRAEL

thousands of years. They passed through Palestine journeying to other parts of the Mideast. Subsequently the term Afro-Asiatic was coined to describe these people. This term can also be deemed appropriate to describe persons including the descendants of Abraham through Jesus, and the disciples that followed Him. The first century Jews, including Jesus and His disciples can be considered Afro-Asiatics; they were not Europeans. The ancient people of the New Testament were not Europeans; so, to equate the modern-day Jews we see today with the Hebrews of the first century Church is a mistake of grand proportions. Having said that, and establishing that ultra-important fact, we have laid the groundwork for pointing out some important persons of color in the New Testament.

The genealogy of Jesus of Nazareth includes four Afro-Asiatic women:

- Rahab, Tamar, Ruth, and Bathsheba – Matthew 1: 1-14
- Jesus being called out of Egypt – Matthew 2: 13-18
- The Queen of Sheba – Matthew 12: 42
- Simon of Cyrene – Matthew 27: 32
- The Jewish pilgrims gathered in Jerusalem for Pentecost – Acts 2: 9-10
- The Ethiopian Finance Minister – Acts 8: 26-40
- Apollos the Jew of Alexandria – Acts 18: 24-25
- The Samaritans – John 4: 7-39
- Apollos the African preacher – I Corinthians 3: 11[119]

Throughout historical scriptural references, Israel is always described as looking like the sons of Ham in their physical appearance. Ham, one of Noah's sons, was a part of the people who repopulated the earth after the Great Flood; mainly in Africa and Canaan. In Hebrew, Ham means black, burnt, and hot. His four sons were: Cush, Mizraim, Phut, and Canaan. They represent the Ethiopians, Cushites, Nubians, Egyptians, Ancient Libyans, Somalians, Canaanites. The descendants of Canaan were the original inhabitants of the land known as Israel. We must remember that up until the construction of the Suez Canal, what we now term the Mideast was actually considered a part of Africa...Northeast Africa to be exact.

Noah's son Shem is the father of the Hebrew Israelite nation. Through his seed came Abraham, Isaac, and Jacob/Israel. Jacob had twelve sons, they were: Reuben, Gad, Simeon, Asher, Levi, Naphtali, Judah, Issachar, Zebulon, Joseph, Dan, and Benjamin. Each of these sons became a tribal nation, and collectively comprised the nation of Israel. Jacob's son of his old age, Joseph, became his favorite son and elicited the jealousy of his older brothers. Their ire with him resulted with Joseph being sold to Arab merchants as a slave. He ended up in an Egyptian prison, which ultimately led to him becoming the Viceroy/governor of Egypt; second in command and authority only to Pharaoh. He was able to warn Pharaoh of the impending famine, and prepare Egypt to be the storehouse that sustained the world during that crisis. As Jacob's sons stood before their brother to receive assistance, they did not recognize him, because the Egyptians and the Hebrews looked alike. Genesis 50: 7-11 describes all of the Hebrews looking like the ancient Egyptians. This mixed multitude at Jacobs burial was thought to be all

CHAPTER SIX: CHARACTERISTICS OF REMNANT ISRAEL

Egyptians; the Hebrews and Egyptians looked alike. This is probably why Pharaoh did not recognize Moses as one of the Hebrew baby boys he had ordered to be murdered. It is why Moses was able to grow up in the house of Pharaoh as Pharaoh's grandson; without being questioned as being a Hebrew.[120] Moses was born a Hebrew. An Israelite from the tribe of Levi.[121] He spent 40 years in the house of Pharaoh[122] and was raised as the Pharaoh's grandson.[123]

It should be apparent by now that after the Flood, the world was repopulated by people of color. Noah was black, Mrs. Noah was black, Japheth, Shem, Ham, and their wives were black African-Edenic peoples. Japheth was the light-skinned brother who left the Fertile Crescent to migrate north, and become the progenitor of the Germanic peoples. Again, this was due to the calcification of his Melanin gland, and his subsequent loss of pigmentation; which was ultimately passed down to his bloodline.

As a final proof of the dark-skinned Hebrews of antiquity being just that, we look at how Jehovah used leprosy to display His power; and at times His displeasure. In Exodus 4: 6-7, when the Ancient of Days is proving Himself to Moses, he turns his hand leprous white. This would have been hard to do if Moses was already white, and not a black-skinned person. When Aaron and Miriam spoke against Moses because he married an Ethiopian, the Most High turned Miriam leprous. What punishment would that have been if she was already white? Leprosy was mentioned in connection with either being a disease or relative to some specific wrong doing, or sin.[124]

In order for us to get a clear picture of what happened to

the Hebrews, we will look at a historical timeline and account as to the events that led to the conquest of the Holy Land; and the lightening of the pigmentation of the Jewish people. This history is critical to understand why the majority of contemporary Jewish people have the complexion they do today; and their geographical dislocation in the world.

As we look at the Germanic tribes in Europe around the fouth century A.D., we find the Ostrogoths, Visigoths, Vandals, Lombards, Alemanni, Burgundians, Jutes, Angles, Saxons, and Franks. These were seminomadic peoples, who herded flocks and tilled the soil, who prized strength and courage in battle. They worshipped many gods, including: Tiw, the god of war; Wotan, the chief of the gods; Thor, the god of thunder; and Freya, the goddess of fertility. Interesting to note is the fact that the names of these deities are preserved in the English days of the week: Tuesday, Wednesday, Thursday, and Friday.

These Germanic people were proud of their heritage as Goths, Burgundians, Franks, and Vandals. They had reddish or blond hair, blue eyes, and were generally powerful in their physiques and of great stature. The men were primarily fighters who scorned labor, loved beer, and relegated all household and agricultural tasks to the women and slaves. Some tribes merged and began to be ruled by warlords who later became kings; and these people had a tendency to choose their warlords from the same family. This practice paved the way for hereditary succession to become the norm in the rulership of these people.[125]

In 105 B.C. German warriors were able to achieve a devastating defeat on a Roman army, however four years later

CHAPTER SIX: CHARACTERISTICS OF REMNANT ISRAEL

a Roman leader was able to outmaneuver the Germans and defeat them. Later, during Julius Caesar's time, German warriors tried to conquer a part of Gaul, but Rome defeated them. The ongoing battle continued during the reign of Augustus Caesar, when Rome attacked German tribes between the Rhine and Elbe rivers, however in 9 A.D. the Romans were defeated in the Battle of Teutoburg Forest. During this battle, three legions were completely decimated. From 161 to 180 A.D., during the reign of Marcus Aurelius, the Romans had difficulty holding off the Germans at the Frontier. This conflict at the Frontier lasted for at least another 120 years.

Some Germans were permitted to enter the Roman Empire, others were captured in war and became Roman slaves. Still others became soldiers of Rome. At some point, the Germans might have turned the subtle infiltration into a full-scale invasion. This happened during the fouth century, with the unsolicited assistance of restless nomads from Asia; called the Huns. These mighty warriors, on swift horses, furiously attacked all tribes in their path. They crossed the Volga River and conquered the Ostrogoths. The Visigoths feared that they would also be conquered, so they implored Rome for protection and sanctuary. The Roman authorities agreed, and promised them land for settlement; as long as they came unarmed.

Both sides failed to keep the agreement, so the Visigoths began sacking Roman settlements. Without land and facing starvation, the Visigoths resorted to who they were; warriors who prided themselves in strength and war. In 378 A.D., the Roman Emperor Valens led a great army against the Visigoths, but the imperial army was defeated, scattered, and the emperor was slain. This battle on the field of Adrianople proved to be one of the most decisive battles in world history; as it rendered the Roman Empire defenseless. It opened the door for German tribes to mobilize their fighting men, round up their herds, and set their destination on Rome's borders; the Hebrew Israelite nation being located within the confines of those borders. The Visigoths reached Rome in 410 A.D. and looted the city dry. Attila the Hun had also invaded the Roman Empire and was threatening to enslave or destroy everybody; Germans and Romans alike.[126]

Added to this incursion of Germanic and Asiatic peoples into the region, there was also an infusion of Slavs. The Slavs were an Indo-European people who had settled north of the Black Sea. They were tenacious, prolific, and maintained their cultural ethnicity despite suffering at the hands of German and Asiatic nomads. These Slavs, who were the ancestors of modern-day Serbians and Croatians, helped to change the ethnic character of the Balkan Peninsula. They helped force the Roman Empire to permit barbarian immigration in her borders and ultimately affect the pigmentation of those members of the Empire who were of a darker hue. Remember that with the ravages of loss in war comes wide scale rape and pillaging; to the victor goes the spoils. These historic events had a definite impact on the pigmentation of citizens in the Roman Empire, the Jews in particular. The infusion of Germanic, Asiatic, and Indo-European genes into the citizenry of these black-skinned people resulted in the lightening of the Hebrew/Israelite nation.

Something else contributed to the composition and

CHAPTER SIX: CHARACTERISTICS OF REMNANT ISRAEL

practices of Judaism and the nation of Israel; the remnant that survived the Germanic, Asiatic, and Indo-European invasion of the Holy Land. The conquest of the Roman Empire ultimately deteriorated into major conflict between Arabs and Christians for control of the Holy Land and the holy city of Jerusalem. The Jews were caught in the middle, and eventually succumbed to the Europeanization of Judaism. Prior to the First Crusades, there were multiple accounts of cooperation between Christians and Jews. There was economic collaboration, with Jews being involved in several industries such as trade, minting, and financial advising. Additionally, Jews and Christians were also involved in social events with one another, even attending each other's weddings.[127]

Many Jews were in danger of being killed, at the beginning of the First Crusade. As the Crusades spread across Europe, there are documented accounts of Christians standing up to protect their neighboring Jews. There were various German cities, in which Jews dwelt, that this took place. Such cities were: Trier; Mainz; and Cologne. Some cities went as far as hiding Jews among their Christian neighbors. The end of the Crusades produced many Jewish and Christians narratives chronicling the cooperative efforts of Christians and Jews during this troublesome time period; even recording martyrdom that took place. This period of death and suffering produced many other narratives; such as: The Chronicle of Solomon Bar Simon; The Chronicle of Rabbi Eliezer bar Nathan; The Book of Remembrance; and The Narrative of the Old Persecutions. The details behind these narratives can all be found in several secondary historical

THE REMNANT CHURCH

resources including: 'Robert Chazan's "God, Humanity, and History"; 'Shlomo Eidelberg's "The Jews and the Crusades." Each of these sources give background to the narratives; and discusses their effects on European Jewry and Christianity.

Robert Chazan also wrote another account entitled "In the Year 1906: The First Crusade and the Jews." This book details changes the First Crusade had on Jewish / Christian relationships. It also speaks to the fact that the Jews were made extremely distinct within the European community because of the Crusades. Additionally, they were now considered to be part of 'the other grouping', such as the atheists and pagans; because of the Crusades. They were no longer considered a part of the general European community. Also, to be considered are the books which tell the story of the Crusader's attacks on Jewish communities, the slaughter of several groups of Jews, and the killings not only being indiscriminatory but without exception. However, a majority of these writings focus on the attempt to regain Jerusalem and the Holy Land from Islamic rulership. Suffice it to say that the First Crusades caused a separation between the Jews and the Christian community physically, mentally, and spiritually. It is commonly believed that this was due to the sheer ferocity and shocking nature of the atrocities against Jews; caused by the Crusades.[128]

As we further explore the state of affairs in remnant Israel, it goes without saying that we must examine the effect of the Holocaust. The aftermath of the Jewish Holocaust had a very deep effect on society in both Europe, and the rest of the world. Its impact has been felt in theological discussions, artistic and

CHAPTER SIX: CHARACTERISTICS OF REMNANT ISRAEL

cultural pursuits, and political decisions. There were major changes in the hierarchy of Jewish spiritual leadership during the Holocaust period. The impact of this period and the subsequent events have much to do with Israel; and her connection to the concept of The Remnant Church.

According to Wikipedia, the Holocaust and its aftermath left millions of refugees; including many Jews who had lost most or all of their family members and possessions. They often faced persistent anti-Semitism in their home countries. The original plan of the Allies was to repatriate these 'displaced persons' to their original countries of origin. However, many refused to return, or were unable to; as their homes or communities had been destroyed. As a result, more than 250,000 languished in 'displaced person camps' for years after the war had ended.

Palestine became the primary destination for many Jewish refugees. This was primarily due to them being unable or unwilling to return to their former homes in Europe. Additionally, there were also restrictions to immigration to many western countries in place. The United Kingdom refused to allow Jewish refugees into the Mandate Territory; because local Arabs opposed the Jews immigration. The Soviet Bloc also made immigration difficult. The Haganah in Palestine, along with former Jewish partisans in Europe formed the Berihah. This organization launched a massive effort to smuggle Jews into Palestine. Eventually, they were able to deliver 250,000 Jews to Mandate Palestine. In 1952 the 'displaced persons camps' were closed. At that time there were more than 80,000 former displaced Jewish persons in America. There were about 136,000 in Israel, and about another 10,000 displaced Jewish persons in other countries including South America, Japan, Mexico, and the continent of Africa.

After the Holocaust there were still a few Jews left in Poland. Others returned from the Soviet Union, those who had survived the camps in Germany also returned. However, due to a resurgence of anti-Semitism in Poland during 1945 and 1946 there was a mass exodus on the part of the Jewish population; due to the majority of the Jews feeling unsafe in Poland. There was a widespread Polish belief that the Jews were supporters of the new Communist regime and the new oppressive Polish state. In fact, two of the three Communist leaders that dominated Poland between 1948 through 1956 were of Jewish ethnicity. As a result, hundreds of Jews were killed in anti-Jewish violence. Subsequently, the mass exodus of Jews from Poland decreased the number Polish Jews from 200,000 to 50,000 in 1950; and only 6,000 by the 1980's. As of 2005, there were about 400,000 Holocaust survivors living in Israel. 40% of them were living below the poverty line. The average rate of cancer among those survivors was nearly two and a half times higher than the national average. Additionally, the average rate of colon cancer was nine times higher than the national average. This is thought to be attributed to the starvation and extreme stress these survivors experienced in the Nazi concentration camps.[129]

Prior to World War II, there was tremendous growth in Yiddish as an official Jewish European language. There were between eleven to thirteen million persons who spoke Yiddish on the eve of World War II. However, beginning with the Nazi invasion of Poland and during the remainder of the war, the

CHAPTER SIX: CHARACTERISTICS OF REMNANT ISRAEL

Yiddish language and culture were almost completely wiped out of Europe. 85% of the victims of the Holocaust were people who spoke Yiddish, approximately five million Jews. There was a dramatic decrease in the Yiddish culture. The secular and religious European communities that used Yiddish in their day-to-day lives were basically destroyed.

From 1939 to 1944, the total physical and spiritual decimation of European Jewry took place. European Jewry had existed for hundreds of years, yet the Nazi attempt at ethnic cleansing drastically impacted the Yiddish culture in Europe. The attack in Poland was so intense because Poland was the heart of world Jewry; with over 3,000,000 Jews residing in that country. The city of Lodz itself had 233,000 Jewish residents; one third of the city's population. Trade, culture, and Rabbinical seminaries were located there. When forced into the ghetto in 1940, forty-five primary schools, two high schools, one vocational school, five pharmacies, and seven hospitals could be found in the confines of that locale. By September 1944 the ghetto population had decreased to only 76,701. They were deported to Auschwitz, and by January 1945 there were only 800 Jews and 70 survivors in hiding remaining there. These 870 were liberated by Soviet troops on January 19, 1945. There were many Jews from Lodz that survived the Holocaust by fleeing to the Soviet Union. By the end of 1946 50,000 had returned to Lodz. Between 1946 to 1950, over half of the city's population left Poland to settle in Israel. There was a second wave of immigration to Israel during 1956-1957, leaving only a few thousand Jews remaining in Poland; and between 1968-1969, nearly all remaining Jews in

Poland had left to settle in Israel. The case was just about the same in Warsaw. There were about 350,000 Jews there who were ordered into the largest ghetto in Poland in 1941. The richness of Eastern European Jewish scholarship, culture, and tradition was accumulated over hundreds of years. Spanish Jewry, which resulted from over five hundred years of growth in Western Europe was never rebuilt; but rather relocated to Sefad and other locales. Similarly, the destruction of Jewish life in Eastern Europe was never rebuilt either. Instead, it relocated to Israel, America, and Western Europe.

It is very easy to recognize the traumatic impact the Holocaust had on the Jewish people, both in Europe and in Palestine. The result was new centres of world Jewry. There was a major shift from pre-war Europe, which was referred to as the Old World, to what became to be known as the New World. This change was reflected in the fact that the Jews had a desire to shed the old image they had in Europe. No longer did they want to be seen as the people who were different and distinct in religion, dress, culture, and speech. They wanted to be seen as being able to assimilate into mainstream society; to blend in so to speak. For example, this could be evidenced by them changing their names and dress upon immigrating to America. Distinctiveness was something relegated to the Old World, and Judaism became something to be practiced exclusively in their homes. The old Jewish life of Europe was now physically and spiritually extinct. After the destruction of Eastern European Jewry, there was low morale and a lack of Jewish pride among the Jews in the New World. They felt that the old Jewish life of Eastern Europe had

CHAPTER SIX: CHARACTERISTICS OF REMNANT ISRAEL

failed and needed to be replaced. That life was represented as an outdated representation of Judaism that needed to become more progressive.[130]

There were numerous Rebbes and Rabbis that began the process of rebuilding Jewish life after the Holocaust. Although this rebuilding took place in a new location, it was a rebuilding nonetheless. There was enormous attention given to academic study and in the study of the Torah. They made an intentional effort to become knowledgeable in every discipline, language, and science in order to respond to people who question the authenticity and logic of the Torah; much like the Sanhedrin of antiquity. These Jewish holy men felt that it was necessary to be knowledgeable about subjects that are inconsistent with the views of Judaism. They sensed the urgency of having a solid world and religious foundation to build the new Jew emerging out of the Holocaust. They felt it was their responsibility to rebuild Judaism and disseminate the former enthusiasm for Jewish life and education for all Jews; especially those with a limited Jewish upbringing. Additionally, these men knew that it was necessary to rebuild morale, and reinstate the Jewish pride that existed before the Holocaust. This was mandatory in order to preserve Jewish continuity after such devastating destruction and tragedy. The result was a concerted effort to establish Jewish day schools, Jewish summer camps, and synagogues in communities worldwide. Rabbis were sent throughout the whole world to offer Jewish education and tradition wherever Jewish communities were found.

Menachem Mendel Schneersohn (Rebbe Rabbi), was

versed in all fields of the Torah and the sciences. He was able to address all types of Jews from all types of backgrounds. He was intentionally building a Jewish infrastructure in every state in America, along with two hundred Jewish centres in Israel, Chabad Houses in over seventy countries. Thus, he was able to re-ignite the spark of Jewish pride in the Jewish nation worldwide. After the Holocaust most Jews thought that their Judaism should be internalized, Rebbe Schneersohn did just the opposite. He instituted public Menorah lightings throughout the world, public Passover Seders and outdoor Lag B'omer parades for thousands of Jewish children on the streets of New York and worldwide. All of these efforts helped rebuild pride and enthusiasm for Judaism in the New World as the centres of Jewry relocated following the destruction of Eastern European Jewry after the Holocaust.[131]

The Remnant Church must be viewed through a Jewish filter; because all of the apocalyptic prophecies in the Old Testament, are written to the nation of Israel. Furthermore, Jesus' description of the end of the age and His second coming was given to His Jewish disciples. Only a minority portion of scripture, dealing with the end of time, is written to the Gentile churches. Therefore, it is virtually impossible to study the notion of a Remnant Church, without recognizing the role the nation of Israel plays in that discussion. In order to get a more in-depth historical perspective on the Remnant Church and the significant role she is to play in motivating Jews to jealousy and acceptance of Messiah Jesus, we must also look at the state of affairs in the world relative to the Jews, and their historical trek from Egyptian bondage to the present day. We will begin our

CHAPTER SIX: CHARACTERISTICS OF REMNANT ISRAEL

journey by starting with the Arab-Israeli War. The 1948 Arab-Israeli War or the First Arab-Israeli War was fought between the State of Israel and a military coalition of Arab states, forming the second stage of the 1948 Palestine war. Relations between Israel and her neighbors never fully normalized following the 1948 Arab-Israeli War.

The remainder of this chapter is extracted from information that is available to the general public. However, it is important to note that this detailed chronology of the nation of Israel is critical to understanding where she stands in the religious, geopolitical landscape. Therefore, we ask that the reader pay close attention to the factors that led to Israel's position in world news; and the nations that impacted her; and continue to affect her. There had been tension and conflict between the Arabs and the Jews, and between each of them and the British forces, ever since the 1917 Balfour Declaration; and the 1920 creation of the British Mandate of Palestine. British policies dissatisfied both Arabs and Jews. The Arabs' opposition developed into the 1936-1939 Arab revolt in Palestine, while the Jewish resistance developed into the Jewish insurgency in Palestine (1944-1947). In 1947 these ongoing tensions erupted into civil war, following the 29 November 1947 adoption of the United Nations Partition Plan for Palestine which planned to divide Palestine into three areas: an Arab state, a Jewish state and the Special International Regime for the cities of Jerusalem and Bethlehem.

On May 15, 1948 the ongoing civil war was transformed into inter-state conflict between Israel and the Arab states. This was due to Israel proclaiming the Israeli Declaration of

Independence on May 14, 1948; without any reference to defined borders. Egypt, Syria, Jordan, and Iraq joined forces and invaded Palestine. Even though Jordan had privately declared that it would not invade Israel, they did. These combined forces took control of the Arab areas and immediately attacked Israeli forces, and Jewish settlements. The fighting primarily took place on the former territory of the British mandate, Sinai Peninsula, and southern Lebanon.

> *"They are not always necessarily living in Jewish communities; and they can be found in countries all around the world."*

This war yielded the State of Israel the area that the UN General Assembly Resolution had recommended for the proposed Jewish state. Additionally, they acquired almost 60% of the Arab state that was proposed by the 1948 Partition Plan. This included: the Jaffa, Lydda and Ramle areas; Galilee; part of the Negev; West Jerusalem; a wide strip along the Tel-Aviv - Jerusalem Road; and territories in the West Bank. No state was created for the Palestinian Arabs; even though 2,000 Palestinian delegates called for the unification of Palestine and Transjordan as a move towards full Arab unity. Although Transjordan garnered control of the remainder of the former British Mandate, and the Egyptian military took control of the Gaza Strip; there was no full Arab unity attained. Around 711,000 Palestinian Arabs became displaced from their homes and became Palestinian refugees. This was due to their former places of residence becoming a part of the State of Israel. At the same time, around 700,000 Jews immigrated to Israel during the three years following the

CHAPTER SIX: CHARACTERISTICS OF REMNANT ISRAEL

war. Many of those emigrant Jews had been expelled from their previous places of Middle East residency; including Lebanon, Syria, Turkey, Afghanistan, India, and Iran; just to name a few. As a result of Israel's victory, immigration of Holocaust survivors and Jewish refugees from Arab lands doubled Israel's population within one year of her independence.

Israel, the Jewish state, currently is home to almost half of the world's Jewish population. Israeli Jews refers to Israeli citizens or residents who are Jews, and also the descendants of Israeli-Jewish emigrants outside of Israel. These Jews are mostly found in Israel and the Western world. They are not always necessarily living in Jewish communities; and they can be found in countries all around the world. These Israeli Jews mostly speak Hebrew, and follow some type of religious Jewish practice. The Jewish population in Israel comprises all Jewish diaspora communities. Some members include: Ashkenazi Jews, Beta Israel, Bene Israel, Karaite Jews, Mizrahi Jews, Sephardi Jews, Moroccan Jews, Algerian Jews, Tunisian Jews, Yemenite Jews, Bukharan Jews, Iranian Jews, Iraqi Jews, Kurdish Jews, and many other groups. There is a wide range of Jewish cultural traditions and a full spectrum of religious observances found within the Jewish population in Israel. There is a lot of mixed ancestry in that population between the Ashkenazi, Mizrahi, and Sephardi Jews. An IDI Guttman Study in 2008 found that a plurality of Israeli Jews identified themselves first as Jews; and second as Israeli. Among Israeli Jews, 72% are Israeli-born. 19% are Jewish immigrants to Israel from Europe, the Americas, and Oceania. The remaining 9% are from Asia, Africa, and the Muslim world.

For many years, Israel's Jewish population continued to grow at an extremely high rate. There was a tremendous amount of Jewish immigration from countries all around the world. Of significant notice was the massive amounts of Jews that immigrated from the Soviet Union. They arrived in Israel in the early 1990's, following the dissolution of the USSR; 380,000 from 1990-1991 alone. They were granted Israeli citizenship upon arrival in Israel; based on The Law of Return. Some 80,000 to 100,000 Ethiopian Jews have been reported to have immigrated to Israel since the early 1980's. Jews from countries around the globe converged on Israel, and claimed her as their homeland. She once again became the citadel for modern day Judaism; and continues to be so until this day.[132]

The current most prominent European countries of origin of the Israeli Jews are as follows:
- Western Europe
- Former Soviet Union and Russia
- Poland
- Ukraine
- Romania
- United States & Canada
- Latin America (mainly from Argentina)
- Hungary
- Czechoslovakia
- South Africa
- Australia & New Zealand
- Germany/Austria

CHAPTER SIX: CHARACTERISTICS OF REMNANT ISRAEL

Since 1948, Israel has been involved in a series of major military conflicts, including the 1956 Suez War, 1967 Six-Day War, 1973 Yom Kippur War, 1982 Lebanon War, and 2006 Lebanon War, as well as a nearly constant series of ongoing minor conflicts. Israel has been also embroiled in an ongoing conflict with the Palestinians in the Israeli-occupied territories, which have been under Israeli control since the Six Day War in 1967, despite the signing of the Oslo Accords on September 13, 1993, and the ongoing efforts of Israeli, Palestinian and global peacemakers.

After the Six Day War, there was another major population boom in the tiny land mass of the State of Israel. With the large influx of Jews from different cultures, the government encouraged the emigrants to "'melt down' their own particular exile identities within the general melting pot of Israeli culture in order to truly become Israelis.

By 1967, Israel assumed that the world would always protect it. The United Nations had a peace keeping force present on the Sinai Peninsula, and the entrance to the Gulf of Aqaba. Even though Egypt did not allow any Israel shipping, or ships sailing to Israel passage through the Suez Canal, Israel felt it could live with that inconvenience. However, Nasser, acting on the advice of his Russian advisors, decided to start a war with Israel. He was persuaded that his army could easily defeat the Israelis. Nasser violated the United Nations agreement between Israel and Egypt after the 1956 Sinai Campaign and crossed his army over the Suez Canal. He then ordered the shipping blockade when no one took action against him. His next escalation was to order the United Nations peace-keeping troops off of Egyptian territory. When they evacuated, there was now nothing between Israel and the large Egyptian army in Sinai moving toward the Israeli border.

Not wanting to face Israel alone, Nasser made an alliance with Syria and Jordan, and ended up with a great Arab army under the control of an Egyptian general. As they became aware of this tri-fold alliance, Israel mobilized her army. The Israeli air force launched a devastating surprise attack that literally destroyed the entire Arab air force; including those forces in Egypt, Syria, and Jordan. It only took under three hours for Israel to destroy about 500 Arab planes. Flying at almost seventy miles over the speed of sound, thereby remaining undetected, Israel decimated the air threat the Arab alliance posed; and gained a tactical advantage. Israel then sent three main tank battle groups into the Sinai to attack the Egyptian front. They smashed the Egyptian army in three days, and over 5,000 Egyptian soldiers surrendered immediately. Before Egypt knew what happened, Israel was at the Suez, with nothing standing between them and Cairo.

Jerusalem was recaptured. Israeli paratroopers captured Ammunition Hill from the Jordanians, outflanked them, and sent them into a full-blown retreat. The Israelis captured the Old City all the way to the Western Wall; the Wailing Wall. The liberation of Jerusalem forced the Jordanian army to completely vacate the West Bank. As they were pounded by the Israeli air force, the Jordanian army and about 100,000 other Arabs added to the ever-growing Arab refugee problem.

CHAPTER SIX: CHARACTERISTICS OF REMNANT ISRAEL

Israel now turned its attention to the Syrians, who had entrenched themselves in the seemingly impregnable fortress of the Golan. Yet, with the aid of the Israeli air force, the ground troops were able to push the Syrians out of their bunkers, system of mines, and batteries of artillery and machine guns; they built into the high ground of that fortress. After capturing the peak of Mt. Hermon, the entire Golan fell under Israeli control. This small Jewish state, which was thought to be on the verge of annihilation, was now seen as an 'imperial power'. Russia instantly broke diplomatic relations with Israel, and the United Nations voted for a cease-fire; which was gladly accepted by Egypt and the Arabs. Israel had seized: the Gaza Strip; the Golan Heights; the Sinai Peninsula; and the West Bank of the Jordan River, including East Jerusalem. In those captured territories, about one million Arabs were placed under Israel's direct control. The subsequent displacement of the civilian population, as a result of the war, would impact the region in a recognizable way. About 300,000 Palestinians fled to the West Bank. Additionally, about 100,000 Syrians left the Golan, and ended up becoming refugees. In countries all across the Arab world, Jewish minority communities were expelled. These Jewish refugees ended up immigrating to Israel or Europe.

After the Six Day War, the whole world now had a new viewpoint and perspective on Israel. Jews worldwide were extremely proud of her, while non-Jews viewed her with enormous resentment. Major resentment even spilled over into the United Nations. In spite of the resentment, Jewish emotions were soaring sky high. Jewish history and Jewish destiny had converged in a brief Six Day War; and suddenly the nation was somewhat feared and respected. Unfortunately, it did not last. To date, the Jewish nation has not reached the level of that emotional high again.

The Yom Kippur War of 1973 proved profitable for Egypt and Syria as they launched attacks to reclaim their lost territories. Israel made peace with Egypt following the Camp David Accords of 1978; and completed a staged withdrawal from the Sinai in 1982. Jordan and Egypt eventually withdrew the claims to sovereignty over the West Bank and Gaza. Israel and Jordan eventually signed a peace treaty in 1994. There were now hundreds of thousands of Israeli settlers in the West Bank. However, Israel evacuated and destroyed the Israeli settlements in Gaza in August 2005; as a part of their disengagement from Gaza.[133]

As we can see from the historical discourse, Israel has been positioned to be the center of geopolitical and spiritual confrontation. She is at the core of conflict between Islam, Christianity, and Judaism. She stands as a source of quarrel between the Arab and non-Arab worlds. She is surrounded by nations that are intent on seeing her demise and total obliteration. Global forces are aligned to orchestrate her complete annihilation. In addition to these natural threats, she is also in the crosshairs of a spiritual enemy that has been on an ongoing campaign to destroy God's chosen people. She continues to be at the center of the events that mark 'the end of the age'; and the return of Jesus Christ. That remnant Israel, the contemporary Jews that remain after Israel was delivered out of Egyptian slavery, continues to play a prominent role in natural and spiritual world affairs. Additionally, she is an obvious component in the events that

CHAPTER SIX: CHARACTERISTICS OF REMNANT ISRAEL

will bring the world to the brink of another worldwide war. She emphatically impacts the role the Remnant Church will play during the end of the period; known as time. Remnant Israel cannot be ignored as we look at the function of the end-time Church, and the difference the Church must play in order to be a viable option to the impending chaos; into which the world will be thrust.

Chapter Seven

Characteristics of the Remnant Church

"And they, continued steadfastly in the apostle's doctrine and in fellowship, and in the breaking of bread, and in prayers. And fear came upon every soul: and many signs and wonders were done by the apostles. And all that believed were together, and had all things common."
Acts 2:42-44

As we begin this chapter, we want to emphatically state that we will once again lean heavily on the timeline recorded in Wikipedia, and the Bible, to assist us as we examine the Remnant Church post the crucifixion. After the initial Sanhedrin persecution of the Remnant Church, subsequent to the crucifixion of Christ, and the Day of Pentecost, 'Why were Jesus' disciples so frightened'? After all, hadn't He told them that after He was arrested, crucified, and put to death that He would come back to life? In fact, yes He had. As a matter of fact, on several occasions Jesus taught His disciples what would happen to Him as His ministry drew to its close. He told them, *"...The Son of Man is going to be betrayed into the hands of men. They will kill him, and after three days he will rise."* Mark 9:31 Why, then, did they flee and act so frightened when He was arrested? One reason is because they didn't really understand what He was saying. They didn't want to embarrass themselves by admitting it. The very next verse makes this clear: *"But they did not understand what he meant and were afraid to ask him."* Mark 9:32 The idea that someone might die, and then come back to life again was so unheard of, that they just could not grasp it.

Another reason, I suspect, is because they were overwhelmed with disappointment by Jesus' arrest. They had hoped He would overcome the power of the Roman government, and establish a new kingdom. Now their hopes of this vanished. They were also filled with fear for their own future. When Jesus of Nazareth was crucified on Good Friday, 30AD, His apostles and disciples must have been very frightened for their own lives. It is quite amazing to realize that, as frightened and as grief stricken as they must have been, they did not attempt to leave Jerusalem to return to their own homes. Instead they stayed for three days, to witness the resurrection of the Messiah.

The apostles didn't completely understand how the Scriptures were to be fulfilled in the resurrection of Jesus of Nazareth, as Jesus Himself would teach the disciples on

Resurrection Sunday.[134] However the Apostles must have remembered the times during the last year of His ministry when Jesus tried to prepare them for what they would be required to face. He did this by warning them that it was necessary that He should die; but He would be raised from the dead. The first prophecy of His passion and resurrection was recorded in *Matthew 16: 21-23*.[135] From then onward, Jesus began to make it clear to His disciples that He was destined to go to Jerusalem. He would suffer grievously at the hands of the elders and chief priests and scribes, be put to death, and be raised up on the third day. Understanding their grief and confusion after the first announcement of His death and promised resurrection, Jesus gave His disciples hope by promising them this:

"In truth I tell you, there are some standing here who will not taste death before they see the Son of man coming with His kingdom."
Matthew 16:27-28

Then He gave them a miracle to strengthen their faith. He showed Peter, James, and John a preview of the resurrection when He took them to the Mount of Transfiguration.[136] There they saw Jesus in His glory together with Moses and Elijah, two great prophets who represented the Law and the Prophets. In essence the revelation of the Transfiguration event was the entire sum of Old Testament salvation history brought face to face with the leaders of Jesus' New Covenant Church; in God's continuing plan for the salvation of mankind. From that point until the last day of His preaching in Jerusalem, Jesus continued to speak of

His passion and resurrection to His disciples,[137] again in *Matthew 20:17-19*,[138] and in John.[139]

Not only did Jesus' disciples know of the prophecy of His death and resurrection, but the chief priests and Pharisees also knew. Jesus told them in His 'sign of Jonah' prophecy which He gave the Jewish authorities.[140] Knowing that Jesus had promised to arise from the grave was the reason the Jewish religious authorities went to the Roman governor Pilate and demanded a Roman guard be placed around Jesus' tomb. The chief priests and the Pharisees went in a body to Pilate and said to him,

Sir, we remember that that deceiver said, while he was yet alive, "After three days I will rise again." Command therefore that the sepulcher be made sure until the third day, lest his disciples come by night and steal him away and say unto the people, "He has risen from the dead…"[141]

Therefore, with Jesus' repeated testimony concerning His death and resurrection, the Jewish people 'knew'. In the promise of His glorification witnessed in the Transfiguration event, the Apostles 'knew'. Even though the Apostles and disciples didn't fully understand, their faith, love, and loyalty was part of their 'staying power' that, despite their fear, kept them in Jerusalem. However, there was something else which allowed Peter, James, John to influence the other disciples to stay in the holy city after Jesus' crucifixion. It was their witness of the Transfiguration that allowed them to do this.

It is essential to understand that religious Jews lived within the context and framework of the Law that Jehovah gave to His people at Mt. Sinai. The Law of the Covenant stated that Sabbath was a day of rest. No work was allowed to be done on the Sabbath.

CHAPTER SEVEN: CHARACTERISTICS OF REMNANT CHURCH

If Jesus' crucifixion was on Friday, it was 'Preparation Day' for the holy Sabbath.[142] Everything associated with everyday life, food preparation, etc. had to be completed before Sabbath day. There was also a ban against traveling on Sabbath day; so, everything had to be done on Friday; 'Preparation Day'. We understand according to Luke's gospel that Mt. Olivet was no more than a 'Sabbath walk' from Jerusalem. According to rabbinic rules in the Mishnah, Jews were limited to walking outside of a walled city by two thousand cubits, or about 0.57 of a mile, on Sabbath. Therefore, most of the disciples could not leave the holy city before sundown Saturday night. The only ones who could leave were the disciples who lived in Bethany; or one of the villages that fell within that prescribed distance.

There was another reason the disciples stayed in Jerusalem though. When an old covenant believer died, his friends were expected to take care of the funeral arrangements, attend the grave, and pray with the family for seven days.[143] The body of the deceased had to be buried the same day; especially someone who died from punishment for a capital offense. If someone was crucified, their body could not stay on the cross overnight; and they had to be buried the same day. They believed since anyone hung on a cross was a curse of God, they were not to bring pollution on the soil which Yahweh their God had given the nation as their inheritance.[144] It was also necessary to treat the deceased with reverence and respect. This was exhibited toward the welfare of the grieving family who survived the deceased. It was known as 'kevod ha-met' and 'kevod he-chai'. In Jewish communities, these two principles provided the basis for mourning death and dealing with it. The family and closest friends of the deceased prepared the body for burial, and also provided a 'meal of condolence' for the bereaved family; known as Se'udat Havra-a.

Another reason the disciples stayed in Jerusalem was to fulfill their obligation to pray with the grieving family. They were required to recite the prayers of 'Tziduk Hadin' and the "Kaddish' during the week long mourning period. The Tziduk Hadin begins with the words of the Song of Moses found in Deuteronomy.[145] The Kaddish, known as the 'mourners' prayer' is an expression of faith in the righteousness of the Ancient of Days, acceptance of His will, and an expression of adoration of Jehovah. The Kaddish has been called 'an echo of the book of Job' since the prayer quotes Job 13: 15

Though He (God) slay me, yet will I trust in Him.

A quorum of ten adults has to be present to offer these prayers, and the initial period of mourning, known as 'Shiva', is to last no less than seven days. Shiva means 'seven' in Hebrew, and the custom is based on Amos 8:10

And I will turn your feasts into mourning...

There are two holy pilgrim feasts that last seven days. They are the Feast of Unleavened Bread and the Feast of Tabernacles.[146] The idea of a seven day mourning period has been a tradition of the Old Covenant peoples for a long time. This concept predates the Sinai Covenant, as evidenced in the account of Joseph mourning for Jacob's death in Genesis 50: 10.

The Apostles remained in Jerusalem in observance of Jewish

CHAPTER SEVEN: CHARACTERISTICS OF REMNANT CHURCH

traditions which obligated them to do so. They were ministering to Mary, Jesus' kinsmen, and the host of other friends who loved Jesus and His family. Their ministry of comfort afforded them the opportunity to be a first-hand witness to visitation of the resurrected, glorified Christ. Although they were witness to the miracle of resurrection, they were still fearful of the Jewish leaders, and had to be bewildered, confused, and terrified by the events that had just transpired.[147] They had just lost their leader and teacher to the cruel, inhumane, rigors of Roman crucifixion. However, there are numerous accounts throughout the Synoptic Gospels which document Jesus' interactions with His disciples; as He communicated His final instructions to them before ascending to His Father. Their initial interaction with Him on Resurrection Day marked the actual beginning of the Church. We offer this for consideration, as they were the first recipients of the salvation that was provided by His disciples on the road to Emmaus, in the locked room where they were assembled for fear of the Jews, by the seashore as they had fished all night in vain, and to Peter, as He instructed him to feed the sheep and the lambs.[148,149,150] There was the encounter with doubting Thomas, and of course their gathering to receive The Great Commission. Therefore, we can see that the Remnant Church that was birthed out of Judaism was charged to go forth with the message of the government of God being manifested among mankind. After witnessing the traumatic death of the Messiah, they saw the

> *"Jesus could have lived in the earth forever, but then the Holy Spirit would not have been distributed to all believers worldwide."*

fulfillment of prophecy; as He was resurrected from the dead. They received their marching orders to evangelize the earth with their eyewitness account of the God of creation walking among men; and the miracles He performed.

Yet, there was another reason why Jesus had to die, be buried, and be resurrected. In addition to having to go through this process to fulfill prophecy; He had to leave this earth so that the Holy Spirit could come. Jesus could have lived in the earth forever, but then the Holy Spirit would not have been distributed to all believers worldwide. Jesus' departure was directly tied to Pentecost, and the fulfillment of Joel 2:28. Without the ascension, there is no Pentecost; as it relates to the availability of the Comforter for believers in Jesus Christ; the Church. As Jesus offered explanation for His departure and encouragement to the post-resurrection first century New Testament Remnant Church, two remarkable transitions took place in their lives. First, and foremost, they had their joy restored to them. Their despondency and distress after witnessing the crucifixion was gone. An excitement and zeal, along with anticipation overshadowed them as they awaited the arrival of the Holy Spirit. The scriptures tell us that they returned to Jerusalem with 'great joy'. They now understood why Jesus had to leave them. Secondarily, and equally as important, they were 'spiritually strengthened'. They were now positioned to turn the world upside down, and become the foundation upon which the Church would be built; Jesus Christ Himself being the chief cornerstone.

> *"They were now positioned to turn the world upside down..."*

CHAPTER SEVEN: CHARACTERISTICS OF REMNANT CHURCH

According to Mark Allan Powell[151] in his work, 'The Crucifixion of Jesus and the Jews', Jesus was crucified as a Jewish victim of Roman violence. On this, all written authorities agree. A Gentile Roman governor, Pontius Pilate, condemned him to death and had him tortured and executed by Gentile Roman soldiers. Jesus was indeed one of thousands of Jews crucified by the Romans. The New Testament testifies to this basic fact; but also allows for Jewish involvement in two ways. First, a few high-ranking Jewish authorities, who owed their position and power to the Romans, conspired with the Gentile leaders to have Jesus put to death. They are said to have been jealous of Jesus and to have viewed Him as a threat to the status quo. Second, an unruly mob of people in Jerusalem called out for Jesus to be crucified. The number of persons in this crowd is not given, nor is any motive supplied for their action; except to say that they had been 'stirred up'. Whatever the historical circumstances might have been, early Christian tradition clearly and increasingly placed blame for the death of Jesus on the Jews, decreasing the Romans' culpability. In Matthew, the Roman governor washes his hands of Jesus' blood while the Jews proclaim, "His blood be on us and on our children!"[152] John's Gospel portrays Jews as wanting to kill Jesus throughout his ministry.[153] Similar sentiments are found elsewhere, including writings by Paul, who, himself a Jew, had once persecuted Christians.[154] The reasons for this shift in emphasis are unclear, but one obvious possibility is that, as the Church spread out into the world, Romans rather than Jews became the primary targets of evangelism; thus there could have been some motivation to let Romans 'off the hook' and blame the Jews for Jesus' death. This tendency seems to have increased dramatically after the Roman war with the Jews in the late 60s A.D.

In any case, by the middle of the second century, the apocryphal Gospel of Peter portrays the Romans as friends of Jesus, and the Jews as the ones who crucify him. Thus, a Jewish victim of Roman violence was transformed into a Christian victim of Jewish violence. For centuries, such notions fueled anti-Semitism, leading to a crass denunciation of Jews as 'Christ-killers'. Contrary to such projections, Christian theology has always maintained that the human agents responsible for Jesus' death are irrelevant: He gave His life willingly as a sacrifice for sin.[155] Christians regularly confess that it was their sins (not the misdeeds of either Romans or Jews) that brought Jesus to the cross.[156] In most liturgical churches, when Matthew's Passion Narrative is read in a worship service, all members of the congregation are invited to echo aloud, crying, "Let his blood be upon us and upon our children!"[157]

According to Wikipedia, after first century Christianity was accepted by the Roman government, it lost its Jewish apostolic leadership and flavor. We must also recognize that Christianity was compromised by the inclusion of pagan sun-god practices into its ceremonies and worship services. Before we travel down this road of exploration, let's look at what happened to Christianity before it was accepted by the Roman government. Rome was not always favorable to Christianity or the idea of there being another king other than Caesar. The historical fact is that Rome's initial interaction with the movement known as 'The Way' began with

CHAPTER SEVEN: CHARACTERISTICS OF REMNANT CHURCH

the persecution of its followers. The story of Christianity's rise to prominence is a remarkable one, but the traditional story of its progression from a tiny, persecuted religion to the established religion in the medieval West needs some debunking. Although in the first few centuries AD Christians were persecuted and punished, often with death, there were also periods when they were more secure. Secondly, the rise of Christianity to imperial-sponsored dominance in the fourth and fifth centuries, although surprising, was not without precedent, and its spread hardly as inexorable as contemporary Christians portrayed it. Christians were first, and horribly, targeted for persecution as a group by the emperor Nero in 64 AD. A colossal fire broke out at Rome, and destroyed much of the city. Rumors bounded that Nero himself was responsible. He certainly took advantage of the resulting devastation of the city, building a lavish private palace on part of the site of the fire. Perhaps to divert attention from the rumors, Nero ordered that Christians should be rounded up and killed. Some were torn apart by dogs, others burnt alive as human torches. Over the next hundred years or so, Christians were sporadically persecuted. It was not until the mid-third century that emperors initiated intensive persecutions.

Why were Christians persecuted? Much seems to have depended on local governors and how zealously or not they pursued and prosecuted Christians. The reasons why individual Christians were persecuted in this period were varied. In some cases they were perhaps scapegoats, their faith attacked where more personal or local hostilities were at issue. Contemporary pagan and Christian sources preserve other accusations levelled against the Christians. These included charges of incest and cannibalism, probably resulting from garbled accounts of the rites which Christians celebrated in necessary secrecy, being the agape (the 'love-feast') and the Eucharist (partaking of the body and blood of Christ). Pagans were probably most suspicious of the Christian refusal to sacrifice to the Roman gods. This was an insult to the gods and potentially endangered the empire which they deigned to protect. Furthermore, the Christian refusal to offer sacrifices to the emperor, a semi-divine monarch, had the whiff of both sacrilege and treason about it. Thus the classic test of a Christian's faith was to force him or her, on pain of death, to swear by the emperor and offer incense to his images, or to sacrifice to the gods.

In the mid-second-century account of the martyrdom of Polycarp, officials begged Polycarp to say 'Caesar is Lord', and to offer incense, to save his life. He refused. Later, in the arena, he was asked by the governor to swear an oath by the 'luck of Caesar'. He refused, and although he was apparently eager to meet his death, beast-fighting had been declared closed for the day and so he was burnt alive instead. General persecutions tended to be sparked by particular events such as the fire at Rome under Nero, or during periods of particular crisis, such as the third century. During the third century the turn-over of emperors was rapid - many died violent deaths. As well as this lack of stability at the head of the empire, social relations were in turmoil, and barbarian incursions were on a threatening scale. The economy was suffering and inflation was rampant. Pagans and Christians alike observed this unrest and looked for someone or something,

CHAPTER SEVEN: CHARACTERISTICS OF REMNANT CHURCH

preferably subversive, to blame. It was hardly surprising that a series of emperors ordered savage empire-wide persecutions of the Christians.[158]

There were certain emperors that were less punitive than others, and did not persecute people for being current or past Christians. For example, even though the emperor Trajan deemed it to be an offense for confessing being a Christian, he did not think that ex-Christians should be persecuted. While it was documented during the fouth and fifth century that Christians experienced sustained vicious persecution at the hands of Rome in the preceding centuries; it should also be noted that there were lulls in the persecution. The lulls were due to the expansionist philosophy of the Roman Empire during the first few centuries. In its expansion, Rome did accommodate new cults and philosophies from different cultures within the countries they conquered. The beliefs included the Persian cult of Mithraism, the Egyptian cult of Isis and Neoplatonism, and the Greek philosophical religion. Paganism actually consisted of a fluid and amorphous collection of belief systems. The Romans just considered Christianity another cult among the many prevalent in the cultures that were included in the Empire. The inclusion of Christianity and Judaism in the empire demonstrates that the Roman religion and government were somewhat accommodating. Even though some cults were actually suppressed, we note that there were also many cults that were singled out for persecution. As there were lulls in the persecution of Christians, there were also some cults that were banned by the Roman Senate because their behavior was un-Roman.

The conversion of the emperor Constantine to Christianity about 312 A.D. had an extraordinary impact on the first century New Testament Remnant Church. He broke the mold of Roman emperors who had traditionally been hostile and indifferent towards the Christian faith. Christianity involved the worship of an executed Jewish criminal, and was very popular among slaves and soldiers; not really suitable to the social status of an emperor. Yet, Constantine embraced it, but on his own terms; which we will explore later. Let's set the stage. Christianity had just emerged from the 'Great Persecution' suffered at the hands of the emperor Diocletian; at the end of the third century. Constantine's conversion was the result of a vision or dream he had during a military campaign against one of his political rivals, Maxentius; at the battle of the Milvian Bridge in 312 A.D. He believed that Christ directed him to fight under the sign of the cross, which actually turned out to be the sign of the Egyptian ankh; and under the banner 'in this sign thou shalt conquer'. Reader, think about the spiritual implications of this. His victory prompted him to serve the Christian God. He sprinkled his army as a form of baptism, and declared them Christian; without any form of repentance whatsoever.[159] So, one has to wonder what supernatural power actually gave Constantine that vision/dream. We are aware that the 'great deceiver' always attempts to counterfeit the acts of Jehovah. The impact this had on the New Testament Remnant Church was substantial, and almost irreversible.

Constantine immediately declared that Christians and pagans would be allowed to worship freely. He restored

CHAPTER SEVEN: CHARACTERISTICS OF REMNANT CHURCH

property that had been confiscated during the Great Persecution. He also restored privileges the Christians had lost during the persecution. However, he did not totally shift to a Christian style of worship. In fact, many of his practices were still pagan; and retained the flavor of sun god worship; which is what Constantine was. In fact, in his new capital, Constantinople, he erected many pagan temples and statues. It is apparent that Constantine did not fully understand what it meant to convert to Christianity. It was not uncommon for Roman emperors to convert to pagan cults and gods; cults which were foreign to Rome. What made Constantine's conversion different was the so-called cult to which he chose to convert. Christianity had become sponsored by emperors and protected by law. However, even though Christianity would remain the official religion of the Roman Empire, it was still subject to attack, and compromise by the inclusion of pagan practices into her worship form. These practices were deemed acceptable by the Roman Catholic ecclesiastical hierarchy.

> *"Constantine immediately declared that Christians and pagans would be allowed to worship freely."*

As stated earlier, Constantine was a sun-god worshipper. He worshiped Sol Invictus. After his victory over Maxentius, he began to implement imperial policy to advance the cause of the god of the Christians. His policies and actions demonstrated his considerable devotion to the Church. The Edict of Milan was published as a result of a meeting of Bishops in 313 A.D.; in Milan, Italy. This edict essentially granted complete tolerance to all religions in the Roman Empire. Christianity benefited the most; and previous persecution victims were granted financial compensation straight out of the royal Roman treasury. Constantine's victory over Licinius in 324 A.D. made him the sole ruler of the Roman Empire. After that time, he became more aggressive in his promotion of Christianity. This was basically manifested by the construction of new churches he built in Rome, and throughout the empire.[160]

The other thing that happened, which in fact favored the New Testament Remnant Church, was Constantine's shift in his attitude towards pagans. He became more hostile and less tolerant. With the exception of those temples dedicated to the Imperial cult, pagan temples had their treasures confiscated and given to Christian Churches; and pagan sacrifice was forbidden. Christian heretic cults also experienced the wrath of Constantine. In 325 A.D., some three hundred bishops met during the Council of Nicaea. As they discussed the state of the Catholic Church, important doctrines were developed to counter "heretic ideas and philosophies." The core belief of the Christian faith was also developed there; which included adopting the concept of the Holy Trinity as the supreme deity. The Roman Church was becoming a powerful and far reaching political institution.

After Constantine's death in 337 A.D., there was a noticeable rift between his sons; Constantine II, Constantius, and Constans. This rift amounted to dissension between differing sects of Christianity. This power struggle also included Constantine II's support of the ancient pagan faith of the Romans. There were many attempts to bring back the ancient religion of the Roman people, and the empire was filled with political instability

CHAPTER SEVEN: CHARACTERISTICS OF REMNANT CHURCH

during this time. After the death of Constantine II, his brothers continued to advance the Christian faith; and many anti-pagan laws were put into place. However, when Julian became emperor in 361 A.D., he made a concerted effort to restore the ancient Imperial cult. He also removed some advantages that Christian priests and churches had previously enjoyed. He then gave these advantages to the pagans instead. Christian teachers lost their jobs. While he did not actively promote open violence against Christians, he did encourage, and promote, the growth of non-Catholic or orthodox sects.[161] These were some of the factors that led to the lulls in the persecution of the New Testament Remnant Church.

The Emperor Theodosius was an ardent Christian. He and his western counterpart Gratian, recognized Christianity as the official religion of the Empire in 380 AD. Both Gratian and Theodosius refused the title of Pontifex Maximus (head priest) and it was bestowed instead on the Catholic pope in Rome. Severe punishments for paganism, and 'heretic' Arianism were religiously enforced; and the established Church prospered. By the beginning of the fifth century, after just four hundred years, the Church had grown from a fledgling mystery cult into a power on nearly equal terms with the Roman emperor himself. Christianity slowly came to dominate the entire western world, and become the major world religion.

In 380 A.D., Nicene Christianity, as a result of the Edict of Thessalonica, issued by Emperor Theodosius I, became the state church of the Roman Empire. The Catholic Church, Eastern Orthodox Church, and Oriental Orthodoxy all claim to be the historical extension and continuation of the state church of the Roman Empire. Theodosius was not quite like Constantine in that Theodosius established a single Christian doctrine as the Empire's official religion. While Constantine, on the other hand, simply established tolerance for the Christian faith; without placing it above other religions and cults. Constantine, however, did preside at the convocations of bishops he convened; but he left the determination of doctrine to the bishops. The Christian doctrine that Theodosius established was professed by both Pope Peter II of Alexandria and Pope Damascus I of Rome.[162]

As we take a further look at the development of the End Times Remnant Church, we find that although Constantine convened various councils of Christian bishops to define the correct teachings of the Christian faith, along with its orthodoxy, schisms persisted to exist within the confines of 'the faith'. These ecumenical councils met throughout the fouth and fifth centuries. In the sixth century, the Eastern Roman Emperor Justinian I, and his Byzantine armies, recovered Italy and Rome from the defeat she had suffered in 410 A.D. and 455 A.D. He was able to hold Rome until 751 A.D. At that time, the Muslim conquests of most of the then Christian world, would begin a mass conversion to Islam in West Asia and North Africa; thereby severely limiting the influence of the Byzantine papacy.

In 527 A.D., Emperor Justinian I established bishops in Rome, Constantinople, Antioch, Jerusalem, and Alexandria. These were assigned to be the leadership of the Imperial Church, and were referred to as 'The Pentarchy'. Each bishop was given the title of 'Patriarch'. However, according to Justinian, the

CHAPTER SEVEN: CHARACTERISTICS OF REMNANT CHURCH

Emperor was the head of the Imperial Church, and the bishops served under his tutelage. Justinian stated that the Emperor had the duty and right to regulate worship, discipline, doctrine, and the theological opinions to be held by the Church. By the time that Justinian was emperor, the churches that are now called the Oriental Orthodoxy had already separated from the Imperial Church of Rome. However, in the west, the churches that practiced Christianity were basically subject to the laws and customs of nations that had no allegiance to the emperor and ecclesia headquartered in Constantinople.

Eastern born popes continued to be loyal to the Eastern Emperor in Constantinople as their political lord. However, they refused to be subject to him, and accept his authority in religious matters. Nor did they accept the authority of the councils he imperially convoked. The last Bishop of Rome that asked the Byzantine ruler to ratify his election was Pope Gregory III in 731 A.D. While the largest portion of the Christian Church was still under the Eastern Emperor's rulership, with the crowning of Charlemagne on December 25, 800 A.D., as Imperator Romanorum, the political split between the east and west became irrevocable; and irreconcilable. The Eastern Roman Empire, the Byzantine Empire, collapsed with the Fall of Constantinople to the Islamic Ottoman Turkish Empire in 1453. This event culminated the many years of the Byzantine Empire losing territory to Islam; and many members of the Eastern Christian Church increasingly living outside of the geographical boundaries of the church of Constantinople.

Due to the missionary efforts of the west, a large number

of churches began to be established outside of the borders of the Eastern Empire. These efforts, along with the evangelization of the Germanic, Pictic, and Celtic peoples resulted in the development of the idea of a universal church. This notion involved the concept of one universal church free from an association with any one particular state or government. This was contrary to the Byzantine East Roman school of thought. They had envisioned the formation of the God inspired and willed perfect world order; as a result of Rome accepting Christianity as her imperial state religion. However, it became extremely difficult for the Eastern bishops to embrace the idea of Christianity without an emperor at the helm. The Church that existed at that time has been labelled with a variety of different designations, or monikers. It has been called the Imperial Roman Church, the Byzantine Church, the Orthodox Church, the Imperial Church, the Catholic Church, and other names. However, it should be noted that the idea of a 'universal church' is still held as a common core belief in the Catholic, Eastern Orthodox, and Anglican Churches.[163]

As we continue to allow Wikipedia to offer us more insight as to additional changes that took place in the Remnant Church after the Protestant Reformation and the subsequent rescue of the Church from Rome and Catholicism; we note the following information. The Lord's Prayer in German Das Vaterunser on a woodcut by Lucas Cranach the Elder during the Protestant Reformation under Martin Luther. The Reformation (from Latin reformatio, literally 'restoration, renewal'), also referred to as the Protestant Reformation, was a schism from the Roman Catholic Church initiated by Martin Luther and continued

CHAPTER SEVEN: CHARACTERISTICS OF REMNANT CHURCH

by John Calvin, Huldrych Zwingli, and other early Protestant Reformers in 16th century Europe. It is usually considered to have started with the publication of the Ninety-Five Theses by Luther in 1517, lasting until the end of the Thirty Years' War with the Peace of Westphalia in 1648. When Luther declared his intolerance and disdain for the Roman Church's corruption, he was destined for exile. In 1521, in the months that followed the Diet of Worms Council, which was designed to martyr him, Luther would translate the New Testament into German for the first time. He translated it from the 1516 Greek-Latin New Testament of Erasmus; and published it in September of 1522. He also published a German Pentateuch in 1523, and another version of the German New Testament in 1529. He would eventually publish the entire Bible in German in the 1530's. To say that he was of extreme importance to the Post Reformation Remnant Church is an understatement.

Although Martin Luther has been given credit for starting the Protestant Reformation in 1517, there were numerous other significant attempts to reform the Roman Catholic Church. Such people as John Wycliffe, Jan Hus, and Peter Waldo, also made reform attempts of the only version of Christianity in the earth at that time. However, it was Luther's challenge of Catholicism's sale of indulgences, non-gospel foundational notion of merits of the saints, and insistence that the Pope had no authority over purgatory, that gave rise to widespread cries for reformation in the belief system known as Christianity. Additionally, the assertion that complete reliance on the Holy Scriptures, and that faith, not good deeds, brings salvation, were the proper sources for a biblical belief system; and were purposed as core tenets of true Christianity. These projected theological changes greatly contributed to the erosion of faith in the Papacy, and helped advance the notion that the Roman Catholic Church was corrupt; and further promoted the questioning of traditional religious acts and practices. The Roman Catholic Church responded with a Counter-Reformation initiated by the Council of Trent. Much work in battling Protestantism was done by the well-organized new order of the Jesuits. In general, Northern Europe, with the exception of most of Ireland, came under the influence of Protestantism. Southern Europe remained Roman Catholic, while Central Europe was a site of a fierce conflict, culminating in the Thirty Years' War, which left it devastated.[164]

Another factor that facilitated the rapid growth of the Protestant Reformation, and significantly impacted the Post-Reformation Remnant Church, was the invention and usage of the Gutenberg Press. The Gutenberg Press, along with the other non-Luther reform uprisings, provided for the rapid dissemination of religious materials and missives. Consequently, the written word of God became available for the laity to read. Johann Gutenberg invented the printing press in 1450. The first book to be printed by the press was a Latin Bible; printed in Mainz, Germany. Gutenberg had unscrupulous business associates who stole control of his business, and literally left him in poverty. Nonetheless, his invention of a moveable printing press made it possible for Bibles and books to be effectively produced, in large quantities, with high quality; in a short period of time.

The first handwritten English language Bible manuscripts

were produced by John Wycliffe, in the 1380's. Wycliffe opposed the teaching of the Catholic Church, which he believed to be contrary to the Holy Scriptures. He was an Oxford professor, scholar, and theologian. He produced dozens of English language manuscript copies for the scriptures. The Latin Vulgate was the only source text available to him, and the team that helped him translate the Bible. The Pope was infuriated by his translation of the Bible into English. Additionally, the Pope did not subscribe to Wycliffe's teachings. He was so furious, that forty-five years after Wycliffe had died, the Pope ordered his bones to be exhumed, crushed to dust, and scattered in a river.

John Hus was a disciple of Wycliffe. He actively promulgated Wycliffe's ideas that people should oppose the tyranny of the Roman Church, and be able to read the Bible in their own language. The Roman Church threatened to execute anyone in possession of a non-Latin Bible. Thus, in 1415, Hus was burned at the stake; with a copy of Wycliffe's manuscript being used as kindling paper to start the fire. Hus' last words were that, "in one hundred years, God will raise up a man whose calls for reform cannot be suppressed." It was almost exactly one hundred years later that Martin Luther nailed his now famous '95 Theses of Contention' onto the door of the Schlosskirche (Castle Church) at Wittenberg, Germany. Martin Luther became the first person to translate and publish the Bible in the commonly spoken dialect of the German people. The Roman Catholic Church also burned seven people at the stake, in the year of Luther's Theses, for teaching their children to say the Lord's Prayer in English rather than in Latin.

THE REMNANT CHURCH

Another great pioneer in the Post Reformation Remnant Church is William Tyndale. Considered to be the spiritual leader of the reformers, he was the first man to ever print the New Testament in the English language. He was a true scholar, a genius, and fluent in eight languages. He is often referred to as the 'Architect of the English Language'. It is a fact that many of the phrases coined by Tyndale are still used in the English language. Tyndale wanted to translate and print the New Testament into English, for the first time in history, using the same 1516 Erasmus text that Luther used to translate the New Testament into German. So, he travelled to Germany to visit Luther in 1525. By the end of that year, he had translated the New Testament into English. Tyndale had been forced to flee England because rumors of his intentions to translate the New Testament into English had been circulated. As a result of this, inquisitors and bounty hunters were constantly trying to arrest him, and prevent his project from coming to fruition. However, in 1525-1526 the Tyndale New Testament became a reality, and the first printed edition of the Holy Scriptures in the English language was made available to the general public.

As soon as the bishops could confiscate these copies, they had them burned. Fortunately, copies trickled through and served to further fascinate the public at large. The Catholic Church declared that Tyndale's works contained thousands of errors, and ultimately torched hundreds of copies that were confiscated by the clergy. The truth of the matter was that they could not find any errors in Tyndale's work. In truth, one risked being burned at the stake if merely caught in possession of one of Tyndale's forbidden books. These aforementioned heroes of the faith were critical to the Post Reformation Remnant Church, and her evolution into who, and what she is in today's world.

Having God's Word available to the public in the language of the common man, English, meant disaster to the Roman Catholic Church. No longer would they control access to the scriptures. If people were able to read the Bible in their own tongue, the church's income and power would crumble. They could not possibly continue to get away with selling indulgences (the forgiveness of sins) or selling the release of loved ones from a church-manufactured 'Purgatory'. People would begin to challenge the church's authority if the church was exposed as frauds and thieves. The contradictions between what God's Word said, and what the priests taught, would open the public's eyes and the truth would set them free from the grip of fear that the institutional church held. Salvation through faith, not works or donations, would be understood. The need for priests would vanish through the priesthood of all believers. The veneration of church-canonized saints and Mary would be called into question. The availability of the scriptures in English was the biggest threat imaginable to the wicked church. Neither side would give up without a fight.[165]

The Remnant Church was significantly impacted after the Protestant Movement. Her members were able to experience a more intimate relationship with their Creator because they were now able to examine the Bible for themselves. Since faith is unquestioning confidence and trust in the word that we have heard from God; believer's faith was now capable of being built to a higher level. As a result of this movement, the Church moved from total reliance on the clergy to communicate to the members what God was saying in the Scriptures. Jesus was recognized as the true mediator between God and man. This meant that people could go to God for themselves; without having to rely on a priest. Individual personal study of the Bible was encouraged, along with personal private prayer. The Bible was no longer only available in Latin, but was now available in English. The doctrine of justification by repentance from dead works and the grace of God and faith in Him became the accepted manner of entering into relationship with Him. Relationship with God was no longer by virtue of being born into the Holy Catholic Church by being sprinkled as a baby. It now required an act of faith, turning from a sinful lifestyle, and turning to Jehovah.

As we make an examination of the state of affairs of the Remnant Church after the Protestant Reformation and her subsequent rescue from Rome and Catholicism, we must note that there were major historical and doctrinal changes; which forever impacted theology and dogma. According to Dr. Bill Hamon, in his book 'The Eternal Church', there were different moves of God to restore certain spiritual gifts to the Body of Christ. These movements included the: Protestant Movement; Holiness Movement; Pentecostal Movement; Charismatic Movement, and Prophetic-Apostolic Movement. These movements facilitated the establishment of certain denominations and the restoration of certain spiritual gifts in the Body of Christ. As we explore these movements, we will discuss the impact these post-Reformation movements had on the Church.

CHAPTER SEVEN: CHARACTERISTICS OF REMNANT CHURCH

1. Protestant Movement

This movement is typically recognized to have begun in October of 1517. During this movement, the Lutheran, Episcopal, and Presbyterian denominations were formed. These were the first effects the reformation of the only then known form of European Christianity had on those following Martin Luther's protest. We say European Christianity because there were still pockets of Semites practicing the Messianic Jewish form of Christianity, who did not succumb to the intrusion of the Roman government into an apostolically governed Church established by Christ; which He left in the hands of His apostles. The first spiritual experience those reformed Catholics experienced was the concept of being justified by faith and repentance versus the notion of being born into the universal Church. This experience resulted in them studying the Bible for themselves, versus relying in a priest to interpret the scriptures for them. It also led to them finding internal peace through the power of personal prayer; as opposed to depending on a priest to pray for them; and giving them absolution for their sins.

2. Holiness Movement

Between 1750 and 1850, water baptism, sanctification (holiness) and divine healing were the three truths restored during the Holiness Movement. These truths comprised the 'faith towards God' concept associated with the Holiness Movement. Baptism by immersion became the standard method of the holiness churches; except for the Methodist church. However, God used the Methodist church to reintroduce the concept of sanctification.

Jehovah used the Christian and Missionary Alliance to restore the truth of divine healing. The 'fruit of faith" was also restored during this movement. Faith towards God produces a fruit of faith in the believer. The Baptists, Methodists, Church of God, Evangelicals, and Christian Missionary Alliance were the major denominations to be birthed during this movement.

3. Pentecostal Movement

This movement restored the revelation and reality of the 'doctrine of baptisms'. The Methodists felt that there was an over emphasis on 'holiness' and as a result of that conflict among the holiness churches, over twenty-three denominations were formed in a seven year period. Among the major ones were: the Assembly of God; the Pentecostal Holiness Church; the Pentecostal Church of God; the Fire Baptized Holiness Church; the United Pentecostal; the Foursquare; and the Church of God in Christ. One of the major distinctions of this movement was the laying on of hands to receive: (1) deliverance; (2) healing; (3) revelation of one's place of ministry in the Church; and (4) the baptism of the Holy Spirit; with the evidence of speaking with 'other tongues' and the interpretation of tongues; as evidenced with Rev. Charles Fox Parham in Topeka, Kansas in December of 1900, and Rev. W.J. Seymour in Los Angeles (Azusa Street Revival) in 1906.

4. Latter Rain Movement

This movement further emphasized the use of the laying on of hands for any and everything other than deliverance and healing. It is noted for the restoration of the doctrine of laying on of hands, with prophecy, for revelation of God's will, calling, ministry, and placement of believers in the corporate Body of Christ. There were no, quote unquote, major denominations formed as a result of this movement. However, the designation of local assemblies as: fellowships; ministerial associations; evangelistic associations were coined. Additionally, the term 'Body of Christ' began to be used when referring to the ecclesia, instead of the 'Church'. This movement reportedly began in February of 1948 as a result of about seventy students at the Sharon Orphanage in North Battleford, Saskatchewan Canada who had begun to study the Bible, fast, and pray.

5. Charismatic Movement

This movement represents a move of God, through the Holy Spirit, to restore all of the manifestations of the previous movements to all Christendom: from Protestants to Catholics; Pentecostals to Lutherans; Eastern Orthodox to Messianic Jews, black, white, rich poor....everyone was now exposed to the 'charisma' of the Holy Ghost and all of His associated gifts and fruits. Beginning with the Full Gospel Business Men's Fellowship International (FGBMFI) in Los Angeles in 1951 through Episcopalian Father Dennis Bennett's forced resignation as an Episcopalian pastor because of his personal testimony of being baptized in the Holy Spirit evidenced with speaking in tongues in 1960 in Van Nuys, California through the beginning of the Catholic Charismatic Movement as four faculty members of Duquesne University in Pittsburgh, PA received a Pentecostal experience in a Protestant Charismatic prayer group in 1967, this movement was having a momentous launch. The concepts of Discipleship, Faith, and Kingdom are among the major foundational teachings of this movement.

6. Prophetic Apostolic Movement

In October of 1988, in Sandestin Florida, at the second Christian International Prophets Conference, the movement was birthed and subsequently launched into what has come to be known as the Prophetic Apostolic Movement. Between the first and second Christian International Prophets Conferences, over 1,500 prophets gathered and were participants in the birth and launch of this great end-times movement. The offices of prophet and apostle were restored as fully functioning gifts of five-fold ministry in the Body of Christ. People such as Bill Hamon. John Sanford, Peter Wagner, Mike Bickle, Dr. Paula Price, Rick Joyner, Cindy Jacobs, Emannuele Cannistraci, Kim Clements, John Eckhardt, David Cartledge, John P. Kelly, Dutch Sheets, Ted Haggard, and many others are among the list of clergy who have risen to be prominent spokespersons, and instructors, for the truths associated with this movement. While there has not been a named denomination ascribed to this movement, many apostolic and prophetic networks have been birthed as a result of the restored truths of this movement.

7. The Advent of Denominations

We must bear in mind that until the Protestant Reformation in 1500, there was only one form of Christianity in the earth; there was no such thing as denominations. There was only the

CHAPTER SEVEN: CHARACTERISTICS OF REMNANT CHURCH

Roman Catholic Church and her sister the Eastern Orthodox Church. These were the only expressions of Christianity available for the world to see. Remember, this came about when Constantine declared Christianity the official religion of the Roman government; and in effect usurped the governance of the first century Church from the hands of the Jewish apostles. According to the nineth edition of the 'Handbook of Denominations' there are currently over ninety-two different denominations representing over two hundred twenty religious bodies or organizations.

8. The Availability of the Bible to the Laity

We must also remember that during the first eight hundred years of the Church, the completed canonized compilation of the Scriptures were only available in Latin; and were only available to the clergy within the Catholic Church. In other words, those people who chose to follow Christianity as a belief system were totally dependent on the priests to tell them what God was saying to His creation. The public's only way of receiving instruction from God was through the man-made system of religion. They did not have a way of securing a direct understanding and relationship with God; as a result of not being able to hear or read what Jehovah was saying to His creation. They could not read the account of God's interaction with the creation because the majority of them could not understand Latin. Additionally, the Latin Bible was not available to the general public; it was only available to the Catholic priests.

The Holiness Movement represented yet another major

shift for the Remnant Church. It helped in the restoration movement of Jehovah to reposition the Church back into right relationship with her founder. The Father was consciously attempting to reestablish one of the basic tenets of the original Church. He was now requiring a conscious awareness of not being able to maintain proper relationship with God without separating oneself from routine religious practices. Being a good person was simply not enough. He was desirous of His people feeling guilty for not agreeing with Him concerning His definition of sin. Jehovah wanted the Church to reflect the character of who He is. According to I Peter 1:16, the command is, 'Be ye holy for I am holy.' As a result of the Holiness Movement, an emphasis on sanctification was birthed. This act was totally dependent on faith towards God. Water baptism by immersion, sanctification or holiness, and divine healing were the spiritual truths that were the focus of this movement. There was a shift from anyone being able to be baptized, including infants and children, to baptism being reserved only for born-again believers. Another major shift associated with this movement was the addition of the idea of experiencing 'conviction' for one's sins. The idea of God making one feel guilty for participating in sinful acts or acts associated with worldly pleasures was a dominant espoused principle.

It should obviously go without saying that the Pentecostal Movement was probably one of the most significant restorative Church movements of the 20th century. The deliberate inclusion of the baptism of the Holy Spirit or Holy Ghost, whichever your preference of calling Him, into the Christian experience represents a substantial stride towards fulfilling one of the mandates of the

CHAPTER SEVEN: CHARACTERISTICS OF REMNANT CHURCH

Great commission given in the gospels of Matthew and Mark. This movement served to catapult the Church back onto the road leading to the place of power it occupied prior to its descent into darkness and powerlessness when Rome usurped the authority of the apostles; who were the God-assigned leaders of the Church. This movement also enabled the believer to operate in the power of God; since 'the baptism in the Holy Spirit' facilitated an 'empowering' of the Christian to live a victorious Christian life; not simply speak in tongues. As a result of the baptism of the Holy Ghost, speaking in tongues, the interpretation of tongues, and pressing the importance of the concept of 'holiness', the Church began to focus on efforts geared toward dealing with social sins, versus the prevailing focus of the day that was geared towards social reform. Although prohibition, slavery, women's rights and masonry topped the list of areas needing social reform, the emphasis of the remnant from the Holiness Movement was more of a concern for the social activities that had been deemed sinful. These included; the movies; smoking cigarettes; drinking; dancing, sporting events, lipstick and the theater. Additionally, the Church focused her attention on fasting, the manifestation of the nine gifts of the Spirit, the doctrine of baptisms, dancing in the Spirit, hand clapping and shouting.

With the advent of the Charismatic and Full Gospel Movements, the Remnant Church moved still closer to her restored place of original power and authority. Still another of the mandates of the Great Commission was being restored; as the Church embraced the practice of the laying on of hands as the standard for imparting the gifts of God to His children. The Church was being moved into a mode where the emphasis was more on stabilizing the people of God; rather than on entertaining them. The focus became equipping the people of God through discipling them unto the Word of God and the Christ of God. The Father was moving His people toward intimate small groups where they would be taught and allowed to have their questions answered and given Biblical explanation. There was a notable shift from high energy emotional preaching to 'flat-footed' teaching. This movement was actually an outgrowth or byproduct of the Latter Rain Movement. The reintroduction of the baptism of the Holy Ghost, the de-emphasis on denominationalism, the introduction of 'teaching vs. preaching', the introduction of 'discipleship' as the method of stabilizing new converts, and the establishment of cell groups or house meetings characterize the major tenets of this movement. One of the most notable outcomes of the Latter Rain Movement and subsequent Charismatic Movement was the practice of the 'laying on of hands' for: healing; deliverance; receiving the Holy Spirit; prophecy for revealing one's place in the Body of Christ; and activation of the gifts of the Holy Spirit. Additionally, psalms, spiritual songs, worship, praise in dance, the arts-drama, mime, and body ministry are associated with these movements.

However, as the Remnant Church continued to march towards her God appointed destiny to be the mirror image of the powerful post-Pentecost Church, there was a problem. This Church that was in the earth as God began to fulfill His promise to faithful father Abraham; and bless all of the nations of the earth through him, did not have to contend with the false gospels that the Remnant Church has to deal with. One might ask, "How does the Church survive all of the false doctrines being perpetrated in the world by the god of this world?" It will take faithful Servant-Warriors of Jehovah, God of the Hebrews, the Ancient of Days to step forward and shoulder the responsibility of fulfilling the Great Commission. It will take disciplined students of the Bible, rightfully dividing the Word of Truth to proclaim and affirm the message of the Gospel. It will take an uncompromising commitment to holiness and the apostle's doctrine to stabilize a world of hedonistic people and carnal Christians. To be sure, there has been an apostasy-like aftermath and negative effect of: the love gospel; the prosperity Gospel; false gospel of carnal Christianity; that implores the Remnant Church to decry these erroneous teachings.

In the 20th century, as the Church struggled to maintain her identity as a holy extension of the organism that the Christ left in the apostle's governance, she was dealt destructive blows in successive order. She had to scripturally combat the deceptive illusions orchestrated by a lovey dovey gospel that perpetuates the myth that one does not need to worry about Jehovah punishing sin and sending people to hell. This mushy gospel dispels the concept of one having to reap what one sows. It absolves people from having to bear the consequences of their actions. It espoused the idea that God is such a loving God that He would not be so punitive as to send His creation to a lake of fire that burns forever and ever. This syrupy philosophy encourages folks to believe that there is no need to fear the wrath of God, because He is such a loving being, that He would not harm a hair on

> *"He doesn't change His mind about blessing us and He has already provided all that we need; as He sees us complete in Christ."*

our head. Therefore, we are free to live a lifestyle that appeases our self-centered appetite. As a result of this, many members of the Body of Christ ended up living lives that did not reflect holiness, nor did they show a marked difference between the ways of God and the ways of the sinful world.

Additionally, the evil one introduced the greed factor into the spirits of the elect. Through the tongues and lives of some susceptible, compromised preachers, he was able to birth a movement that placed emphasis on the ability of the Almighty to bless His children with material wealth and things. The focus of the believer's walk with God shifted from seeking and knowing the face of God to seeking and knowing the hand of God; as He blesses them with the desires of their heart. Even though it is His desire for us to prosper and be in health; even as our soul doeth prosper; that is a conditional promise. Our prosperity and health is directly proportionate to how well our soul is succeeding; how well our thought life, emotions, and will (volition) is growing and thriving in the things of the spirit...in how are we succeeding in allowing the Word of God to influence these areas. This inerrant gospel also wrongly purports that the measure of our spirituality and the move of Jehovah in our lives is indicated by how many material acquisitions we have achieved. It also sets one up to believe that if they have not acquired the accumulation of wealth that society deems to indicate success; that God must not be moving in one's life. They must have

CHAPTER SEVEN: CHARACTERISTICS OF REMNANT CHURCH

some sort of spiritual deficiency that makes it impossible for God to bless them. Consequently, this ideology has duped the saints into believing that they can influence the blessing of God in their lives by 'sowing seed' into the ministry of certain people and organizations. Under the misrepresentation of the idea of reciprocity, these ministers and ministries have been able to pillage the finances of the Church by convincing them that if they give to God's ministry then He will reciprocate and give them financial blessings and physical healings. Yet scriptures tell us that the promises of God are yea and amen; and that the gifts of God are without repentance. He doesn't change His mind about blessing us and He has already provided all that we need; as He sees us complete in Christ.

Add to all of this the negative impact of a doctrine that excuses the believer from succumbing to the appetite of the flesh, and you have the recipe for a compromised, deceived, ineffectual body of people; having no real power to combat the forces of darkness. This gospel that elevates satisfying sensual emotions above meeting spiritual requirements produces a Church that has little sensitivity to the Holy Spirit, a basic inability to be led by Him, and a lack of morals and mores; thereby causing it to closely resemble the 'world' that Jehovah is actually trying to reconcile. This carnal Christianity produces a believer that is preoccupied with operating in the 'soulish' realm of their thinking, feelings, and what they want to do. It positions pleasing their feelings above pleasing the commandments and statutes of Elohim. By adhering to the notion that if it feels right do it, they disregard the idea of dying to oneself and living unto God. The idea of self-sacrifice is thrown out the window, as the evil one seduces the believer to buy into the 'I will'. The 'I will' is the very concept spoken of in *Isaiah 14: 12-15*, when Lucifer expressed it five times; which resulted in him being cast down out of heaven. The danger of this deceptive philosophy is that it leads people to serve and please themselves instead of serving and pleasing God.

It is plain to see that these destructive false doctrines of the 20th century left the Remnant Church in a state where it had to wage spiritual battle on behalf of a larger body of professing Christians who believed they were absolved from having to bear the consequences of their actions. The compromised, deceived, conformist Church believed that there was no need to fear the wrath of God, because He is such a loving kind being, that He would not send His creation to a devil's hell. These doctrines shifted the focus of the believer's walk with God, and from seeking to know God, to seeking what they could get from Him. They were also led to believe that the measure of their spirituality and the move of Jehovah in their lives could be measured by how many material acquisitions they have. Satan duped the saints into believing that they could purchase God's blessings by 'sowing seed' into ministry. They came to a place where they elevated satisfying sensual emotions above meeting spiritual requirements. The Remnant Church had to intercede for a compromised organism that closely resembled the 'world' it was trying to help God redeem.

The Church has come a long way from what started out as the first century post-Pentecost New Testament Church. She has endured the loss of her apostolic Jewish leadership, as she

CHAPTER SEVEN: CHARACTERISTICS OF REMNANT CHURCH

was kidnaped by the Roman government; and underwent fifteen hundred years of Catholicism. She has managed to navigate through the upheaval of the Protestant Reformation; and the Bible being made available to the laity in languages other than Latin. She has survived the metamorphosis associated with all of the restorative movements of the Holy Spirit; as He re-established(Added hyphen to "reestablished") gifts, graces, and helps to the Body of Christ. The Body of Christ has been forced to overcome the false gospels Lucifer has successfully seeped into the Church; as he continually attempts to undermine the purity of the message given to the world by Yahweh. Yet, the Church now faces her most challenging task; as she prepares to minister to the world at the end of the age. As she prepares to answer questions, provide ministry, and cope with the hopelessness of the creation as the cataclysmic events unfold that will herald the second coming of Christ; she is challenged. The Remnant Church must throw down the gauntlet, and draw a line in the sand, to accept the responsibility of being the untainted representative, and ambassador, of the power of God. She must refuse to conform, refuse to be deceived, and refuse to compromise the principle of holiness; upon which the first century New Testament Church was built. She must demonstrate the character of the Most High God Jehovah, in order to qualify as the legitimate replacement to the compromised form of Christianity which currently exists. The Remnant Church must shoulder up under the weight of the cross that she has chosen to bear, if she is to operate in the power, authority, and functionality necessary to accomplish the purposes of God; as He closes out time and ushers in eternity.

Chapter Eight
All things in Christ

"Giving thanks unto the Father, which hath made us meet to be partakers of the inheritance of the saints in light: Who hath delivered us from the power of darkness, and hath translated us into the kingdom of his dear Son: In whom we have redemption through his blood, even the forgiveness of sins: Who is the image of the invisible God; the firstborn of every creature: For by him were all things created, that are in heaven, and that are in earth, visible and invisible, whether they be thrones, or dominions, or principalities, or powers: all things were created by him, and for him"
Colossians 1:12-16

"For in him dwelleth all the fulness of the Godhead bodily."
Colossians 2:9

Christ is looking for a body of believers that has matured and grown into His image. He is looking for a people who are not tossed to and fro' by every wind of doctrine. His body must reflect the height, depth, and width of who He is.

The Remnant must be like Christ was; the visible image of the invisible God. She must be the flesh manifested in the Word; so that when the world looks at her, they see Christ and Him alone. The Remnant Church must have the ability to impact the religion and politics of the contemporary United States; as well as the rest of the world. She must be committed to following the Apostle's doctrine and caring for her members. The Remnant Church must serve as a call for the compromised Church to return to its first love and its original form. She should prompt the contemporary Church to do an about face, as far as her adherence to tradition. She should be compelled to return to her initial mission in the earth; making disciples of the nations.

As the Remnant Church herself returns to the power and position of the first century Church, there should be a substantive change in the quality of ministry and teaching she provides. She must shift her focus from entertaining the Church to equipping and empowering the Church. The Remnant Church must be as fervent and focused as those first century believers who had lived in the physical presence of the Messiah; and witnessed the life-changing miracles He had performed. She must model the behavior and focus of those first century believers. Just as the first century Church called the Jews to come into compliance with the principles of the Kingdom of God in order to attain proper relationship with Jehovah; the contemporary Remnant

CHAPTER EIGHT: ALL THINGS IN CHRIST

Church must do the same. The Remnant Church must compel the contemporary Church to come subject to the principles of the Kingdom of God. The Remnant must influence the compromised Church to forsake the false teachings of the "prosperity gospel," the "name it and claim it gospel," and the "love gospel" and return to the true gospel; as its standard of operation. It is only the true gospel message of Jesus the Messiah that has the ability to convert sinners on the road to hell, and change them into born-again believers.

It is only when the Remnant Church comes into correct position vertically, as it relates to her relationship with Jehovah that she will be in a correct position horizontally with the Body of Christ in the earth. Then and, only then, will she be empowered to affect this kind of influence on religion and the compromised Church in the United States, and world-wide. It is only when Christ is truly allowed to be the Lord and Master that governs the body of believers, known as the Church, that the anointing that empowers the Kingdom of God will be able to affect the changes necessary to bring the compromised Church in alignment with the agenda of the Father. It is only then that the purposes of God for the "ecclesia" will operate in accordance with the dictates of God, versus the dogma and doctrines of men.

The Remnant Church must serve as an alarm to warn the officials of the government about the danger of the New World Order. She must educate the world about the severe consequences of a one world government; and a one world economy. The Remnant Church must fight to maintain the sovereignty of the United States. She must protest America throwing her allegiance in with the other nations that will comprise the ten nation confederacy; which comprise the entity known as the Beast. She must ensure that the correct teaching, as to who the anti-Christ really is, sounds with unmistakable clarity. As the devil seeks to impose a hedonistic agenda on unsuspecting Americans, the Remnant Church must stand strong for the Christian values upon which this country was founded. She must implore U.S. politicians to refrain from endorsing those ungodly principles and practices that open the floodgates for the minions of hell to oppress the people of God. The Remnant Church must minister to keep Lucifer from possessing those who are not sealed and protected by the Holy Spirit. Deliverance ministry must become the standard operating protocol and practice for the Body of Christ. The Remnant Church must exert Godly influence on the people who control the reins of power and run the government of our country. In order to do this, the "Remnant" must be operating in the power of the Spirit and be an uncompromised vessel for the Spirit of God to flow through.

As the world continues its downward spiral into a constant time of crisis, there must be "crisis leaders." These ministers and believers must be trained and equipped to deal with the demonic onslaught that will be leveled against the inhabitants of the world. There must be people of God who have expanded influence and the ability to capture the ear of those in political power. These Christians must be able to communicate with, and relate to, people in all levels of government. These crisis leaders must be uncompromised. They must be well versed in the Scriptures and able to relate current world events to Biblical prophecy. The

Remnant Church must be uncompromisingly and operationally holy to help secure the future of the nation, and the world. She must be prepared to aggressively wage war, as the forces of evil associated with the Beast, anti-Christ, are unleashed on the inhabitants existing at the end of the age.

It is extremely important that the Remnant Church have the ability to influence the religion and politics of the contemporary nation state of Israel. In order for all of Israel to be saved, the Remnant Church must be

> *"The grafted branch must be able to provoke the chosen root to return to her proper relationship with Jehovah; by accepting the way prophesied of by John the Baptist."*

able to make the chosen ones of Israel jealous of the relationship the Gentile Church has with the God of the Hebrews, the Ancient of Days. The grafted branch must be able to provoke the chosen root to return to her proper relationship with Jehovah; by accepting the way prophesied of by John the Baptist. The anointing of God must be so prevalent on the Remnant Church, that His presence in her and endorsement of her is unmistakable. The requirements of the compromised Church to return to the principles of "holiness before God and man" is mandatory for the purposes of God to be accomplished with His chosen people, Israel. For it is only when the manifested presence of God is on display in the converted Church, which has morphed into the Remnant Church, that the nation of Israel will remember the special place they hold in God's heart. They will then yearn for His presence in their midst again; as He was in the days of old. They will be desperate for His manifested presence as He was with the Ark of the Covenant; and the Holy of Holies in the Temple in Jerusalem. The Remnant Church should remind Israel that salvation is of the Jew first, then the Gentile. She must encourage Israel to remember that as Abraham's descendants, they are the recipients of the covenants of promise; salvation being one of those promises. The Remnant Church must serve as a voice to call Judaism to accept its Messiah, Jesus of Nazareth; the crucified Christ of God. She must be a cheerleader for the Jews to assume their rightful place as God's chosen people, for the completion of God's plan for the Church cannot happen without Israel. The Remnant Church needs to serve as a wake-up call for the nation of Israel to prepare itself for the Battle of Armageddon. Israel must be made to realize that her future destiny is directly linked to her relationship with Jesus Christ. For all things are in Him. The culmination of the age is in Him. The victory over the devil is in Him, and Israel's defeat over all of her enemies is in Him.

> *"It is extremely important that the Remnant Church have the ability to influence the religion and politics of the contemporary nation state of Israel."*

As traditional Protestant Christianity witnesses the radical changes taking place within the emerging Remnant Church, there should be a profound character changing transformation occurring inside her halls of tradition. The dogmas and doctrines of traditional historical religion should feel the fire of urgency the Remnant Church exudes; to capture the inhabitants of the world for Christ. Tradition is required to give way to Christ. The culmination of everything that Jehovah has for His creation is found in Christ; not in the traditions of men. Every denominational foundation and doctrine must yield to the superiority of Christ and the knowledge of Him. It is in Him that we move and have our being. The remnant's air of expectancy for His second coming, and return, should spark a similar spontaneous flame within the very fiber of the reformation movement that rescued the gospel from the governance of Rome. The active move of the Holy Spirit within the Remnant Church must attract the attention of our traditional institutions of worship; and motivate them to replicate the objective of the emerging remnant's mission to bring in this last, great harvest. The commitment of the Remnant Church, to help fulfill the time of the Gentiles, should create an infectious itch in traditional Protestant Christianity. This itch can only be satisfied by their active engagement in the spiritual warfare necessary to make this a reality. The movement that began the restoration process of the Church from the "dark ages," can ill-afford to ignore the work of Father; as He manifests Himself in this last great restoration movement.

The fullness of God, and His intended purpose for the Creation, is embodied in Christ Jesus. The destiny of mankind can only be completed in Him, and by Him. As one song writer put it, "Christ is my all in all." Every question that can ever be posed is answered in Christ. He is Alpha and Omega, the beginning and the end; and everything in between. His incursion into our time and space represented the love of the Father in eternity; to make provision for our salvation, and the defeat of our enemy. Everything that mankind needs is found in Christ, as He is the vehicle God used to restore man's broken relationship with his maker. Jesus is the fulfillment of God's promise to Abraham to bless all of the nations of the earth. Jehovah has always intended to have a people who dwell in close communion to Him. Jesus is the way for the Creator of mankind to intimately dwell inside of His creation; He is Jehovah's self-fulfilling prophecy. Christ is the manifestation of God's plan for the age...

"That in the dispensation of the fullness of times he might gather together in one, all things in Christ, both which are in heaven and which are on the earth, even in him." Ephesians 1:10

As mankind races towards the end of the age and the second coming of Christ, there will be distinct signs that earmark the end of time, as we know it. While these signs may not initially be clearly apparent to the Protestant Church and the Catholic Church, the display of the power of God within the remnant will be undeniable, and irrefutable. This display of the power of God will make it impossible for these organizations to ignore the validity, and authority of the Remnant Church. The influence the emerging Remnant Church will have on traditional Protestantism and Catholicism will contribute to the greatest revival that will happen in Christendom; as time prepares to merge with eternity. There will be God-fearing Catholics who come into a personal relationship with Jesus Christ as a result of the ministry of the Remnant Church. There will also be compromised Protestants who rededicate themselves to the principles of holiness. The evidence of the move of God among His remnant will be a major contributing factor in the salvation of many in the Holy Roman

Catholic Church; and the renewal of backslidden Christians. Many agnostics and atheists will find their way to the foot of the Cross, as a result of the movement of the Holy Ghost in the Remnant Church.

Many of the monotheistic and polytheistic world religions will stand in awe and amazement as they witness a demonstration of the power of Jehovah, God of the Hebrews, as He works through His Remnant Church. They will observe the fruit of His efforts as He uses the remnant to move His chosen people to jealous action. His utilization of the remnant will cause Israel to seek a reunification with the Great I Am in the way He has prescribed; Jesus, the Christ of God. Those belief systems, that promise providing a connection with the creator, will stand in astonishment as Father Yahweh moves heaven and earth to demonstrate the fullness of Christ being manifested in the Remnant Church. As those world religions seek to stake their claim at being a true religion, the manifestation of the power of God, through the Body of Christ, will serve notice of their ineffectiveness, false essence, and false nature. In their attempts to validate their worth, they will be confronted, and challenged, by the awesome strength of a mature body of believers in Christ. As full trust in Christ, as the hope for deliverance, and connection to the only true higher power, fills the earth, recognition of all things being dependent on Jesus will pervade the thinking of humanity. False religions, compromised and deceived lifestyles, and non-believers in the supernatural will all be overwhelmed by the power of God being demonstrated in the all-encompassing reality of all things in Christ. They will have to bow in submission to the presence, and power, of the Father, Son, and Holy Ghost. As the Remnant Church proclaims the message of the fullness of God embodied in His sacrifice of the Christ, while simultaneously bringing clarity to the foundational truth of Jesus' superiority in all things, the Spirit of God will draw tens of millions to the saving knowledge of Jesus Christ.

International politics will also be impacted by the Remnant Church as she comes to a measure of the stature of the fullness of Christ. When the Church arrives at her predestined position of being the embodiment of the power of God in His earthly tabernacle, she will effect change in the governments of the nations. She will exert the influence of the King of kings, and Lord of lords. The Remnant Church will truly exercise the influence of Christ, as His delegated authority and designated representative in the earth. She will operate as an ambassador for the Kingdom of Heaven. With Christ as her Lord the Remnant Church will seek to exert the principles of the government that is taking place in the Kingdom of Heaven and the Kingdom of God, upon the governments of the earth. Even as the people in Biblical times took note that the disciples had been in the presence of Christ, even so the nations will recognize the believers who exemplify that the fullness of Christ is in them. When it's all said and done, the governmental rulers of the nations will not be able to deny the authority of the Remnant Church. She will occupy a place of prominence because of the power of Christ in her midst.

As the world experiences the increasing chaos that will accompany the end of the age, they will look for hope and divine intervention. The fullness of Christ in His remnant will provide that hope and intervention. Christ will be recommended as the solution to all things. Whether the problems are physical, emotional, financial, psychological, medical, or educational; Jesus will be the initial solution prescribed to remedy the issue. Prayer and help from Jehovah will no longer be the last ditch solution, but will become sought as the primary source of assistance.

The Remnant Church will evolve into an organism that becomes all things to all men. Her display of power will be continually observable for all to see. As well as affecting religion and international politics, she will also have a direct effect on non-Christians. This remnant will operate at a time when the Body of Christ has been fully restored to her place of apostolic authority. She will be operating in the same vibrant strength as the first century Church. Signs, wonders, and miracles will be the supernatural natural norm at operation in the Bride of Christ; the Remnant Church. While the world is reeling from the effects of the satanic revival and revolution at the end of time; non-believers will be searching for a way of escape. Non-Christians will be seeking refuge from the release of wickedness in the earth. They will have begun to realize the reality of satan, evil, demons, satanic oppression and possession. This realization will happen because God's desire is that none should perish, but that all should come to repentance.

"The Lord is not slack concerning His promise, as some men count slackness, but is longsuffering to us-ward, not willing that any should perish, but that all should come to repentance." II Peter 3:9

THE REMNANT CHURCH

He allowed the fullness of the Godhead to be manifested in Christ.

Beware lest any man spoil you through philosophy and vain deceit, after the traditions of men, after the rudiments of the world, and not after Christ. For in Him dwelleth all the fulness of the Godhead bodily.
Colossians 2: 8-9

Every good and perfect thing that Jehovah desires for His creation is wrapped up in Christ. The relief from evil that non-Christians will seek, will only be found in Christ. He is the be all and end all to every crisis non-believers will face at the end of the age. He is the solution the Remnant Church will propose to non-Christians, as they seek refuge from the demonic attack they will be experiencing. As the Remnant Church posters herself for the battle of the ages, she will shine forth as the agent of Christ's mission to deliver us from evil.

The Remnant Church exists to denounce and destroy Ecumenical Christianity. The Ecumenical Movement is a vehicle that recommends going to a one world religion. The United Nations, which was created and is controlled by The Council on Foreign Relations, is highly involved in bringing to fruition a One World Religion, as part of a New World Order. The New World Order is the forerunner system of government for the coming Antichrist. These past decades have seen the founding of the World Council of Churches after World War II and the increased activity of the National Council of Churches in the United States.[166]

CHAPTER EIGHT: ALL THINGS IN CHRIST

Ecumenism a religious movement that seeks to unite all Christians and bring the various denominations together in mutual cooperation. The word comes from the Greek 'oikoumene', which means "the whole inhabited world." Christians should be "eager to maintain the unity of the Spirit in the bond of peace." I therefore, the prisoner of the Lord, beseech you that ye walk worthy of the vocation wherewith ye are called. With all lowliness and meekness, with longsuffering, forbearing one another in love; Endeavoring the keep the unity of the spirit in the bond of peace. Ephesians 4: 1-3

Christ's desire is that we may all be one, just as the Father, is in Him, and He is in the Father. So, biblically, Christians should pursue unity with one another. How does this apply to the contemporary ecumenical movement?[167]

Neither pray I for these alone, but for them also which shall believe on me through their word; That they may be one; as thou, Father, art in me, and I in thee, that they also may be one in us: that the world may believe that thou hast sent me. John 17: 20-21

Jesus said, "I am the way, the truth, and the life; no man cometh to the Father but by me." The modern ecumenical movement often goes beyond uniting Christians and seeks to connect Protestants, Catholics, and non-Christian religions. Modern ecumenical leaders promote "interfaith dialogue" with Mormons, Islamists, Hindus, Buddhists, Wiccans, Universalists, and a variety of New Age belief systems. Such efforts are at odds with the concept of Christian unity as presented in Scripture. While there is room for discussion with those outside of

THE REMNANT CHURCH

Christianity; to accept all religions as equally valid is to deny the uniqueness of Jesus and the Christian faith. For example, recent attempts to bridge differences between Protestant and Catholic theology have included joint statements on salvation and the inspiration of Scripture. To sign a statement that compromises core biblical teaching is dangerous. Doctrines such as salvation by grace alone[168] and the authority of Scripture[169] should not be compromised for the sake of a synthetic unity.[170]

The foundation for this ecumenical trend has been laid and built upon over many years. We saw the beginning of institutional ecumenism in the 1960's, with The World Council of Churches. This is an organization of mostly liberal mainline Protestant denominations who denied such essential doctrines as the inerrancy of Scripture and a literal, bodily resurrection of Christ. For years, Evangelicals distanced themselves from this institutional ecumenism because of the unsound theology of the groups involved.

Today, however, that spirit of compromise has invaded Evangelicalism. The recent Catholic-Evangelical accord is an example of such compromise. In this accord, Evangelicals compromised essential doctrines such as justification by faith alone and the sufficiency of Scripture in order to unite with Roman Catholics on issues such as abortion and school prayer.[171]

The Ecumenical Movement is a prelude set up for the one-world religion, one world economy, and one world government the beast will seek to initiate as an answer to the economic collapse of world markets.

This collapse will be the impetus for the nations of the world to seek an entity or person to save it from total destruction. Enter

CHAPTER EIGHT: ALL THINGS IN CHRIST

the beast...that ten nation confederacy that will claim to be the world's savior. With access to the tracking system that monitors world population, The Beast 666 computer was reportedly located in Brussels, Belgium, and with the consent of the world's governments, the beast will be positioned to make everyone take its mark. This bar code on a computerized microchip, with human flesh compatibility, is already in existence. As far-fetched as this scenario sounds, it is 100% within the realm of possibility. The international stock market crash of 2008 should have served as an example of how easy it will be for the world to accept this type of global intervention. The Remnant Church must cry loud and spare not, against the dangers of a one world religion. An ecumenical church will make it too easy for the beast / anti-Christ spirit to invade the earth and deceive the nations into receiving this counterfeit religious organization. Contrary to the popular saying, all roads DO NOT lead to Rome. The Bible states that there is a way that seems right unto man, but the end thereof are the ways of death. The mature, unified Body of Christ is obligated to wage a counterattack against the dangerous concept of an ecumenical church.

Jesus is the cornerstone and foundation on which the structure of the Church is built. It is His Church. The Church is firmly fit together to function synergistically as a cohesive unit. Her aim is the same as Jesus' incursion into time from eternity. Her single focused purpose should be the same as His was and is, "to destroy the works of the devil." Every function that the Remnant Church seeks to represent and operate can be seen in Christ. He is the perfect model that the Church must emulate;

THE REMNANT CHURCH

all things in Him. Being the head of the Body, it is He who sends signals to the Body as to how they should operate. Jesus Christ is the spiritual embodiment of what the Remnant Church should be. This Church should be actively engaged in the deliverance, healing, and prophetic ministries. She should represent the aggregation of God's people who are called together as citizens of the Kingdom of God.

The Remnant's focus should be on worshipping God and carrying out His agenda in the earth for His creation. God's purpose has always been to have a people who maintain intimate fellowship with Him; and serve as His delegated authority and designated representatives in the earth. Separation from the world's morals, and values must be inherent in the Remnant's nature and character. The Remnant Church has to be absolutely separated from unrighteousness and worldly immorality. The Church is married to Christ; she must maintain devotion and faithfulness to Him. She must totally love Him and constantly develop and increase her intimacy with Him. There must be spiritual fellowship among the members of the Remnant Church. Unity in the Spirit, baptism in the Spirit, love and care for one another, a free flow of the gifts and fruits of the Spirit is mandatory; if the Remnant Church is to reflect the character of Christ for the world to see. The Remnant Church is an extension of the army of heaven; waging spiritual warfare on earth. She uses the sword of the spirit and the Word of God to battle against Satan, his army, and sin. The Remnant Church is the foundational pillar for truth, and must operate in all the truth that Messiah Jesus brought into our sphere of time, from

CHAPTER EIGHT: ALL THINGS IN CHRIST

His sphere of eternity.

In addition to being God in the flesh, Christ is: the Great High Priest; the only mediator between God and man; the Great Shepherd; King of the Kingdom; the accurate Prophet; and the Anointed One. The Remnant Church must also function in some of these capacities. She must serve as a priest and go to God on the people's behalf. She must not only be able to give an accurate prophetic word, but she must be able to go to the people on God's behalf. The Remnant Church must be able to lead the sheep to the place where the grass is green and the waters are still; a place of healthy, edible, and digestible teaching. This Church must be able to govern its members with the anointed administration of the Holy Spirit of Jehovah. Since all things are in Christ, the Remnant Church must be as Christ was and is. Her character must be: holy; righteous; just; guileless; sinless; spotless; innocent; gentle; forgiving; merciful; and humble.

> "This Church must be able to govern its members with the anointed administration of the Holy Spirit of Jehovah."

Although the Church is comprised of many members, it is the Father's desire that we all come to the unity of the faith, and of the knowledge, or appreciation, of the Son of God. She must grow into a perfect, or mature man; or member. She must grow unto the measure, or limited portion we can attain of the stature, or maturity of the fullness, of that which is put in to be the piece that fulfills the full fullness of Christ. So, the Remnant Church must be delivered from the dogmas and doctrines that cause us to be divided along ideological differences. Denominations have more in common than they have differences. The differences in the way we worship should not be enough to keep us divided. We must forge a united front to combat the forces of darkness. The Church can never come forward conquering victorious as long as we remain splintered among man-made dogmas and interpretations of scripture. We must learn to be all things in Christ. Every member has a role to play, but our goal has to be singular. We must be more focused on waging war against the kingdom of darkness than we are on proving the "rightness" of our denominational dogma and doctrine. Our goal has to be to blend our spiritual and physical resources into one spiritual armory; to battle the prince of darkness and his emissaries.

The aggressive engagement in active spiritual warfare of the Remnant Church will have a direct impact on the timing of the second coming of Christ. While we are well aware that the time and season of His coming is in the Father's hand, we are also aware of the part the Church plays in God's timetable. As we move towards the fulfillment of 'The Time of the Gentiles', we will see an increase in demonic activity in the earth. As time comes to a close and the devil realizes that his time is short, he will accelerate his efforts to ensnare people and corral them into hell. We will see The Great Tribulation unfold and the enemy of our soul wage war against the saints and prevail against them. As this onslaught of evil is unleashed upon the inhabitants of the earth, saints world-wide will begin to intercede for the Church and the residents of the sphere of time. Deliverance will become more commonplace in our local assemblies. Active engagement of the people of God against the kingdom of darkness will become

CHAPTER EIGHT: ALL THINGS IN CHRIST

the rule, versus being the exception. Although our efforts will be valiant and ongoing, (according to scripture) they will not be totally successful. For the Bible all tells us that the beast was given power to war against the saints; and to prevail against them. We cannot overlook this fact. The Lord of Lords and King of Kings intervenes right in the nick of time and saves the people of God; the Remnant Church. Subsequently the second coming of Christ will be directly impacted by the level of warfare the Remnant Church is waging against the beast and his minions. Therefore we can see why it is imperative for the Remnant Church to mature and grow up. She must blossom into the uncompromised, non-conflicted, Body of believers manifesting the power and character of her head, Jesus Christ. She must be properly equipped to wage spiritual war against the fallen angels and demons that will fight on Satan's behalf. The only way this can happen is if the Remnant Church becomes all things in Christ.

THE REMNANT CHURCH

Chapter Nine

Those of us who are alive and remain

"For this we say unto you by the word of the Lord, that we which are alive and remain unto the coming of the Lord shall not prevent them which are asleep. For the Lord himself shall descend from heaven with a shout, with the voice of the archangel, and with the trump of God: and the dead in Christ shall rise first: Then we which are alive and remain shall be caught up together with them in the clouds, to meet the Lord in the air: and so shall we ever be with the Lord. Wherefore comfort one another with these words."
I Thessalonians 4:15-18

"Behold, I shew you a mystery; we shall not all sleep, but we shall be changed, In a moment, in the twinkling of an eye, at the last trump, for the trumpet shall sound, and the dead shall be raised incorruptible, and we shall be changed. For this corruptible must put on incorruption, and this mortal must put on immortality."
I Corinthians 15:51-53

THE REMNANT CHURCH

The Remnant Church is a concept that is critical for the compromised, deceived Church to understand and accept. She is an organism, a living entity, that remains in the earth after the wrath of God has been poured out on the devil, his minions, and those who have chosen to follow him. The "remnant" is a concept that is currently being discussed in Christendom, and is actually gaining acceptance among those who are tired of "church as usual." The idea of there being a group of believers who separate themselves for a higher, more intense, form of ministry is rapidly gaining popularity within the Body of Christ. This cadre of "servant warriors" must consecrate themselves in an extraordinary manner, if they are to truly be effective in carrying out the mission of this entity known as The Remnant Church. They must have the same level of commitment and consecration as those monks in Nepal; who thirty years ago, were able to melt snow in a circumference ten feet around themselves. The believers who have chosen to be a part of the remnant must be equipped to actively participate in deliverance ministry on an on-going basis. They must not only know how to "get in the Spirit"; but they must also be willing to stay in the Spirit. They can ill-afford to operate in the flesh or according to their sensual, secular knowledge.

The Remnant Church must possess the same intestinal fortitude the Israelites had, as they isolated themselves in Goshen, while Jehovah poured out His wrath on the inhabitants of Egypt. We need to begin to understand that the Jew's release from bondage, and ultimate freedom, was as a result of the plagues experienced by the Egyptians; while the Hebrews remained unscathed. The

CHAPTER NINE: THOSE OF US WHO ARE LIVE AND REMAIN

fact that the Jews were unaffected by the plagues made Pharaoh want to remove them from his country. Understanding this, we can further comprehend why it is necessary for the Church to be prepared to go through the Great Tribulation. Though the idea of being on the earth as the wrath of God is poured out on humanity is extremely unpleasant, it is consistent with His manner of dealing with mankind all throughout history. Additionally, if God removes the Church and His Spirit from the earth before the Great Tribulation, then who will be in the earth to lead non-believers to Christ during the Tribulation? Who will be there to help insure that "all of Israel will be saved?"

Those who are alive and do remain until God raises the dead in Christ and changes the living mortals into the living immortals, are essential to the evangelization of Jews and Gentiles alike. They are to be key pieces in God's plan to redeem humanity during the most devastating time it will ever experience. The Remnant Church is a critical part of the puzzle, as God's plan for the end of the age unfurls with cataclysmic impact upon the world. She is a key player in the strategy to provoke Israel to jealousy, and an acceptance of her Messiah; Jesus of Nazareth. The Remnant Church is the stabilizing mechanism Jehovah has chosen to provide a refuge and shelter for those seeking salvation during the Great Tribulation. She is a part of the "witness" that will serve to demonstrate the power of God to deliver, even in the midst of seemingly impossible circumstances.

There is a vital need for us to realize that according to scripture, there is going to be a remnant that remains in the earth until the dead in Christ rise from the grave. According to Scripture, not man's doctrine, that great catching away, or rapture, doesn't happen until the sound of the "last trump." It is only then that the dead in Christ shall rise. For those who are in the earth until the dead in Christ rise, there are apocalyptic events that will have taken place. Those saints will have experienced and lived through these happenings. So, one of the first things we must do, as we search for biblical truth concerning this concept, is to determine when the dead in Christ rise. What is the time period in which this occurrence happens? In the process of us taking a hard look at the timing of the resurrection of the dead in Christ, we will notice a laundry list of cataclysmic events that have taken place. If we are to truly gauge what has transpired up until their resurrection, we must maintain an open mind. We cannot approach this topic with preconceived notions about the rapture and the second coming of Christ. We must be totally open to accept what the Scriptures say about this event. We can ill-afford to allow doctrines conceived as rebuttals to the truth of the Word of God, to frame our viewpoint of how God plans to end the ages. So, as we close out this book with this final chapter, we will take a microscopic view of this controversial topic.

> *"We can ill-afford to allow doctrines conceived as rebuttals to the truth of the Word of God..."*

It is also imperative to do a word study on the word "last" as it is used in these prophetic scriptures referencing the "rapture." These scriptures also deal with the resurrection of the dead and those of us who remain. As we do so, we find out that this word "last" speaks to the finality of that trumpet. It is the last one that sounds. There are no more trumpets that will sound

CHAPTER NINE: THOSE OF US WHO ARE LIVE AND REMAIN

after that one. What does that mean for those who are alive and do remain? It means that if they are alive at the sound of that last trump, they have lived through and experienced everything that happened with all the trumpets that preceded that trumpet. It means that they have experienced everything that happened on the earth and in the heavens as those other trumpets were sounded. It means that they have lived through the Great Tribulation and the war that the "beast" has waged against the saints; in which the beast prevailed. It means they have witnessed and lived through the martyrdom of the saints. It means they have escaped being a part of the great number that John saw. They have avoided being one of those who have come up out of great tribulation; whose robes are washed white in the blood of the Lamb.

Revelation 7: 9-17 gives us the account of the saints John saw, coming up out of the Great Tribulation, after the Jewish servants of God were sealed. Those sealed servants being comprised of the members from the twelve tribes of Israel. After those servants are sealed and the multitude coming up out of the Great Tribulation are revealed, then the seventh seal is opened and the seven angels are given the seven trumpets. As we take note of *Revelation 11: 15-19*, we see the sounding of the seventh trumpet; the last one. Paying particular attention to *verse 18*, we see that this is the time that the dead are judged.

"And the nations were angry, and thy wrath is come, and the time of the dead, that they should be judged, and that thou shouldest give reward unto thy servants the prophets, and to the saints, and them that fear thy name, small and great; and shouldest destroy them that destroy the earth."
Revelation 11:18

THE REMNANT CHURCH

This is when the dead in Christ shall rise. This is when those who are alive and do remain are changed in a moment, in the twinkling of an eye. This is the time of the seventh trump; the last trumpet. The last trump sounds after the Great Tribulation. The Remnant Church survives the Great Tribulation, she navigates her way through it; much like the first century Church survived in the Catacombs during the Roman persecution. For further clarification we should look at:

"Immediately after the tribulation of those days shall the sun be darkened, and the moon shall not give her light, and the stars shall fall from heaven, and the powers of the heavens shall be shaken: And then shall appear the sign of the Son of man in heaven: and then shall all the tribes of the earth mourn, and they shall see the Son of man coming in the clouds of heaven with power and great glory. And He shall send His angels with a great sound of a trumpet, and they shall gather together His elect from the four winds, from one end of heaven to the other." Matthew 24: 29-31

It's plain to see that Jesus doesn't gather His elect until after the Tribulation of those days. The tribulation of those days is a direct reference to what was stated in the *21st and 22nd verses* of that same chapter.

"For then shall be great tribulation, such as was not since the beginning of the world to this time, no, nor ever shall be. And except those days should be shortened, there should no flesh be saved: but for the elect's sake those days shall be shortened."
Matthew 24:21-22

So, first the Great Tribulation, then the "catching away" of

CHAPTER NINE: THOSE OF US WHO ARE LIVE AND REMAIN

the Remnant Church. There are many different views concerning the Great Tribulation. How long will it last? Who will be affected by it? However, if anyone has the 411 on the Great Tribulation, it would be safe to say that Jesus does. Therefore, we offer *Matthew 24: 14-22* and *Matthew 24: 29-31* for your consideration.

There are three primary opinions, and groups, concerning the Great Tribulation and the rapture. The largest group belongs to the Pre-Tribulation opinion. They believe that the rapture will happen before the seven year Great Tribulation. The next largest group belongs to the Mid-Tribulation opinion. They believe that the rapture will happen midway into the Great Tribulation; or three and one half years into that occurrence. The smallest group belongs to the Post-Tribulation opinion. They believe that the rapture will happen at the end of the Great Tribulation.

It is interesting to note however, that prior to the Council of Trent, held in Northern Italy during 1545-1563, there was not even any discussion about a seven year tribulation period. The Council of Trent was a Roman Catholic attempt to refute the accusations of the Protestant Reformers. It produced a Jesuit based strategy to move the second coming of Christ from the last day, to a period in front of a seven year Great Tribulation. Prior to this ecumenical council of the Catholic church, it was commonly believed that the "catching away" of the Church, the second coming of Christ, would happen at the end of time; the last day.[172] John Nelson Darby, the father of Modern Dispensationalism, was a strong promoter of a Pre-Tribulation rapture. He strongly influenced Cyrus Ingerson Scofield. Scofield, who was the publisher of the popular Scofield

Reference Bible, injected large doses of Futurism, pre-tribulation Jesuit-based philosophy, into the footnotes of his Bible. This Bible became extremely popular in American Protestant Bible schools; such as Moody Bible Institute and Dallas Theological Seminary. So, this Jesuit spawned theory to reposition the second coming of Christ from its initial Bible-based location at the end of time, to a location directly in front of the Great Tribulation with a questionable time period of seven years; was successfully launched in the United States.[173]

As it pertains to Jesus' prophecy about the Great Tribulation in the 24th chapter of Matthew, He states that the sign to look for, as an indication that we are about to enter the Great Tribulation, is the Abomination of Desolation spoken of in Daniel.

"And after threescore and two weeks shall Messiah be cut off, but not for himself; and the people of the prince that shall come shall destroy the city and the sanctuary; and the end thereof shall be with a flood, and unto the end the war desolations are determined. And he shall confirm the covenant with many for one week; and in the midst of the week he shall cause the sacrifice and oblation to cease, and for the overspreading of abominations he shall make it desolate, even unto the consummation, and that determined shall be poured upon the desolate."
Daniel 9:26-27

There are those who believe that the Abomination of Desolation has already been fulfilled. They refer to the carnage created by Antiochus IV Epiphanes from 168-167 B.C. and the Roman general Titus in 70 A.D. as evidence of the fulfillment. Nonetheless, as we note that Jesus associated the Great Tribulation

CHAPTER NINE: THOSE OF US WHO ARE LIVE AND REMAIN

with the Abomination of Desolation, neither of these events could be the fulfillment of that prophecy since they both deal strictly with the Jewish people. The account in Revelation, speaking of those coming out of the Great Tribulation, describe this multitude being comprised of all nations, kindreds, peoples, and tongues.[174]

Considering the Abomination of Desolation as a future event mandates that two things happen in the nation of Israel. First and foremost, it will be necessary to have the Temple rebuilt on the Temple Mount in Jerusalem. Secondarily, it will be necessary for Israel to reinstitute live animal sacrifice as a part of their daily worship in that Temple. Contemplate the following facts:

There has been a movement and continuous effort to rebuild the Temple since 1967. Shortly before the reunification of Jerusalem in 1967, an ad appeared in the Washington Post calling for Jews worldwide to unite to rebuild the Temple of God in Jerusalem.

Jewish priests in Israel have been in training to perform live animal sacrifice since 1992. Live animal sacrifice has been practiced in remote parts of Israel since 2004. In 2018, two live animal sacrifices were performed at the base of the Temple Mount in Jerusalem. The stage is set for the conditions to open the door for the Abomination of Desolation to take place. All that is needed is for the anti-Christ and Beast to appear on the world stage. Just be on the lookout for the beginning of the construction of the Third Temple in Jerusalem. A prominent Jewish architect stated that with current technology, the Temple could be completely constructed in about eighteen months.

Please bear in mind that Jesus said that He would raise up those who will receive everlasting life at the "last day"; and that His coming would be after the Great Tribulation. If the Church is raptured out before the Great Tribulation, and if the Holy Spirit is removed before the Tribulation and the anti-Christ is revealed....then how will people be saved during the Great Tribulation? If there is no Body of Christ to spread the gospel message, and no Holy Spirit to convict and draw people to repentance and translate them into the family of God, the Church....then how does the salvation process happen during the Great Tribulation? If these two ministries are not in place after the Great Tribulation, then how does the great multitude in Revelation, that John could not number, get drawn to the cross of Christ; the sacrificial Lamb of God?

Those who are alive and do remain unto the second coming of Christ are truly the Remnant Church. They are those whom the Spirit of God has left in the earth to be a witness of the Gospel that has the power to deliver creation from eternal destruction in a devil's hell. The Remnant Church has been empowered to be a safe haven for those who have been converted to Christ, as a result of the Great Tribulation. Those who remain are a part of the Church that has been committed to perfecting holiness. They have found out that holiness is the only way to be empowered to be sustained through the Great Tribulation. They are those who have abandoned their agenda and exchanged their purpose for His purpose. They are sold out to being a part of the labor force that truly brings in the "last harvest." They are the

CHAPTER NINE: THOSE OF US WHO ARE LIVE AND REMAIN

Remnant Church who are serving as ministers of reconciliation and ambassadors of the Kingdom of God in the earth. In the midst of catastrophic chaos and confusion, they are committed to be witnesses of the saving grace of Jesus Christ.

Members of this assembly are those who have been trained in spiritual warfare. The Remnant Church has her spiritual weapons mastered and on point, by way of use and discernment. Those who are alive and do remain are those who have acclimated their behavior to a heavenly standard. They have spent their salvation experience walking and living by the boundaries of the Kingdom of God. Therefore they are those who will not experience cultural shock as they transition from time into eternity. The Remnant Church will easily blend into the invading Army of Heaven, as it accompanies the King of kings and Lord of lords upon His return. As the dead in Christ rise and our mortal bodies are changed into immortality, we will meet our Savior in the air. The scripture says, "So we will ever be with Him." As He continues His journey from eternity into the sphere of time for the second time...we will be with Him. As He executes the Father's final judgment and attack against the kingdom of darkness...we will be with Him. As Jesus carries out the Father's promise of victory for the covenant people of the Most High God Jehovah, the Remnant Church will be with Him.

> *"The Remnant Church has been empowered to be a safe haven for those who have been converted to Christ, as a result of the Great Tribulation."*

The Remnant Church that is alive and remaining at the last day will be battle tested. This aggregation of believers will have survived persecution and the Great Tribulation. They will have remained "faithful and focused" on enduring to the end, in order to finish their mission. These stalwart Christians will have remained faithful and not become a part of the great apostasy. As a result of their steadfastness, they will be qualified to join the invading forces of the Army of Heaven. Their unwavering determination to destroy the works of the enemy will result in their successful spiritual functioning; and make room for them to join their comrades in arms. The Remnant Church will seamlessly and effortlessly blend into the attacking force of the eternal saints Yeshua is bringing to execute judgment and wrath on the prince of darkness. This remnant will be adept, skillful warriors; vested in fasting, prayer, sanctification, and holiness. They will be well capable of wielding the weapons of spiritual and natural warfare against the forces of darkness. This Remnant Church will be bold, fiery servant warriors of the Ancient of Days who are intent upon engaging in the spiritual warfare necessary to accomplish the purpose of God on the last day. They will be willing warriors who don't need to be coerced into fighting the forces of satan. The Remnant Church will be those who readily yield themselves to God as vessels available to be dispatched as combatants in the war of evil; willing to fight satanic forces on one hand, and restore lost humanity on the other. Those of us remaining will be the sanctified, consecrated, holy and righteous ones who have not taken the mark of the beast, nor bowed to his image.

It is important to note that it is not called 'the mark of the anti-Christ', it's called 'the mark of the beast'. There is a very

CHAPTER NINE: THOSE OF US WHO ARE LIVE AND REMAIN

important reason for that. In order for those who do remain and are alive to effectively function in their intended capacity, it is imperative to differentiate between the beast and anti-Christ. The fact is that there is a marked difference between the two. The term anti-Christ used five times in the Scriptures, by the Apostle John, translates to the Greek word 'antichristios'. The meaning of this word is, "an opponent of the Messiah." John did truly recognize that one would come and oppose Christ and try to purport himself to be 'the Christ'. However, when the Apostle was speaking in the second and third chapters of I John, he was writing to wayward first century Post Pentecost disciples. These errant and rebellious disciples had:

- Denied that Jesus existed in eternity before time began
- Left the Church and did not continue in the Apostle's Doctrine
- Denied the Father and that Jesus IS the Christ Messiah
- Began teaching the false doctrine of Gnosticism and that access to God could be acquired by a means other than acceptance of Christ Jesus
- Denied the Trinity; and that Jesus was God manifested in bodily form;
- Become the enemy and antagonist of Christ
- Denied and repudiated Christ
- Seduced Christians and led them away from sound doctrine and truth[175]

According to Steve Wohlberg, author of "End Times Delusions" & "Truth Left Behind, A Study Into The Left Behind

Deception," as a result of the Council of Trent in the 1500's, a Jesuit priest and doctor of theology, Francisco Ribera published a commentary on the book of Revelation in 1590. He relegated John's vision to a period happening at the end of time. He asserted that AntiMessiah or The Antichrist would be a single evil person received by the Jews; who would rebuild Jerusalem. This was birthed out of the Catholic Church's determination to refute the Protestant Reformers claims that the Roman Catholic Church and the Pope himself were in fact the Antichrist.[176]

It is extremely important for us to realize that the "spirit" of antichrist has been released into the earth since the days of the twelve Apostles. If we ignore this fact, we minimize the danger of those groups, organizations, and people who possess that spirit. The danger that exists is that if we are so focused on identifying one single person as the Antichrist, we will fail to see all the other people and organizations that are in fact antichrist (against Christ) & possess the spirit that is "preparing" the world to accept that single person who will come on the scene and be received as a savior and answer to civilization's quest for world peace.; and a true identification a "higher power." We must fight the temptation to identify the one person who is the Antichrist, while ignoring all the destructive agents possessing the "spirit" of antichrist; which are undermining the spiritual fabric of Christianity. Satan would have us to focus on all the acts of the beast as the works of the Antichrist. Why would we choose to call the beast something that God has not called him? The fact is that there are a number of persons, social organizations, and governmental agencies that are currently working, both

CHAPTER NINE: THOSE OF US WHO ARE LIVE AND REMAIN

separately and collectively to deceive and destroy God's chosen people, the Jews; and God's redeemed people, the Church. We must acknowledge and understand that there are spiritual forces aligned against God's purpose. They have an agenda that is anti-Jewish and anti-Christian. They are seeking to implement a New World Order that is intent on destroying Judeo-Christian principles world-wide.

We find it noteworthy that the Apostle John, the Revelator, the only author to use the term antichrist never used it once in another book he authored, the book of Revelation. The Book of Revelation is considered the exhaustive blueprint for the end of time and the events that happen during the Great Tribulation; yet the word "Antichrist" fails to appear there. Instead, we find the word "the beast" used in reference to the acts the modern Church attributes to the anti-Christ.[177] We submit that ten nations will align themselves with the Beast; and the Beast will destroy the Catholic Church. These ten nations will control the world economy.

Let's take a look at how Apostle John describes the works of the beast, which the Church has erroneously attributed to the anti-Christ. Reader, please note that these works and descriptions are specifically attributed to the beast of Revelation. The beast is:
- Allowed to speak great blasphemies against God
- Miraculously healed
- Given authority to do whatever he wants for three and one half years
- Allowed to wage war against God's people
- Given authority to rule over every tribe, people, language and

nation
- Allowed to conquer God's people
- Worshipped by all the people in the world
- Is demonstrated to have the allegiance of the people who worship him, because the false prophet (the second beast) commands the people to receive the mark of the beast on their right hand or forehead; and they obey that command[178]

The people of the world give the beast their allegiance. He slanders God's name, His dwelling, and His people. The beast exhibits contempt, insult, and lack of respect for Jehovah God. An addition to all of this, the beast claims the attributes of God for himself. It should be plain to see that the reality of our battle against anti-Christ is now, as opposed to some distant time in the future. Our battle in the future is against the beast.

> *"The Remnant Church will in no way be afraid of deliverance ministry."*

Those who are alive and do remain will not shy away from spiritual confrontation. The Remnant Church will in no way be afraid of deliverance ministry. Instead, she will be positioned for a full frontal attack; knowing that to die is gain. She will be confident in the power at work within her; because she knows she is untainted and uncompromised. She is not conflicted; she knows her role and who is in charge of the attack. These saints will not be those who doubt their ability to be used by God. They will not have a compromised relationship with our Savior, encumbered by sin, and deceived by the forces of darkness. Nor will they be conflicted as to what their purpose is.

CHAPTER NINE: THOSE OF US WHO ARE LIVE AND REMAIN

Conversely, they will be resolute in their relationship with God and tenacious on the battlefield for our Lord. They will be on point, and in alignment with the purposes of Jehovah; resolute in their determination to endure until the end.

The Remnant Church will know her place in God, and in the Body of Christ; and be assured of her destiny to accomplish Jehovah's expected end for her. She will be obedient to the commands of the Holy Spirit and Messiah Jesus as the Army of Heaven marches forward. She is confident that she is a part of those who will be added to that great uncountable number that came up out of the Great Tribulation. Additionally, she wholeheartedly believes that she will be added to the myriad of angels also found in this invading force from heaven. She will be welcomed by the patriarchs of old who died in faith that God would keep His promise and send the Messiah. The disciples that suffered and died at the hands of the Roman government will extend their welcome to this Remnant Church; as she joins the ranks of that great heavenly host being led by the King of kings.

As we ponder joining the ranks of this heavenly host, we lean on the Scriptures located in I Corinthians 15:51-55 and I Thessalonians 4:13-5:2 as the basis for our brief discussion. The scriptures in the 15th chapter of 1st Corinthians primarily deals with several things:
- Resurrections.
- The resurrection of the dead.
- The resurrection of the body.
- Earthly bodies vs. heavenly bodies.

While the scriptures in the fouth chapter of 1st Thessalonians primarily deals with these followings things:
- The second coming of Christ.
- The hope of the resurrection.
- When Jesus comes back again, God brings back with Jesus all the Christians who have died.
- The dead in Christ will rise first to meet Him in the air.
- Then those Christians who are still alive will be transformed and meet Jesus and the dead in Christ who have risen in the air.[179]

The second coming of Christ is usually commonly referred to as either, "The Day of the Lord" or "The Last Day."[180] Jesus is coming again to gather His own and bring judgment on the ungodly.[181] Please note that the Scriptures never refer to multiple comings of Christ that go beyond His first and second advents. The Bible equates the gathering of believers with second coming of Christ. There is no mention in the scriptures of a third or fouth coming. Everything that is associated with the second coming of Christ happens simultaneously. Therefore we must understand that everything that is associated with His second advent happens at the same time..."the Last Day."

Those who remain until the resurrection of the dead will have a chance to participate in all of the glory associated with the "last day." We are reminded of the words of Jesus as He tells of when He will give the fullness of eternal life to those who receive Him as Savior. He plainly states when He will give that eternal reward.[182] As the dead in Christ rise, the Day of the Lord will be

CHAPTER NINE: THOSE OF US WHO ARE LIVE AND REMAIN

in full effect. The judgment of the world will be beginning as we who are alive are transformed into our celestial bodies. As the creation shakes and quakes at the coming of the Lord, and nature reverberates as her creator once again steps onto the world scene; the Remnant Church is part of His supporting cast. We are there to witness the culmination of the ages. We step onto the world stage with Him, as the Bride of Christ; the New Jerusalem where the Spirit of God dwells. We represent the conclusion of the sphere time, and are a sign that "the fulness of the Gentiles" has been accomplished. The time to receive God's forgiveness and salvation is now finished. It's time for Him to receive all of His holy people...The Jewish Church and the Gentile Church; the Body of Christ. The time of His grace has come to an end. It is now judgment time. The final trumpet has sounded and heaven is coming to earth; but only after every vestige of evil has been eradicated. The Remnant Church stands poised to be a part of Jehovah's final solution to the "sin problem."

In conclusion, those members of the Remnant Church who remain, and are alive at the second coming of Christ, are people who have chosen to make themselves available to help evangelize those who have experienced the Great Tribulation. They also understand that God's plan for redemption started with the Jews and will conclude with the Jews. The Remnant Church accepts the fact that Messiah Jesus was always predestined to be of Jewish descent; and that the first century New Testament Church was always predestined to be an outgrowth of Judaism. She appreciates that the choice of the Hebrew people to be the progenitors of the patriarchs and Messiah was not an afterthought of Jehovah; as He decided on how to deal with what happened in the Garden of Eden. These Christians comprehend the evidence that the Church originated out of the Jewish people, was shared with the Gentile world, and will ultimately stand as the vessel that once again houses God's chosen people; when all of Israel shall be saved.

The viewpoint that the first century New Testament Church was birthed out of Judaism, with her foundation being built upon Jewish apostles and prophets, Jesus Christ Himself being the chief cornerstone is critical. It is essential in order for the Remnant Church to fully understand the role she plays in the redemption of the nation of Israel, as it experiences the Great Tribulation. To be a member of this Church, to be alive and remaining at the second coming, will not be popular, convenient, or glamorous. It will require a person to have such a serious commitment to Christ, that they are willing to lose their life. It will be similar to the persecution the first century Church received at the hands of the Jews and Roman government. This persecution will serve as a screening filter to help determine who is serious enough about their commitment to change their lifestyle to conform to the level of holiness needed to function in this capacity. A high level of holiness is compulsory to differentiate the Remnant Church from the contemporary deceived, conforming, compromised Church.

In addition to being willing to minister to non-Jews, those who are alive and do remain until His coming must be willing to minister the Gospel to the Jewish nation. Paul reminds us that there will be a remnant of Jews who will be instrumental in accomplishing the evangelization of Israel. Those Jews will first have to believe that Yahweh's covenant promises are yet extended to His chosen people. Even though the Jews had refused to accept their Messiah, Jesus of Nazareth, God still had intentions of making salvation available to the Jews. These remnant Jews and the Remnant Church represents an assurance that God will always leave Himself a "witness." He will always allow a portion to remain who will reflect His nature and purpose. Jehovah utilizes those who remain to represent Him, as reflected in their possession of the holiness and integrity necessary to influence non-believers to accept His accepted form of salvation; in Jesus Christ. In the midst of Tribulation calamity, these two remnant groups represent groups who will not bow to worldly pressures, ethics, and behaviors. It is a reminder that the Remnant Church is only a recipient of God's covenant promises because of her relationship with the nation of Israel. It is only because the Remnant Church has been grafted into the commonwealth of Israel that she can boast of inclusion into provisions of Jehovah's grace, holiness, and power.

Therefore, it is imperative to recognize that those Gentiles who are alive and do remain are intrinsically related to the people of Israel. It is mandatory to acknowledge the Remnant Church's inherent Jewish foundation; and inescapable attachment to God's chosen people. To attempt to do otherwise is ludicrous. It is also obligatory for the Remnant Church to interpret apocalyptic prophecies through a Jewish filter; having the nation of Israel as the central focus of those prophecies. Jehovah is making abundantly clear, on many different platforms, that His plan for the end of the age and the Church cannot come to pass without Israel playing a major part in it. The Remnant Church must intentionally correlate her root to the rock from which she springs...Israel; the Jewish nation. It is impossible to examine eschatological truths without admitting the fundamental Hebrew composition of the prophets, apostles, disciples, supporting cast, and central figure of this great ensemble of characters. In its birth, the first century Church was unearthed out of Judaism; as Jehovah released her from the bondage of the Law. At the end of the age, the Remnant Church helps to once again exhume the nation of Israel from her captivity to the Law.

God's chosen people always exist by election or selection. Those who are alive and do remain have either been elected or selected by God. The Remnant Church does not "will" herself into existence, but rather exists at the pleasure and will of Jehovah. She doesn't accidentally come forth, trip into purpose, or stumble into destiny. Those who are alive and do remain are a deliberate, ordained, selected group of people. They have a pre-ordained purpose, a pre-planned course of action, and a predetermined destination. They exist as an extension of God's continual plan to perfect the Church, and ensure that she lives up to His original purpose for her.

Despite the constant attempts, and success, of the enemy to pollute what God has intended to be a reflection of His holiness, there will always be a portion of the original group that refuses to bow down, refuses to compromise, and refuses to accept the deception. Those who are alive and do remain are those people. Although the Remnant Church has the option to accept the

CHAPTER NINE: THOSE OF US WHO ARE LIVE AND REMAIN

demonic concessions, compromise is not an option for her. For her, non-compromise is the only option. The question is not so much whether we recognize or accept the impending existence of the Remnant Church. The question is whether or not we recognize and accept the "significance" of those who are alive do remain at the catching away of the Church. Do we understand their ministry in calling Jews and Gentiles to repentance during the Great Tribulation? Whether or not we recognize the existence of the Remnant Church does not invalidate her being, or discourage God from causing her to emerge. God will not allow anyone or anything to prevent His will from being accomplished. He is undaunted by the world's refusal to accept the salvation provision He has established, or to allow His prophetic word to be fulfilled. He is impervious to the world's unbelief or lack of acceptance of the notion of a Remnant Church. He realizes that there must be a body of believers in place who are not influenced by this world system. He is absolutely certain that there must be a group of people who will not buy into the satanic compromise. He also allows that the emergence of those who are alive and do remain, the Remnant Church, is paramount to dispelling the idea that He is okay with compromise. She helps dispel the impression that He is in agreement with a Church that will not stand her ground on scriptural issues; one that chooses to be non-offensive and lukewarm on controversial issues. The Remnant Church is vital to conveying His message of holiness.

> *"God's chosen people always exist by election or selection."*

Those who are alive and do remain will have been

responsible for ushering in the great end-times harvest of Jewish converts to Christ. This cataclysmic event alone will change the course of human history. Again, we must bear in mind that the end times Remnant Church will be the vehicle that sparks Israel to jealousy. She will be the voice that reminds the Jews that salvation was initially to the Jew first; then to the Gentiles. Those remaining in the earth, during the Tribulation, will be the catalyst to finally understand that Christianity is the grown-up child of Judaism. The Church started with the Jews and will end with the Jews. The time is fast approaching when all of Israel will be saved. The Church has become a part of them; in totality. Her destiny is linked to them. Where they go, so goes the Church. We are simply amazed that some theologians want to separate the prophetic promises made to Israel from the prophetic promises made to the Church. The Church has no promises save the ones that are associated with the Jews.

With the emergence of those who are alive and do remain, the Remnant Church, the compromised, deceived, conformist Church will no longer be in a position of power to block the move of the Holy Ghost in the body of Christ. The compromised Church will not be able to hinder the ministry of those who have been duly empowered to be God's designated representative and delegated authority in the earth. The Remnant Church will be duly authorized to do battle against the kingdom of darkness; and intent on doing just that. The emergence of the Remnant Church represents a return to the fiery vigor and vitality that was present in the first century remnant; as the Spirit of God made Himself available to dwell in as many earthy bodies as would receive Him. She represents a well-oiled fighting machine, with a single driven focus to wreak havoc upon her arch-enemy, the devil; as she helps bring in the Jewish and Gentile harvest during the Great Tribulation.

When Jeus returns, He will be looking for a Church that resembles the one He deposited in the earth when He left. He will be searching for those who are alive and do remain that are without spot or blemish; like the ones He fashioned on the Day of Pentecost...when He returned in the form of the Holy Spirit to dwell in the earthen temples of the ecclesia. Our returning Savior will be looking for a Church that is walking in the power and authority that replicates that which was in the Church birthed at that Pentecost; as a pronouncement of His power. The Lion of the tribe of Judah will be in pursuit of a body of believers that are casting out demons, defying natural science, and standing as "servant warriors" of the Most High God Jehovah; the Ancient of Days. He will be hunting those who have given all things in common, and are committed to evangelizing their own world as a daily lifestyle. He will be seeking those who are the quintessence of the principles of the Kingdom of God in the earth. He will be trying to find those who are accurately representing His image in the earth. He will be looking for those who are an embodiment of His message of "no compromise," "no conformity," and "no surrender to seducing spirits or different gospels." He will be in pursuit of those who have gone, given, preached, told, and worked; whose colors are unmistakably clear. He will be looking for us...The Remnant Church!

Endnotes

Chapter One

1 Edict of Toleration 311 A.D., Edict of Milan 313 A.D.
2 Revelation 12:9
3 Revelation 13:4, 7, 12-15; Revelation 19:20; Revelation 20:7-10
4 II Peter 2:1-2; II Timothy 4:3-4
5 II Kings 25:11; Jeremiah 37:13-14; Joshua 22:22; II Chronicles 29:19; II Chronicles 33:19; Jeremiah 2:19, 8:5
6 Acts 21:21; II Thessalonians 2:3
7 "Holman Bible Dictionary"; Holman Bible Publishers; Nashville, TN
8 Jeremiah 23:1-3; II Kings. 21:11-15
9 Genesis 7:11-22
10 Genesis 19:29-30
11 Genesis 45:1-46
12 Genesis 15:7-1
13 I Kings. 18:10-20
14 Daniel 6:7-23
15 Daniel 3:1-30
16 Judges 7:1-25
17 Isaiah 7:3
18 Jeremiah 23:3; Ezekiel 14:22; Amos 5:15; Micah 5:7; Zechariah 8:12

Chapter Two

19 John 1:11-12
20 Ephesians 2:20-22

21   The Crusaders, Volume 11; published by Chick Publications, Chino CA; "Sabotage," Page 19

22   "Constantine" by Ramsay Mac Mullen; published by the Dial Press; Crosscurrents in World History Series, New York, 1969, Page 72

23   "The Eternal Church" references; notes page 2; by Dr. Bill Hamon; Destiny Image Publishers; Inc., Shippensburg, PA

24   "The Eternal Church"; pg. 94-95; by Dr. Bill Hamon; Destiny Image Publishers, Inc.; Shippensburg, PA

25   "Church History," Vol. 1; Newman

26   "Which Bible?" by David Otis Fuller, D.D., Institute for Biblical Textual Studies, 2233 Michigan Street, NE, Grand Rapids, MI 49503; "God Only Wrote One Bible" by J. J. Ray, The Eye Opener Publishers, P.O. Box 7944, Eugene, OR 97401; "Manuscript Evidence" by P. S. Ruckman, Bible Baptist Bookstore, P.O. Box 7135, Pensacola, FL 32534; "The King James Version Defended" by Edward F. Hills, Th.D., Order from the Eye Opener Publishers, P.O. Box 7944, Eugene, OR 97401

27   "Constantine" published by Ramsay Mac Mullen; Page 112

28   The Crusaders, Volume 11, published by J.T.C., Chino CA, "Sabotage," Page 23

29   "The Two Babylons" by Hislop; published by Loizeaux Bros.; Neptune, NJ; chapter entitled 'The Mother of the Child

30   Romans 9th, 10th, & 11th chapters

31   Isaiah 10:20-27

32   Romans 11:25-27

33	Romans 11:26-32
34	Romans 9:22-27
35	Romans 11:11-24
36	Romans 11:25-27
37	Matthew 24:11-14; II Timothy 4:1-4; II Thessalonians 2:3; I Timothy 4:1
38	Genesis 16:1-16
39	Genesis 21:9-21
40	Ephesians 2:11-22
41	Galatians 3:26-29
42	Genesis 1:27-28
43	Hebrews 9:22; Lev. 17:11
44	Galatians 3:26-29
45	Matthew 10:34-39; Luke 12:51
46	Haggai 2:7-9
47	Romans 1:16; Acts 13:44-48
48	Luke 3:23-38
49	Genesis 5: 1-32
50	Exodus 12:29-36
51	Genesis 41:25-41
52	Exodus 12:37-42
53	Exodus 12:24-28
54	I Kings. 11:1-10
55	I Kings. 11:29-40
56	Hebrews 7:11-17
57	Joel 2:17-27
58	Romans 11:4-5; Romans 11:25-26
59	Leviticus 10:1; Numbers 26:61

60 John 20:19-23
61 Acts 1:1-8, 15-16; Acts 2:1-4
62 Acts 2:9-11
63 Wikipedia – The Free Encyclopedia
64 Wikipedia – The Free Encyclopedia
65 Theopedia – An Encyclopedia of Biblical Christianity
66 Theopedia – An Encyclopedia of Biblical Christianity
67 Theopedia – An Encyclopedia of Biblical Christianity

Chapter Three
68 Revelation 11:15
69 Ephesians 1:4; Revelation 13:8
70 Genesis 12:1-3
71 www.About.com; Christianity; Jack Zavada
72 Wikipedia – The Free Encyclopedia
73 Wikipedia – The Free Encyclopedia
74 Isaiah 53:12; Mark 15:27-28; Galatians 3:13; Deuteronomy 21:23
75 Wikipedia – The Free Encyclopedia
76 "The Two Babylons" by Hislop; published by Loizeaux Bros., Neptune, NJ

Chapter Four
77 Genesis 3:15
78 Acts 2:38
79 Proverbs 14:12
80 Acts 2:28
81 Acts 10:1
82 Acts 11:18

83   Acts 11:25-26
84   Acts 14:11-15
85   www.Bible.org – New Testament Repentance: Repentance in the Gospels and Acts
86   Mark 1:12-15
87   "The Eternal Church" by Dr. Bill Hamon; Destiny Image Publishers, Inc.; Shippensburg, PA
88   I Peter 1:14-16

Chapter Five

89   Baker's Evangelical Dictionary of Bible Theology
90   Easton Bible Dictionary; Baker's Evangelical Dictionary of Bible Theology
91   "In Bishop's Corner"; 'The Rapture'; Bishop Ronald D. Roston, D. Min.
92   The Open Bible
93   Wikipedia – The Free Encyclopedia
94   www.Gotquestions.org
95   Daniel 9:27; Daniel 11:31; Daniel 12:11
96   Revelation 13;1-3; Revelation 13:11-14
97   Revelation 13:7
98   Daniel 9:7
99   Daniel 11:31; Daniel 12:11
100   Revelation 13:15-17
101   Matthew 24:15-21
102   Matthew 24:20-30
103   "Numbers in Scripture" by Ethelbert W. Bullinger; Kregel Publications; Grand Rapids, MI
104   Acts 1:15-17
105   Wikipedia – The Free Encyclopedia
106   "A Course in Miracles"; The Foundation for Inner Peace;

Huntington Station, N.Y. Lesson 228, p. 461

107 "A Course in Miracles"; The Foundation for Inner Peace; Huntington Station, N.Y.

108 "Hidden Dangers of the Rainbow" by Constance Cumbey; Huntington House Inc; Shreveport, LA 71107

109 "Hidden Dangers of the Rainbow" by Constance Cumbey; Huntington House Inc; Shreveport, LA 71107

110 The Encyclopedia Britannica

Chapter Six

111 Numbers 16:1-14

112 Ezra 2:20

113 II Chronicles.6:6-7:16

114 I Chronicles 22:14

115 Acts 21:37-38

116 Dr. Gene Rice, Professor of Old Testament, Blacks in Biblical Antiquity, American Bible Society

117 Dr. Gene Rice, Professor of Old Testament, Blacks in Biblical Antiquity, American Bible Society

118 Dr. Gene Rice, Professor of Old Testament, Blacks in Biblical Antiquity, American Bible Society

119 Dr. Cain Hope Felder, Professor of New Testament Language and Literature at the Howard University School of Divinity in Washington D.C., which appeared in the 'African American Jubilee Bible, published by the American Bible Society (1999)'. Scripture citations are from the New Revised Standard Version. "THE PHYSICAL APPEARANCE OF ANCIENT ISRAEL THE HEBREWS & THE SONS OF HAM. And the sons of Ham, Cush, Mizraim & Phut & Canaan." "Genesis 10:6"

120 Dr. Cain Hope Felder, Professor of New Testament

Language and Literature
121   Exodus 2:1-3
122   Acts 7:23
123   Exodus 2:6,10
124   "History of Egypt" by George Rawlinson
125   Wikipedia – The Free Encyclopedia
126   Wikipedia – The Free Encyclopedia
127   Wikipedia – The Free Encyclopedia
128   Wikipedia – The Free Encyclopedia
129   Wikipedia – The Free Encyclopedia
130   Wikipedia – The Free Encyclopedia
131   Wikipedia – The Free Encyclopedia
132   Wikipedia – The Free Encyclopedia
133   Wikipedia – The Free Encyclopedia

Chapter Seven
134   Luke 24: 26-27; 24:44-47
135   Mark 8:31-33; Luke 9:22
136   "Hidden Dangers of the Rainbow" by Constance Cumbey; Huntington House Inc; Shreveport, LA 71107
137   The Encyclopedia Britannica
138   Matthew 17:1-8; Mark 9:2-8; Luke 9:28-36
139   Mark 9:30-32; Luke 9:44-45
140   Matthew 20:17-19; Mark 10:32-34; Luke 18:31-33
141   John 12:31-33
142   Matthew 12:38-40
143   Matthew 27:62-63
144   Mark 15:42; Luke 23:54; John 19:31
145   John 11:17-31
146   Deuteronomy 21:22-23
147   Deuteronomy 32:4

148   Exodus 23:14-15; Leviticus 23:6-7, 34, 39; Numbers 28:17; 29:12; Deuteronomy 16:16
149   Wikipedia – The Free Encyclopedia
150   Luke 24:32
151   John. 21:15-17
152   Luke 24:52
153   "The Crucifixion of Jesus and the Jews" by Mark Allan Powell
154   Matthew 27:25
155   John 5:18; John 7:1; John 8:37
156   I Thessalonians 2:14-15; Philippians 3:5-6
157   Mark 10:45; John 18:11
158   Romans 5:8-9; I Timothy 1:15
159   Matthew 27:25
160   Wikipedia – The Free Encyclopedia
161   Wikipedia – The Free Encyclopedia
162   Wikipedia – The Free Encyclopedia
163   Wikipedia – The Free Encyclopedia
164   Wikipedia – The Free Encyclopedia
165   Wikipedia – The Free Encyclopedia

Chapter Eight
166   www.The Modern Apostate Ecumenical Movement jesus-is-savior.com/False Doctrines/ecumenical_movement.htm
167   Vatican II and the Ecumenical Movement - www.usccb.org/.../ecumenical-and-interreligious/vatican-ii-and-the-ecumenical-movement.cfm
168   Ephesians 2:8-9
169   I Timothy 3:16-17
170   Should a Christian be involved in the ecumenical movement?, compellingtruth.org/ecumenical-movement.html

Chapter Nine

171   The Modern Apostate Ecumenical Movement.... www.jesus-is-savior.com/False Doctrines/ecumenical_movement.htm

172   "End Time Delusions" by Steve Wohlberg; Destiny Image Publishers, Inc; "End Times Ministry" by Bishop Ronald D. Roston, D. Min; Suber Media Group

173   "End Time Delusions" by Steve Wohlberg; Destiny Image Publishers, Inc; "End Times Ministry" by Bishop Ronald D. Roston, D. Min; Suber Media Group

174   Revelation 7:9-17

175   "In Bishop's Corner"; 'The Rapture'; Bishop Ronald D. Roston, D. Min.

176   "In Bishop's Corner"; 'The Rapture'; Bishop Ronald D. Roston, D. Min.

177   Revelation 13:1-9; Revelation 13:11-18; Revelation 14:9-11; Revelation 15:1-2

178   "In Bishop's Corner"; 'The anti-Christ'; Bishop Ronald D. Roston, D. Min.

179   I Thessalonians 5:1-6; II Peter 3:9-14; John 6:38-40, 44, 54; John 12:48

180   Matthew 24:21-31

181   Matthew 25:32-46

182   John.4:7; John. 14:9; John. 9:21

WORK CITED

Bible. English. New Living Translation. *Holy Bible, New Living Translation.* Wheaton, Il, Tyndale House Publishers, 1996.

"Bible.org | Where the World Comes to Study the Bible." *Bible.org*, bible.org//.

britannica. "Encyclopedia Britannica." *Encyclopædia Britannica*, 2024, www.britannica.com/.

Bruce Manning Metzger, and In The. *Holy Bible : New Revised Standard Version : Containing the Old and New Testaments with the Deuterocanonical Books.* Peabody, Mass., Hendrickson Bibles In Conjunction With Oxford University Press, 2008.

Butler, Trent C. *Holman Bible Dictionary.* B&H Publishing Group, 1991.

Cain Hope Felder. *Race, Racism, and the Biblical Narratives.* Fortress Press, 23 May 2023.

Crossin, John. "Vatican II and the Ecumenical Movement | USCCB." *Www.usccb.org*, 2012, www.usccb.org/committees/ecumenical-interreligious-affairs/vatican-ii-and-ecumenical-movement.

Cumbey, Constance E. *The Hidden Dangers of the Rainbow.* Huntington House Publishers, 1983.

David Otis Fuller, and Benjamin George Wilkinson. *Which Bible?* Grand Rapids, Mich., Grand Rapids International Publications, 1972.

Davis, Blair. *Christianity and Comics.* Rutgers University Press, 15 Mar. 2024.

Easton, M G. *Easton's Bible Dictionary.* 19 Aug. 2017.

Elwell, Walter A. *Evangelical Dictionary of Biblical Theology*. 2nd ed., Grand Rapids, Mich., Baker Books ; Carlisle, Cumbria, 2001.

Ethelbert William Bullinger. *Number in Scripture*. Kregel Publications, 1895.

Foundation For Inner Peace. *A Course in Miracles: Combined Volume*. Foundation For Inner Peace, 2008.

Gideons International. *The Holy Bible : New International Version*. Lutterworth, England, The Gideons International In The British Isles, 2012.

GotQuestions.org. "Bible Questions Answered." *GotQuestions.org*, Apr. 2002, www.gotquestions.org/.

Hamon, Bill. *The Eternal Church*. Destiny Image Publishers, 28 July 2011.

Hills, Edward F. *The King James Version Defended*. Eye Opener Publishers, 1 Feb. 1984.

Hislop, Alexander. *The Two Babylons*. Loizeaux Bros., 1959.

Life Application Study Bible : New Living Translation. Carol Steam, Illinois, Tyndale House Publishers, Inc, 2016.

MacAuthor, John. *The MacArthur Study Bible*. Thomas Nelson, 5 Nov. 2013.

MacMullen, Ramsay. *Constantine (Routledge Revivals)*. Routledge, 17 June 2014.

Newman, Albert H. *Manual of Church History*. Legal Street Press, 1931.

Rawlinson, George. *History of Ancient Egypt, by George Rawlinson, ...* S.E. Cassino, 1881.

"Should a Christian Be Involved in the Ecumenical

Movement?" *CompellingTruth.org*, www.compellingtruth.org/ecumenical-movement.html.

Strong, James. *Strong's Exhaustive Concordance of the Bible*. Peabody, Ma, Hendrickson Pub, 2012, www.christianbook.com/strongs-exhaustive-concordance-updated-edition-kjv/9781598563788/pd/563788. Accessed 22 Dec. 2019.

The Holy Bible : King James Version. Peabody, Ma, Hendrickson Publishers, 2014.

"The Modern Apostate Ecumenical Movement." *Jesus-Is-Savior.com*, 2024, www.jesus-is-savior.com/False%20Doctrines/ecumenical_movement.htm. Accessed 13 Aug. 2024.

"The Modern Apostate Ecumenical Movement." *Jesus-Is-Savior.com*, 2024, www.jesus-is-savior.com/False%20Doctrines/ecumenical_movement.htm.

Trevor Gervase Jalland. *The Open Bible*. Church Literature Association: London, 1938.

Wikipedia. "Wikipedia, the Free Encyclopedia." *Wikipedia*, Wikimedia Foundation, 15 Jan. 2001, en.wikipedia.org/wiki/Main_Page.

Winston, James C. *The Original African Heritage Study Bible : King James Version : With Special Annotations Relative to the African/Edenic Perspective*. Iowa Falls, Iowa, Word Bible Publishers, 1998.

Wohlberg, Steve. *End Time Delusions*. Destiny Image Publishers, 28 Jan. 2005.

Theopedia.com, 2019, www.theopedia.com/.

ADDITIONAL SUGGESTED READINGS

1. "The Mystery of Iniquity" by Michael J. Rood
2. "End Time Warriors" by John Kelly & Paul Costa
3. "Israel, The Church, by Dan Juster & Keith Intrater & The Last Days"
4. "The Rise of Babylon" by Charles H. Dyer
5. "Battle for Jerusalem" by John Hagee
6. "The Last Days According to Jesus" by R. C. Sproul

www.ingramcontent.com/pod-product-compliance
Lightning Source LLC
Chambersburg PA
CBHW070045080526
44586CB00013B/917